Housing and Social Policy

This book looks at the changing nature of housing policy in the UK and how it relates to the economy and society generally. Contributors to the book consider the effects of market forces and state action on low-income households, different social classes, women, minority ethnic groups, and disabled people. It is argued that housing is a key focus for economic development, for social justice, for everyday lived experience, for class struggle, for gender and racial divisions, for organising the life course, and for physical and social regeneration.

A key theme of the book is that, although housing is inextricably bound up with all aspects of our lives, we experience it in very different ways, depending on our social status, our spatial location, and our own physical, mental and financial characteristics. Contributors emphasise not only the differences among individuals, however, but also how the pattern of these differences can be understood through a focus on housing in particular. In this way, what appears to be a uniquely individualised experience can in reality be understood as a product of a complex web of interactions of different kinds, which assumes a relatively concrete shape in the context of housing. Categories of class, gender, race, disability and age are therefore shown to intersect while, at the same time, housing policy itself merges imperceptibly with other kinds of policy, such as economic, family, health, education, crime, and environment policy, under the 'catch-all' title of 'regeneration'. Consequently, both housing experience and housing policy lose their specificity and become generalised as well as individualised.

The book contains a number of original findings and arguments, which should be of interest to both housing academics and policy makers, as well as to students of housing and social policy. New material is presented on the nature of housing and social inequality in relation to class, race, gender and disability, and new theory is developed on the causes of housing policy change, the 'place' of housing in relation to other policy fields, and the possibilities of transformative residence-based community politics.

Peter Somerville is Professor of Social Policy and Head of the Policy Studies Research Centre, University of Lincoln. He has extensive experience of housing as a practitioner, teacher and researcher and has published widely on housing, social exclusion and community development. **Nigel Sprigings** is Lecturer in Housing at the School of Environment and Life Sciences at the University of Salford. He has extensive experience of housing as a practitioner as well as more recent experience as a teacher and researcher. Both Somerville and Sprigings have taught professional courses for the Chartered Institute of Housing Professional Qualification.

Housing and society series
Edited by Ray Forrest, School for Policy Studies, University of Bristol.

This series aims to situate housing within its wider social, political and economic context at both national and international level. In doing so it will draw on the full range of social science disciplines and on mainstream debate on the nature of contemporary social change. The books are intended to appeal to an international academic audience as well as to practitioners and policymakers – to be theoretically informed and policy relevant.

Housing and Social Change
East–West perspectives
Edited by Ray Forrest and James Lee

Urban Poverty, Housing and Social Change in China
Ya Ping Wang

Gentrification in a Global Context
Edited by Rowland Atkinson and Gary Bridge

Housing and Social Policy
Edited by Peter Somerville with Nigel Sprigings

Forthcoming:
Managing Social Housing
David Mullins, Barbara Reid and Richard Walker

Housing Structures
Shaping the space of twenty-first century living
Bridget Franklin

Housing and Social Policy

Contemporary themes and critical perspectives

Edited by Peter Somerville
with Nigel Sprigings

Routledge
Taylor & Francis Group

LONDON AND NEW YORK

First published 2005
by Routledge
2 Park Square, Milton Park, Abingdon, Oxon OX14 4RN

Simultaneously published in the USA and Canada
by Routledge
711 Third Ave, New York, NY 10017

Routledge is an imprint of the Taylor & Francis Group

© 2005 Peter Somerville and Nigel Sprigings, selection and editorial
material; individual chapters, the contributors

Typeset in Times and Frutiger by
HWA Text and Data Management, Tunbridge Wells

British Library Cataloguing in Publication Data
A catalogue record for this book is available from the British Library

Library of Congress Cataloging in Publication Data
Housing and social policy : contemporary themes and critical
perspectives / edited by Peter Somerville and Nigel Sprigings
        p.   cm. – (Housing and society series)
    Includes bibliographical references and index.
    1. Housing policy–Great Britain. 2. Great Britain–Social policy–1979–
I. Somerville, Peter. II Sprigings, Nigel. III. Series.
HD7333.A3H6769 2005
363.5′0941–dc22   2004017249

ISBN 0–415–28366–3 (hb : alk. paper)
ISBN 0–415–28367–1 (pb : alk. paper)

Contents

Contributors

Charlie Cooper is Lecturer in Social Policy at the University of Hull. He previously worked for a number of years in the housing association sector before moving into higher education. Charlie's current research interests are primarily around conditions of domination within British social policy and the harm these generate. He also has avid affections for Sheffield United and African music.

Malcolm Harrison is Reader in Housing and Social Policy at the University of Leeds. He has published widely on housing policy, particularly in relation to ethnicity and 'race'.

Jo Milner is an honorary research fellow based within the Scott Sutherland School, Robert Gordon University. She has an inter-disciplinary research, teaching and practice based background, which spans disability studies and housing policy, especially as they relate to housing quality and design.

John Pierson is a Senior Lecturer in the Institute of Social Work and Applied Social Studies at Staffordshire University. He is editor of *Rebuilding Community: Policy and Practice in Urban Regeneration* (2001) and the author of *Tackling Social Exclusion* (2001). He is currently writing a volume on neighbourhood practice, *Going Local*, which is to be published in 2005.

Kesia Reeve is a Research Fellow in Housing in the Centre for Regional Economic and Social Research at Sheffield Hallam University. Since completion of her Doctoral thesis on 'the squatters movement in London 1968–1980' she has researched extensively on housing issues. Particular areas of interest include homelessness and the housing needs of vulnerable groups, and understanding housing market change.

Joan Smith is a Reader in Social Research at London Metropolitan University, and Director of the Centre for Housing and Community Research. She has extensive experience in running research teams in the field of homelessness, deprivation and children/young people.

Contributors

Peter Somerville is Professor of Social Policy and Head of the Policy Studies Research Centre at the University of Lincoln. He is author of *Social Relations and Social Exclusion* (2000) and co-editor of *Race, Housing and Social Exclusion* (2002).

Bill Spink has been actively involved in housing for over forty years. After a career as a housing practitioner with several northern local authorities he took up appointments in Further and Higher Education which culminated in his role as Senior Lecturer in Housing and Management Studies at the University of Lincoln. A Fellow of the Chartered Institute of Housing and holder of a Master's degree in Business Administration he now does part-time work for universities and local authorities.

Nigel Sprigings has been a Lecturer in Housing at the University of Salford since 1996. Prior to that he had twenty years in housing practice including homelessness, estate management, area improvement and other aspects of housing sector service delivery.

Claire Worley is currently undertaking her PhD on community cohesion at the University of Huddersfield, where she also teaches social policy. She has a specialist interest in the relationship between gender and ethnicity in community regeneration, and has several publications arising from community based research in the field of homelessness and regeneration.

1 Introduction

Nigel Sprigings and Peter Somerville

Ideally, one aim of any book with the title 'Housing and Social Policy' should be to consider, explicate and evaluate the ways in which housing interventions by governments help to achieve social policy objectives. This task would include elucidation of alternative policies that government may have rejected but the broad remit would be the housing aspects of the full range of social policy. Obviously, the scope of such a book would be encyclopedic. This may be one of the reasons why previous books on the subject have tended to concentrate primarily on the nuts and bolts of housing service delivery in the public sector, often linking housing needs issues with other welfare services. Clapham *et al.* open their book 'Housing and Social Policy' with the statement that their

> book focuses on two key relationships: that between housing policy and social policy, and that between the provision of housing and the provision of other welfare services such as the health service, the education system, the personal social services and the social security system
>
> (Clapham *et al.* 1990: ix)

This places housing policy squarely amongst the welfare services with an emphasis on public provision in its various forms. The definition of social policy they use covers 'the areas of consumption in which the state plays a central role' and they recognise that this is 'not uncontroversial'. But the emphasis is on consideration of the way welfare services 'interact' to achieve social objectives. This leads to considerations of community care and homelessness policies and practices in some detail. Such an approach meets a particular need for students and practitioners wanting to understand recent social policy and the changes this imposes on, or requires of, their organisations.

The aim of this book is different in that it will try to see social policy more widely than welfare provision. Social policy in this light includes a wider range of interventions across all sectors not just the public sector. While this requires consideration of some nuts and bolts issues that are not commonly covered in such a book (for example, strategies to tackle anti-social behaviour or house design for disabled people), it also creates the opportunity to evaluate those policies and practices in the light of social theory. This is where we hope the book offers an original perspective that will give it an audience wider than that focused on housing and directly related welfare services. Consequently, there are some notable absences from the main content, such as homelessness or community care, while other core issues usually found in housing policy books, such as the right to buy and its impacts, are not addressed in any great detail. These issues are well covered in other books: for example, on homelessness see Hutson and Clapham (1999), Kennett and Marsh (2000); on the right to buy see Malpass and Murie (1999).

Instead the chapters consider aspects of social policy with a housing focus but informed by social theory as it relates to the topic area. This approach not only provides an explanation of what policy approaches have achieved but also allows for the development of critical understanding of the subject area through elucidation of social theory debates that have driven or resulted from those policies.

Housing is ubiquitous in that, in some form, it is generally accepted to be essential to all the nation's residents at every stage (or some stages) of their lives. Even travellers have occasional call on permanent housing provision and are partially provided for under homelessness legislation. Housing policy, however, as a form of welfare policy, is not ubiquitous. A change of housing policy, such as significantly reducing the supply of public housing, as happened in the 1980s, may not impact directly on the majority of individuals in the country unless they need council housing and find it in short supply. Of course, many people never need to call on the supply of council housing as they live their lives in privately owned homes, tied housing or privately rented housing. Government policy has more influence on our housing circumstances than might at first be imagined (see Spink, this volume) but this does not alter the fact that, for many people, housing policy impacts on them only indirectly and often over time. An example of this would be where government failure to stimulate supply across all sectors causes cyclical increases in the value of owned homes (see below). Another would be the current availability of a three bedroom semi-detached house in suburbia that may have depended on a long forgotten construction subsidy from the 1930s.

Lowe (2004) cites research illustrating how different national housing structures interact closely with other areas of social policy such as health and pensions. High housing ownership economies have higher inflation over time[1] and tend to more marketised provision of welfare services whereas low home ownership economies tend to be more state welfare oriented in other provision too. There may be a chicken and egg factor here but, given the links between ownership and capital accumulation through inflation, the social and economic reach of housing-related policies is one of the key factors in determining personal and economic well-being. Renters tend to become relatively poorer, for example, in a system that generates unearned wealth for owners. That the owners benefit from social policy may not be immediately obvious to them but is vital for their personal economic gain.

The importance of the housing sector to national economic performance is a key message of the reports issued by the recent Barker Review of Housing Supply (Barker 2003, 2004). Barker states clearly that 'a weak supply of housing contributes to macroeconomic instability and hinders labour market flexibility, constraining economic growth' (Barker 2004: 1).

In seeking ways to understand the operation of the current market(s) for housing and making proposals for increased flexibility the Barker Review considered both the public and private sectors. It assessed land release and planning practices and policies, and considered the economics of the building industry and its responses (or lack of supply responses) to increased housing market demand as well as the factors that generate demand and the consequences of a prolonged period of under-supply. In making recommendations on the topics within its brief it acknowledged the need to 'strike a balance' between a range of social policy goals such as

- greater economic stability and economic growth;
- adequate and affordable housing for a growing population;
- meeting the aspirations of individuals as to the amount of space, the location and nature of housing to be provided;
- efficient allocation of resources, in particular land; and
- environmental and amenity considerations.

(Barker 2004: 12)

The broad economic role and context that Barker places first on this list is crucial to understanding housing and social policy even for those of us who doubt the ability of economists to fully represent issues such as aspirations, environment and amenity in human life.

Except in the immediate postwar years of 1945 to 1949, growth in home ownership since the First World War has always outpaced the growth in public provision. When it finally became the dominant (as well as the favoured) tenure in the early 1970s, the implications for the economy of the country as a whole were enormous. Arguably, the policy of promoting ownership while the supply industry failed to meet growing demand (Hamnett 1999; Barker 2004) led to a volatile market. Barker argues that a range of factors contributed to this supply failure including planning controls, land banking by builders, inefficiency compared to the European construction industry and a culture of risk aversion in the building industry. Whatever the cause(s) the resulting price volatility affects the economy so extensively that Britain's membership of the European Monetary Union (EMU) now substantially depends on our ability to exercise control over these historically unstable housing markets. As Barker states:

As well as the significance of housing supply for national economic well-being and individual welfare, housing supply is highly relevant to the issue of membership of Economic Monetary Union (EMU). In 2003, HM Treasury published its assessment of the five economic tests and 18 supporting studies. The assessment of the five tests concluded that: '... the incompatibility of housing structures means that the housing market is a high risk factor to the achievement of settled and sustainable convergence'.

The study shows that low housing supply responsiveness could have contributed to the greater trend increase in real house prices in the UK. The study also noted that UK households had greater ease of access to additional equity resulting from house price rises. Together, these characteristics meant that increases in house prices tended to have a stronger influence on consumer spending than in many other countries.

(Barker 2003: 1)

The organisation of the housing market in the UK itself tends to encourage lack of responsiveness to changing demand and general inefficiency in the housebuilding industry. Barker presents evidence that builders, under the current system, can maximise profit by holding land back from development (thus benefiting from a restrictive planning system; relaxation of this system is advocated as a stimulus to supply), that volatility itself restricts supply (as a 1 per cent shift in price can make an 8 per cent difference to profit so builders are cautious and favour shortage), and that inefficiency arises because profits can be achieved without efficiency gains. Barker even claims that the quality of our new housing suffers as a result of the failures in the operation of the market (Barker 2003: 94). This occurs when old stock of low quality is not cleared from the market but instead serves to hold down prices in the second-hand market thus impacting on the quality of new provision for first time buyers for which old stock is a direct price competitor. Builders presumably hold down the price by reducing quality rather than increasing efficiency. The evidence presented in the Barker Review is that many consumers are dissatisfied with the quality of the product and would not buy again from that supplier.

Seeking a simple analysis of the volatility of the housing market is doomed to failure, partly because of the range of social policies and personal choices/aspirations that impact upon it. Nevin *et al.* (1999) have identified drivers of housing markets, operating at a minimum of four distinct levels:

- *National level* where increased mortgage availability has led to increased accessibility of ownership in the new and second-hand housing markets. Housing benefit changes have created new 'markets' for rented housing across the private and social sectors. Aspirations to ownership have increased, with accessibility resulting in changing perceptions of social rented housing and its residualisation, thus reducing demand for housing funded directly through public spending. Economic and labour market restructuring has created inequalities of income and job security, which impact on households' ability to achieve housing aspirations. This same labour market restructuring affects patterns of migration by moving attractive jobs to some regions (Massey 1995) while reducing the ability of households to move (Barker 2004). National policy has rejected demolition programmes as either a supply or quality control mechanism, with clearance programmes falling from a peak of 70,000 per year in the 1970s to less than 2,000 per year by the turn of the century (www.odpm.gov.uk). Improvement grant contributions to the private sector have declined from their mid-1980s' peaks back to 1970s' levels.

- *Regional level* where decentralisation of population and employment has resulted from some of the above national drivers. Significantly the populations of the major cities have been declining for some time with patterns of suburbanisation and increased travel to work distances/patterns.

- *Local authority level.* This is an administrative rather than 'natural' area but it has significance where historic patterns of housing provision by type (terraced housing, flats) or tenure (the predominance of social renting) show significant divergence from national norms or averages. For example, Manchester has the lowest proportion of owner-occupied stock outside London. These patterns of provision have impacted on housing demand within the boroughs as a whole but have amplified effects at …

- *Local level* where neighbourhoods can be dominated by unpopular tenures or house types and where significant proportions of housing can be old and in poor condition. These neighbourhoods can fall into rapid decline where old/failing infrastructure and eroded employment bases can combine with poor services and facilities to create very poor areas with little inward migration or investment. (Nevin *et al.* 1999: 4–8)

Traditionally, housing policy has been discussed in terms of meeting government identified, or locally assessed, 'housing needs'. Policy discussion of the concept of housing market(s) has developed alongside the growing dominance of owner occupation as the main housing tenure in the UK. Obviously, there are different sub-markets, reflecting the different tenures, but the main market is now for owner-occupied housing, with drivers generally accepted to be:

- health of the economy as reflected in personal income growth affecting demand;
- the level of supply which should increase with demand in a well functioning market but with overall supply actually rising between 1 per cent and 2 per cent per year;
- demographic factors such as population levels, household formation, and migration within and across UK borders.

Many economic analysts have studied the cycles of boom and slump in the UK housing market and have given us some understanding of the national patterns and processes. Hamnett, for example, first establishes that there is a longer-term relationship between house prices and household incomes, and then attempts to understand the shorter-term house price cycles in the light of this longer-term relationship. He argues that house prices rise in line with earnings rather than with retail prices because 'housing has a high and positive income elasticity of demand. In other words, for a given increase in income, people are likely to devote a high proportion to housing' (Hamnett 1999: 14).

> Broadly speaking, house prices rise over time because housing is a key element of household consumption and, as incomes rise, people are both willing and able to put a substantial proportion of their income into buying a house or moving up-market to a larger, more desirable and usually more expensive home. As already noted the number of home owners has risen from four million immediately after the Second World War to 16 million today. Supply [of new housing] is largely fixed in the short term as the building industry only builds 150,000 to 200,000 units a year (about one per cent of the owner occupied stock) and planning restrictions mean that the supply of land is limited, particularly in south-east England, which tends to push up house prices. Although over six million houses have been transferred to owner occupation from private and social renting, since the war demand for home ownership has exceeded supply.
>
> (Hamnett 1999: 17)

With regard to the causes of house price cycles, Hamnett argues that 'booms are triggered by changes in the number of people in the key first-time buyer age groups, by increases in real income and mortgage availability' (Hamnett 1999: 12). He then maps the major house price booms, beginning with that of 1971–2, with evidence pointing to two causal factors:

> The first was a demographic shock…The 25–29 age group grew sharply in size from 1971 to 1973 … With a static supply of housing, prices began to rise rapidly, assisted by Barber's early 1970s Conservative credit boom which made borrowing far easier than hitherto.
>
> (Hamnett 1999: 24)

This boom began in London and south-east England and spread, with a slight lag (about twelve months), to the regions. The house price/earnings ratio rose from 3.25 in 1970 to 4.95 in 1973. After the ensuing slump, house building fell back, as did house sales (transactions), with the house price/earnings ratio declining to 3.34 by 1977.

Each cycle has been characterised by essentially the same pattern. At the start of each upturn, real incomes tend to rise faster than house prices and the house price/income ratio is at or below its long term historic norm of 3.5. As the volume of sales rises, any overhang of unsold property on the market begins to dry up and (as housing supply is largely fixed) prices begin to rise quite sharply. The house price/income ratio rises and, as the cycle nears its peak, house prices rise ahead of incomes to the point where the ratio becomes unsustainably high and prices stabilise and fall in real terms. Subsequently, as incomes continue to rise, the house price/earnings ratio falls back until the conditions are in place for a new boom.

(Hamnett 1999: 24)

The later booms followed the same pattern, with the house price/earnings ratio rising to 3.82 in 1978 before falling back, and to 4.43 in 1989 before falling back. It is worth noting at this point that Barker has identified a *fall* in the supply of new owner-occupied housing over recent years (along with a long-term fall in public supply since the 1980s) rather than either the traditional stability Hamnett refers to or the increase (in response to demand) that market economics would predict.

Other housing economists have commented on the failure of existing economic modelling techniques. For example, Maclennan says:

There is no more or less complex econometric model available which accurately tracks and explains the 10 year history of the housing market. Changing financial sector behaviour, shifts in government policies, the importance of expectations and confidence are not only difficult to model but, further, 'causality' becomes elusive when they are happening about the same time.

(Maclennan 1994: 13)

Housing policy, as an element of social policy, is constrained by the lack of understanding of its causal elements at national and local level. This may be particularly important if 'markets' are relied upon to replace an interventionist public housing supply policy as has happened over time in the UK, and some of the discussion in this book is an analysis of this trend to marketisation.

So, a reduced supply of housing does not necessarily result in a reduced demand. However, if demand remains constant while supply falls, the inevitable consequence is rising prices. This puts house prices further and further out of the reach of lower-income households. Continuing government intervention is therefore required in order to ensure that such households can access affordable housing (to buy or rent), for example, through income support (such as housing benefit and Supporting People funding – see, for example, Spink or Milner, this volume) or through supply measures (such as key worker homes in south-east England, housing market renewal and other regeneration initiatives), and to mitigate the social and wider economic effects of these housing market inefficiencies.

Of course another possible policy response to shortage is direct public spending for public provision. Barker identifies in her review a need for:

> An increase in supply of social housing ... of 17,000 homes each year ... to meet the needs among the flow of new households. There is also a case for provision at up to 9,000 a year above this rate in order to make inroads into the backlog of need.
>
> (Barker 2004: 5)

The interaction of ownership, private rental and social rental is one of the little understood factors in this overall demand and supply relationship, although it is often assumed that ownership and social rental (in particular) are not substitutable goods.

The chapters that follow explore particular social policy aspects of this dynamic housing market, which sometimes even drive elements of it. This is not always about direct funding and provision, as will be shown. Governments apply a variety of intervention mechanisms to an expanding range of policy objectives such as sustainable communities, economic development, meeting needs, improving access and so on. For example, the government directly sets standards of housing in all sectors, with the current drive to achieve the Decent Homes Standard (ODPM 2002) running alongside moves to establish registers of private sector landlords (but see Milner, this volume). All these areas have social policy content.

The edges of the housing and social policy jigsaw are hard to identify, and the direct causal links, which policy makers would love to find in order to achieve their objectives through precisely targeted interventions, remain elusive. Also, while housing policies may be initiated under one government the full impacts of initiatives may not be felt until many years and several governments later. To take a simple example, more than twenty years after tenant involvement became a statutory requirement in the Housing Act 1980, many social landlords are still struggling to identify effective and appropriate methods for consulting and involving tenants in decision-making. Such consultation is intended to increase the quality of public services by making them more responsive to those who use them (Walsh 1995) but this remains largely an aspiration rather than a reality.

The changing nature of housing policy is the subject of Chapter 2. For students and newcomers to housing policy issues this chapter sets the scene and directs readers to more detailed historical and contextual sources should they need them. Partly because of the slow rate at which structural changes occur in housing provision or service delivery as a result of policy change, this historical context is essential for anyone wishing to understand why current structures exist in their present form.

Without such an understanding, housing and social policy changes can seem simply arbitrary. For example, the legislators of the early 1970s may not have had a detailed conception of the actual route that would lead to social housing sector landlords being dominated by Boards of Management. However, their use of the Housing Corporation for the promotion and funding of housing associations from 1974 has led directly to the variety of social housing organisations seen today, all with Boards of Management ostensibly controlling their direction and purposes.

An often forgotten driver for this policy was to bring UK housing provision more into line with the rest of the European Union, where social housing is rarely under the direct control of elected local government. The UK's various housing-focused convergence policies have been a long and winding road and, as Chapter 5 points out, class struggles may still affect the eventual outcome.

Chapter 3 approaches the issue of social justice in housing. Traditionally, such approaches consider the distribution of housing as a good in order to achieve greater equality. This approach seems to begin with a massive assumption as to what social justice is. This does not take any account of varying political and popular approaches to social justice. At one time socialists suggested nationalising housing stock but now policy is often driven by people who see markets as the only way to secure just distribution of housing 'goods' or who see welfare as part of complex systems of social punishment.

The approach of this chapter is to consider some of the more significant political philosophies that impact on housing and social policy. These philosophies are then applied to the very specific problem of managing anti-social behaviour in public sector housing. The chapter explores the reasons for the emphasis on policy interventions in public sector housing and finally attempts to evaluate a specific policy initiative by asking whether the initiative seems socially just. The question is answered in light of the particular political philosophies outlined in the chapter. One of the reasons for this approach is that it will, hopefully, open up discussion of how policy interventions can be evaluated in terms of their social justice outcomes. But it also highlights how policy interventions are already premised on assumptions that are rarely explicit in discussion of the problem or the solution and how these assumptions in themselves can create injustice.

Of course all human beings make assumptions about situations and events. It is part of the way we seem to make responses to situations that arise in our lives. One of the key factors in our immediate responses to events or incidents is where they take place. Does an incident of anti-social behaviour, for example, elicit a different response when it occurs outside an expensive bar in the City of London from when it occurs outside a pub in the East End? Are people in different places expected to invest similar amounts of time in their 'communities'? And, however we may respond quickly as individuals calling on our prejudices about places, do we really expect policy makers to devise policy on the basis of those prejudices about places?

Chapter 4 explores residential experience and the efforts of social policy to respond to or use that experience. Particularly, it focuses on the way 'popular perceptions of place…have influenced social policy interventions in Britain' (Cooper, this volume). Drawing on social theories of folk devils and moral panics (Cohen 1972) the chapter highlights how disadvantage can be seen as deviance and deviance can be seen as dangerous. This labelling in turn shapes the responses of policymakers, which sustain the social relations between the advantaged and the disadvantaged.

There was a time when this would have been described as a class issue. Although the demise of Eastern Bloc socialism temporarily undermined class analysis there has been a revival in discussion of class as a powerful way of understanding social structures and social status within those structures. Traditionally, class discussion was caricatured as a Marxist approach. An equally powerful analytical tool in social theory was the Weberian theory of class and class creation. Chapter 5 uses these contrasting ideas of class to understand changes in the housing system in Britain and the role of housing management in an increasingly managerialist environment where social policy is more about delivery than about objectives. Here it is important to understand the different class positions of the different actors and the roles they play in sustaining existing class relations.

Chapter 5 explores the continuing relevance of social class to discussions of housing and argues that housing and tenure play an important role in creating and sustaining class identity. Classical and contemporary social theory are drawn upon to support the argument. Furthermore, it is shown that class struggles, such as by Defend Council Housing, may still influence housing policy despite the alleged irrelevance of class in the modern world. The chapter ends with a consideration of class in the context of regeneration and sustainability policies affecting housing and neighbourhoods.

A logical continuation of this discussion about modern conceptions of class is a consideration, in Chapter 6, of the impact of social policy on ethnic minority groups, again focusing on housing. It has been argued that race issues are class issues. Whether or not this argument is accepted there is evidence of continuing disadvantage in the housing circumstances of ethnic minority households although the chapter argues that there have been substantial changes in that both the 'research and policy preoccupations differ from those of the past' (Harrison, this volume). Again issues of social sustainability arise and policies affecting ownership of housing in 'downmarket' areas are discussed. The chapter ends by highlighting the need to continue testing policy against likely differential impacts when implemented. This is a central element of evidence-based policy that has been developing in other policy areas such as health and should be introduced more widely.

Other key equality issues for housing and social policy are those of gender and disability, which are covered in Chapters 7 and 8. Chapter 7 addresses gendered housing needs and routes into homelessness as well as the potentially differential impact of recent housing and homelessness legislation. Arguing that housing has often not been central enough to social and welfare policy debates about gender, the chapter presents evidence of the increased housing needs of women resulting from traditional care roles and then demonstrates the impact of some policies on this set of housing needs.

Concentrating on homelessness and domestic violence the chapter draws on research to demonstrate the continued need for social housing provision of good quality to meet the needs of homeless women with children and women fleeing violence. Government policy has fluctuated rapidly in this area but has remained reluctant to grasp the nettle of the continuing need for social housing provision to meet emerging and continuing needs.

In Chapter 8, housing, disability and social policy issues are considered, concentrating on the changing role of design in meeting the needs of disabled people as understanding disability as a social policy issue changes. Important in these developments has been the role of groups in challenging the stereotypical assumptions of 'normality' and the impact this has had on design and services. Ultimately this is an issue of housing quality and 'inclusive' design. The historical development of understanding of the issues and changing policy responses ends with a discussion of the implications of the Disability Discrimination Act 1995.

The idea of government policy responding (or not responding) to changing needs and aspirations is explicit in most chapters. Chapter 9 considers a particular aspect of direct individual or collective response to the failure of policy initiatives to meet specific localised needs. Squatting has attracted a lot of journalistic attention from time to time as it is often presented as an activity that undermines social conventions and property contracts for ownership and occupancy. The discussion of squatting activity presented here adds to understanding of the variety of squatting movements and locates these movements within the context of recent social theory. While much of the latter argues against the continued relevance of class in the modern world (Beck 2003 and Giddens 1994 are cited as examples of this trend), the chapter demonstrates that squatting movements continue to have their roots in the material needs (such as for housing) that define class differences.

Government attempts to meet material needs for housing without substantial house-building programmes have tended to concentrate on 'urban regeneration'. Chapter 10 returns us to some of the broader themes and social policy issues that were raised at the start of this introduction. The fate of places, on whatever scale but especially at neighbourhood level, is determined by a range of factors in much the same way as the performance of housing markets is determined by the overall economy, wealth distribution, demographic change and so on. In fact the drivers are often the same, because the qualities of a particular locality for working in or sending children to school are very similar to the qualities affecting the demand for housing in that locality.

Urban regeneration policy developed as a result of the perceived failure of the housing led programmes of the 1970s and 1980s to change the fate of places in any lasting way. Renewing or replacing housing makes significant improvements to the local infrastructure but it tended not to create jobs for local people and was certainly not a long-term replacement for the loss of traditional industries. As a result some neighbourhoods have been 'regenerated' several times without creating the substantive shift in the quality of the social, economic and physical environment that was hoped for.

Urban regeneration programmes now attempt to concentrate on economic and social factors that led to or sustained decline in specific locations. Chapter 10 analyses this change in emphasis of social policy in regeneration and argues that housing has a central role. This chapter also provides another perspective on the government's communitarian agenda and its attempt to create participation and citizenship at the centre of 'community'. Lastly the chapter asks whether the experience of the individuals living in regeneration areas is the same 'holistic' experience as the policy makers and professionals are trying to deliver.

Chapter 11 concludes the book with a consideration of the achievements of New Labour housing policy both in its own terms, namely, the four main types of housing policy it designated, and in light of the contributions included here. In making the plea that 'the market must be made to work for the people, and not the other way round', the chapter indicates what we see as a fundamental failure of New Labour's extension of the Thatcherite project to replace 'policy' with 'markets'. That is, that policy becomes identified with what markets can provide, and meets the needs only of those who can access the market (which is by its nature exclusionary). Making markets work to achieve social benefits requires at least as much clarity and direction in social policy as making state provision work. The chapter attempts to provide such clarity by returning to the theme of social justice and considering how policy could be made to change so that people's needs would be better met.

Notes

1 In the Barker Review, the three countries with the highest average house price inflation are the countries with the highest levels of owner occupation (UK, Spain, Ireland) (Barker 2004).

References

Barker, K. (2003) *Review of Housing Supply: Securing our Future Housing Needs. Interim Report – Analysis*, London: HM Treasury/HMSO.
—— (2004) *Review of Housing Supply: Delivering Stability: Securing our Future Housing Needs*, London: HM Treasury/HMSO.
Beck, U. (2003) *Risk Society: Towards a New Modernity*, London: Sage Publications.

Clapham, D., Kemp, P. and Smith, S.J. (1990) *Housing and Social Policy*, London: Macmillan.

Cohen, S. (1972) *Folk Devils and Moral Panics*, London: Paladin.

Giddens, A. (1994) *Beyond Left and Right: The Future of Radical Politics*, Cambridge: Polity Press.

Hamnett, C. (1999) *Winners and Losers: Home Ownership in Modern Britain*, London: UCL Press.

Hutson, S. and Clapham, D. (ed.) (1999) *Homelessness: Public Policies and Private Troubles*, London: Cassell.

Kennett, P. and Marsh, A. (eds) (1999) *Homelessness: Exploring the New Terrain*, Bristol: Policy Press.

Lowe, S. (2004) *Housing Policy Analysis: British Housing in Cultural and Comparative Context*, London: Palgrave.

Maclennan, D. (1994) *A Competitive UK Economy: The Challenges for Housing Policy*, York: Joseph Rowntree Foundation.

Malpass, P. and Murie, A. (1999) *Housing Policy and Practice*, 5th edn, Basingstoke: Macmillan.

Massey, D. (1995) *Spatial Divisions of Labour: Social Structures and the Geography of Production*, 2nd edn, Basingstoke: Macmillan.

Nevin, B., Lee, P., Goodson, L., Murie, A. and Phillimore, J. (1999) *Changing Housing Markets and Urban Regeneration in the M62 Corridor*, Birmingham: CURS/University of Birmingham.

Office of the Deputy Prime Minister (ODPM) (2002) *Sustainable Communities: Building for the Future*, London: HMSO.

Walsh, K. (1995) *Public Services and Market Mechanisms: Competition, Contracting and the New Public Management*, Basingstoke: Macmillan.

2 What has the state ever done for us?

A review of the state's role in influencing the UK's housing market 1800 to 2003

Bill Spink

Introduction

Housing, unlike health, education and the benefits system, does not readily appear to rely on the commitment and contribution of the state to ensure its provision and distribution, so it is easy to minimise the state's contribution to Britain's housing situation. Whereas health, education, benefits, etc., continue to be provided primarily by the state, albeit with an increasing contribution by the private sector in distributing these services, housing is largely left to the market to provide. As Lansley suggested:

> [housing] … contrasts with other areas of social policy such as education and health where governments have adopted a much more comprehensive and embracing approach. Housing hovers somewhat unhappily between the status of a social service and a private good.
>
> (Lansley 1979: 17)

In 2004 perhaps only those who live in council houses will acknowledge that the state has had any direct involvement in the way in which they are housed; a few more may, perhaps, recognise that they are able to meet the rent of their accommodation through the benefits system. However, when one investigates the way in which we live a little deeper, it becomes apparent that the majority of families have, in some way, directly benefited from the state's intervention into the unfettered operation of the market. The purpose of this chapter is to dig a little deeper so as to demonstrate the impact of government policy on almost all aspects of the nation's housing – the quantity, quality, location, cost and tenure of our homes. Whilst the diminishing number of dwellings owned and let by local authorities may still be the most obvious example of state action, this chapter highlights the fact that the housing situation of remarkably few of us has been untouched by some aspect of the government's social and/or economic policy. Historically, the state's role has gone much further than a direct intervention, via the local authorities, of building council homes: it has influenced both the supply of housing and the demand for various forms of housing; it has directly involved itself in where new homes may be built and has determined the standards to which they will be built; it has offered financial inducements to people to build, to modernise or convert their homes; and it has provided financial aid to individuals to enable them to access accommodation and continue to meet their accommodation costs once they have settled.

Figure 2.1 shows the way that housing numbers and tenure have developed during the last 100 years or so. From this, one can identify two remarkable features: the overall number of dwellings has more than doubled and the tenure of our housing has changed dramatically. Whereas for centuries beforehand rented housing was the tenure of the average family the growth of home-ownership during the twentieth century has resulted in this tenure becoming the 'norm', with over two-thirds of the population now being owner occupiers. Despite the enormous direct contribution by the state in the form of council housing, adding over six million new dwellings to the nation's stock during the twentieth century, by the beginning of the twenty-first century the number of rented homes stood at a lower level than a century before.

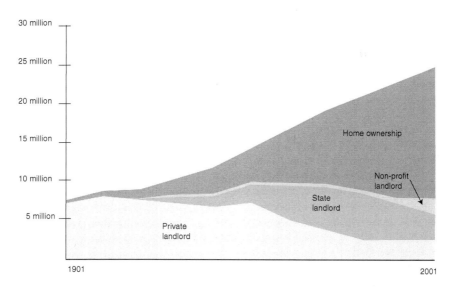

2.1 Tenure trends in Great Britain 1901 to 2001 (derived from a variety of census data)

Although government policies have played a considerable role in shaping these outcomes, this role has not always been quite that which was intended. As Hill (1983) has indicated, some social policy may not be introduced with welfare objectives in mind, and some government activity, for example in economic policy, may have a significant impact on welfare and individual well-being. Clapham *et al.* (1990) recognise that housing policy may be considered, simply, part of economic policy in that it is concerned with issues of quantity, quality, and cost, but they counter this view by indicating that state intervention in the housing field is multi-faceted and that housing policy should be regarded as:

> ... any form of intervention in housing production, distribution or consumption that affects the location, character and availability of homes, or the rights associated with housing occupancy – irrespective of the ownership of property, land or the means of production.
>
> (Clapham *et al.* 1990: x)

Therefore, this chapter reviews some of the major interventions and impacts of state action on the supply of, or demand for, housing regardless of whether the policy outcomes were, necessarily, intended to be 'housing policies'. Taking this approach enables a critical analysis, from a variety of perspectives, of the rationale behind state action.

The first part of this chapter is largely descriptive and offers a review of some of the major interventions by the state that have impacted on housing supply or demand. Later on, some of the reasons why the government may act and why certain approaches may be adopted will be discussed. However, before attempting to identify both the justification for action and evaluating the impact of that action, it may be helpful to establish the broad parameters within which the state may attempt to intervene.

Doling (1997) has suggested that 'one way of looking at policies is to regard them as attempts by governments to bring about changes in the behaviour of all or some actors, be they private individuals or organizations such as firms' and goes on to define six broad forms of strategic approach – non-action; exhortation; regulation; taxation; subsidy; and provision – each of which offers a different form of approach for government. However, Doling emphasises that, whilst each is very different from the others, 'they are not mutually exclusive and, in practice, are often implemented in combinations' (Doling 1997: 40).

In each of Doling's policy approaches (other, of course, than non-intervention) the state has the option of intervening in order to influence either the supply of housing (by seeking to increase the quantity and/or quality of housing) or by taking action to affect demand (by aiding or influencing individuals to access housing). During the last 200 years we have seen each of these approaches (that Doling identifies) being used by a government at one time or another, either individually or in combination with other policies. A further influence on the state's choice of intervention is the ease and cost of their policy choice. At the planning stage the overall cost of each policy option must be considered in the context of other government policies, particularly in respect of taxation and overall public spending, and against any ideological concerns over the role of both public and private sector. We can, therefore, further categorise the state's policy options in terms of the actual level of intervention – does a policy involve a heavy commitment to funding and /or high levels of administration to deliver or police? The different policy options are summarised in Table 2.1.

It is important to note that this typology is intended only as a convenient means of classification, and its use does not indicate allegiance to any particular theoretical perspective. Examples of each of the forms of intervention will now be reviewed in turn and their contribution to the current form of the nation's accommodation identified.

Non-intervention

Without the involvement of the state, the supply of housing and access to it is totally reliant on the market, with some additional numbers being achieved via self-provision or by contributions from philanthropists. This is the situation that existed in the UK until the mid-nineteenth century, often referred to as the 'laissez-faire' approach to housing. Such a non-interventionist approach is one in which the government literally 'leaves it be' and does not intervene in the market in any form. In this approach, new supply relies upon individuals either constructing their own homes or paying someone else to do this for them.

Table 2.1 Policy options available to the state (after Doling 1997)

Supply side interventions	Non-intervention *Demand side interventions*

Low level intervention:
    Exhortation
    Regulation (via control,
        planning and taxation)
	Low level intervention:
	    Exhortation (i.e. consumerist
	        policies)
	    Regulation (via taxation and
	        citizens' rights)

Middle level intervention:
    Tax allowances for producers
    Subsidies to producers
	Middle level intervention:
	    Tax allowances for purchasers
	    Grants and subsidies for
	    purchasers

High level intervention:
    State provision
    Overall state control of markets
	High level intervention:
	    Individual financial aid packages
	    (i.e. rebates and housing benefit)

During much of the UK's history this is exactly how the government dealt with housing – it was a matter for the individual who might be able to gain assistance from others (family, co-operative, employer, church or charity) in obtaining a home. Whether this attitude, of non-intervention, was as a result of some formal consideration by government is a matter for conjecture – if the government deliberately chose not to intervene in the housing market then one must consider this a policy. However, it seems more likely that those who formed the government of the time never regarded housing as an issue for the state to consider, though the ownership and use of land was an issue for some time before any form of housing intervention. Only after the turn of the nineteenth century were there signs that housing might be a matter that concerned government, and a debate began to emerge as to both whether the state should intervene and, if it does, how it might act.

The reasons for this apparent indifference prior to the nineteenth century are relatively straightforward; Britain's economic and urban development had been slow and the power held by landowners was substantial. The UK economy was, initially, based on agriculture and the population had grown relatively slowly, from around 2 million at the time of the Norman Conquest to around 5 million at the turn of the seventeenth century. Decisions made by parliament recognised the interests of the parliamentarians and their electorate – for to be a politician or an elector you had to be an adult male landowner. It can, therefore, come as no surprise that the major role of the state was seen to be security and defence so as to maintain the status quo in the UK and protect national interests in the new commonwealth that its merchants explored.

This status quo was, however, disturbed by the operation of market forces. Advances in technology facilitated the industrialisation of production and had a dramatic impact on both the form and location of employment during the eighteenth and nineteenth centuries. The old cottage industries and smallholdings were replaced as the former agrarian economy rapidly switched to a more urban centred, wage oriented system in which factories were created in locations where convenient power sources and raw materials existed. Whilst some of the new factory areas were established around existing towns, cities and labour markets, many more sprang up wherever the entrepreneur found it convenient. New towns and cities were created as entrepreneurs built their factories and adjacent housing to accommodate their workers whilst others speculated by building homes for rent or by establishing businesses to serve the newly arriving population.

The problems encountered during this period of laissez-faire are well illustrated by a number of texts (for a detailed description, see Burnett 1980). Without state intervention property owners were free to utilise their land and property in any form that they wished. During the eighteenth and nineteenth centuries houses were built on land as a speculative venture in order to provide rented homes for the factory workers who needed to be close to their source of employment. In other cases the factory owners built homes for their workers as part of their total development. The motive for much of this development was profit. In very few cases was any real consideration given to either the longer-term adequacy of the development or its effect on the general environment.

Consequently, although there were a number of notable exceptions during the nineteenth century (the model dwellings movement, the industrial philanthropists and, later, the five-percent philanthropists), much of the housing created during the period of laissez-faire was of very poor quality, lacking in any of the facilities which we now regard as essential, and usually crowded together in order to maximise land use. In addition, as the owner of each plot of land was free to determine the use to which the land was put, the resulting development was often a mixture of houses and industry/commerce, with no planning of streets, sewers, water supply etc.

Despite the dangers of such an environment, pollution and contagion, disease, high mortality rates, and almost non-existent health care, the population continued to expand and the availability of waged employment attracted a substantial number of immigrants, particularly from Ireland. The state's role had, by now, expanded to provide basic measures to alleviate absolute poverty by way of the Poor Laws (dating from 1601) and the operation of the Speenhamland Justices' Act, but the complete lack of building and sanitary standards provided an environment that encouraged the spread of disease. Cholera arrived in 1831 and the government finally found it necessary to intervene by giving itself the power to compulsorily enter into any home in order to cleanse and fumigate (Cholera Act 1832). From this time the state became increasingly involved in the way that its citizens lived. However, the forms of intervention have varied over time.

Looking back on the period of laissez faire, given the existence at the time of both a tax and an electoral base in which a small minority of the population (property owners) played a predominant part, it is not really surprising that governments did not intervene in the housing market. However, should there have been a desire to intervene, the implementation and administration of any policy would have posed severe problems to the limited and varied nature of local administration that existed at the time.

Supply side intervention

(1) Low level intervention – exhortation and regulation

The UK's experiences during the nineteenth and twentieth centuries demonstrate the problems connected with the adoption of a non-interventionist approach. Although the state accepted no moral or financial responsibility for housing and public health it became clear (as suggested by Merrett 1979: 29) that this laissez faire approach contained the seeds of its own destruction. Simply 'sitting back' and allowing an unfettered free market to operate presents a number of problems, not least those caused by the predominance of decision-making by private individuals based on short-term self-interest over any longer-term considerations of a more general public interest. Thus the rapid urban expansion was fuelled by the potential for short-term profits for individuals at the possible expense of longer-term public health issues for a wider population.

The reasons for lack of state intervention before the mid-nineteenth century were the absences not only of any real commitment by the nation's leaders but also of any comprehensive administrative structure to oversee and implement an interventionist policy. Furthermore, any form of intervention required public expenditure and this had to be funded from tax income – drawn largely from the same property owners as were eligible to elect the state's leaders and who owned much of the property with which the regulation would be concerned.

It is not, therefore, surprising that the very earliest interventions by the state could be described as *exhortation*, in which the efforts of individuals and voluntary bodies to produce better accommodation were championed by the state. Philanthropists such as Robert Owen, who, with David Dale, had established a new 'model' community at New Lanark during the last decade of the eighteenth century, had shown what could be done and their philosophies inspired others (such as Ackroyd, Cadbury, Lever, and Salt) to develop further communities during the next century. The examples that these 'industrial philanthropists' set were further developed by a series of voluntary bodies such as the Society for Improving the Condition of the Labouring Classes (formed in 1844), and other builders of 'model dwellings', and their ideals were championed by a number of prominent politicians of the time – some such as Ackroyd, Shaftesbury, and Waterlow being actively involved in some of the development. However, whilst exhortation cost the state nothing, only the rich could afford to make meaningful charitable contributions, and some of the industrial philanthropists may have had more pragmatic objectives (economic or political) than simply seeking to improve living standards (see Spink 1998). Potential housing suppliers were offered improved alternatives to what had come to be accepted as the norm but there was little incentive to encourage them to spend extra money to adopt better standards.

Perhaps the most basic form of state intervention is one of *regulation*, and this provides some of the earliest examples of government intervening in the supply of housing. In its most basic form, regulation involves the state, at either national or local level, setting minimum standards and attempting to ensure that providers adhere to these. Such regulation may be promoted through voluntary codes of practice or through a legally enforceable structure in which house builders and/or house owners are required to comply with state-set minimum standards for both housing construction and the built environment. The advantage of such an approach is that the financial responsibility for meeting the state-set standards rests entirely with the private builder and/or owner rather than with the general taxpayer whose financial commitment is restricted to funding the enforcement process. The major disadvantages of such a system are the problem of funding and administering the enforcement process and the fact that the builder passes on the extra cost to the end user of the dwelling.

Commencing around 1850, the earliest examples of state regulation of housing standards were those introduced to deal with the worst effects of the overcrowded and insanitary conditions resulting from unfettered urban expansion. However, the first attempts by the state to intervene in an attempt to set minimum standards were not universally supported:

> In our condition suffering and evil are nature's admonitions; they cannot be got rid of; and the impatient attempts of benevolence to banish them from the world by legislation, before benevolence has learned their object and their end, have always been productive of more evil than good.
>
> (*The Economist* 1848 cited by Merrett 1979: 9)

Nevertheless, despite the vested interests of many of its representatives in property ownership, the government passed the Public Health Act 1848, which required certain minimum standards of layout, design and building standards.

Although the new approach was often patchily introduced and enforced, it did begin the process that is today reflected in planning legislation and in Building Regulations that prevent landowners doing whatever they wish with their property. The early 'model byelaws', introduced by local Boards of Health and local authorities, enabled these bodies to refuse the construction of new dwellings unless they were built to an acceptable standard and allowed for the width of roadways and sanitary facilities to be considered by the enforcing body. For the first time, commencing in 1848, the state took on the responsibility of limiting land owners' rights in the longer-term interests of the nation, though whether this intervention was to protect the individual from exploitation and/or disease, whether it was to ensure that employers had a supply of healthy labour, or whether it was to protect the law makers (from revolution or disease) is debatable.

Subsequently, over the next twenty years or so, the state gave itself significantly greater powers, via the Shaftesbury, Cross and Torrens Acts, to deal with housing by removing the very worst of the existing stock through clearance and closure policies. Many of these approaches went further than regulation (see below).

Another form of regulation is rent control. Here, the state's role is one of specifying the maximum levels of rent that landlords can charge. The cost to the taxpayer is, as with the regulation of housing quality, limited to that of enforcing the process, with landlords having to meet the cost of any difference between the permitted maximum rent and the actual cost of provision. As shown below, the introduction of such a policy in the UK came about partly as a consequence of the state's earlier intervention in relation to the quality of housing.

During the last half of the nineteenth century increasing regulation by the state improved the standard of new homes but also pushed up their cost – better quality houses built to a lower density meant that builders needed to charge more simply to 'break even'. An expanding population and the impact of the closure or demolition of the worst housing led to increased demand for new, better, housing whilst increasing wage rates, for a time, meant that workers could afford the rents required by landlords. By the beginning of the twentieth century, however, economic recession resulted in wage rates failing to keep up with other costs and fewer families could now afford the rents charged on new properties. Consequently, demand for new housing fell and supply dropped correspondingly, as money was directed towards investment opportunities that could produce a better financial return. As the supply of new properties diminished, landlords of existing properties found that their dwellings were in greater demand and sought to increase rents accordingly.

What finally triggered government action was the rise of profiteering by private landlords in the First World War. Consequently, the Rent and Mortgage Restrictions Act was passed in 1915, effectively preventing any further increase in either rents or mortgage interest rates for the duration of the war. This intervention broke new ground in seeking to limit the price that could be demanded by a property owner. Many changes have since been made to the system, and several governments have tried to extricate themselves from this form of intervention, but the principle, that the state can intervene in setting the level of rents charged, has continued, in some form, to this day. Now, however, rent control affects only a few longer serving tenants, via the benefits system.

In conclusion, state encouragement to providers to implement improvements to both the quantity and quality of the nation's dwellings does not necessarily conflict with free market principles and, to a certain extent, is still based on the concept of demand as a measure of acceptance. In contrast, regulation imposes state control over the operation of housing markets by determining, on behalf of the individual, what is acceptable and what is not acceptable. However, regulation also requires the state to monitor and administer the rules and, therefore, involves a bureaucracy to oversee its operation. The cost of such state intervention must be borne by both the taxpayer and the end-user of the property (perhaps the same person), as taxes must be raised to fund the monitoring and enforcement process, and the provider needs to pass on the increased costs of compliance to the consumer in order to stay in business. Additionally, the regulation process is a 'negative' policy in that it prevents the worst excesses of the market (and so discourages some providers from becoming or staying involved) but does nothing positively to encourage the adoption of new practices.

(2) Middle level intervention – state aid to production

If the state wishes to create more accommodation of a better standard, it needs to introduce something that will encourage specific action rather than just inhibit alternative activity. If regulation is the 'stick' that punishes a failure to conform, the introduction of state aid can be seen to be the 'carrot' that is offered to induce co-operation. Many countries have found that, in order to ensure that the market produces goods that the state deems to be necessary to achieve its social, economic or even political objectives, then it needs to become more actively involved in managing the process. The introduction of state aid to encourage producers/ suppliers to do what the state requires represents a substantial increase in the state's role as well as dramatically increasing its costs. However, such an approach may still be regarded as cheaper (to the taxpayer) than the state doing the job itself. Offering inducements to producers/suppliers may also be regarded as more acceptable to those opposed to state intervention than taking supply out of the hands of the private sector altogether. Such inducements can involve either grants or subsidies to housing suppliers (land owners, builders, developers and/or landlords) in order to encourage them to act in a specific fashion, or amendments to the provider's tax situation by allowing certain activities to be set against tax or taxed at a more advantageous rate.

In the UK the state's earliest involvement in direct aid packages to housing suppliers came at the conclusion of the First World War and was a direct response to the problem caused by the lack of new building. One-off grants were offered to builders prepared to construct new housing to the same standards as those expected of housing that local councils had begun building at that time (see next section). As a result of the Housing (Additional Powers) Act 1919 private builders, who committed themselves to building new homes to the standards set by the Tudor Walters Committee, could claim a one-off lump sum of between £130 and £160, whether the house was to be subsequently sold or rented. Although this system was later abandoned it set a precedent for later action. Subsequent legislation allowed the payment of Exchequer subsidies to private builders in line with those being paid to local authorities for developing their own housing. The Housing Act 1923 provided local authorities with a subsidy of £6 per dwelling per year payable for twenty years, and a one-off lump sum payable to private builders of £75 was considered to represent the net present value of the local authority's subsidy.

Similar incentives have continued since the early twentieth century, with central and local government initiatives being directed at encouraging action, not just in house-building, but also in employment creation and business expansion, by the payment of grants and subsidies or by the making available of inexpensive land and premises to attract the sort of development that the state (locally or nationally) desired. Perhaps the most obvious example of the use of such aid packages to encourage housing development can be seen in the expansion of the housing association movement, which is now responsible for well over a million dwellings.

The housing association movement traces its roots back to the philanthropists who provided housing for the less fortunate on charitable grounds. For many years these voluntary or charitable bodies were eligible for state loans at preferential rates, but their contribution to new housing provision was small. With the passing of the Housing Act 1974, however, the government committed itself to funding much of the cost of housing association development, and the movement expanded rapidly (see Cope 1999 and Malpass 2000). This Act introduced substantial building grants calculated to reduce the association's loan repayments to a level that could be funded by rents, and these rents were, themselves, limited to a 'fair rent' set by one of the state's Rent Officers. From the 1970s the housing association movement has been increasingly regarded as the main provider of new social housing and, despite significant changes in their funding systems resulting from the Housing Act 1988, their contribution to the nation's housing continues to grow. However, this growth is at a cost: forced to find significantly larger amounts of money themselves in order to fund their activities, associations have had to substantially increase rents, and many smaller, specialist organisations have had to merge with larger and richer associations. At the same time, new associations are still being formed in order to receive housing transferred from an increasing number of local authorities.

Whether the housing association movement should be regarded as part of the state apparatus or whether it is truly independent (as the 1987 White Paper indicated) is contentious – certainly the majority of associations were set up by volunteers under no formal pressure to do so. However, the housing associations that have been established in recent times to take control of property transferred from local councils clearly owe their existence to state action, as do many of the other associations established since 1974. Even those bodies that date from before the introduction of state aid probably owe their continuing existence to the availability of substantial amounts of public money to support their development. Consequently, although a much smaller proportion of housing is now provided directly by the state, the government maintains control over its development and management via the state-established and funded Housing Corporation, which monitors each housing association's performance and only approves new projects and channels funds toward activities that comply with the government's policy objectives.

(3) High level intervention – state provision and state control

Undoubtedly, the state's most dramatic and obvious intervention in the housing field is through direct provision – by acquiring land and building new homes or by acquiring property for clearance, development, refurbishment or rent. Whilst many governments have accepted responsibility for removing the worst of the slums, few have embarked on the building of so many state-owned dwellings as did the UK during the twentieth century. Whilst the cost of direct intervention in supplying dwellings is considerable this approach may be perceived by government as being the only way in which it can both maintain control over the process of meeting its intended objectives and reap the full political advantage from providing much needed new housing.

Whilst most western nations followed the path of offering financial aid to 'socially acceptable' developers who operate separately from the state (similar to the UK's housing association system), the UK chose, beginning in 1919, to develop housing directly by harnessing the resources of the local authorities in each area.

> Local authorities, who already had experience of implementing public health measures, were seen by the central state as easier to control than private or voluntary sector organisations.
>
> (Burden *et al.* 2000: 168)

Despite strong opposition from supporters of the free market and existing property owners, the government first sanctioned local authorities to subsidise the building of new houses for rent towards the end of the nineteenth century and then, in 1919, effectively required them to do this. Whilst the Housing of the Working Classes Act 1890 allowed local councils to build, the so-called Addison Act of 1919 required each local authority to take on the responsibility of reviewing the housing needs of its area and submitting proposals to respond to these needs. Perhaps, most importantly, the 1919 Act also provided substantial financial support for each local council's house building programme. This subsidised building programme, coupled with the earlier regulation of rents and building in the private sector, marked a significant trend in housing policy and one that proved difficult for successive governments to abandon (see Malpass and Murie 1999: 36).

Although changes in the subsidy levels and changes in emphasis (building for general needs or to respond to some other perceived problem such as overcrowding, unfit housing, special needs etc.) occurred at regular intervals, what started in 1919 continued for over fifty years. The principle of this policy was that local authorities were encouraged to resolve local housing problems by building affordable housing for rent, with the cost of this venture being shared between the tenants, central government (i.e. all tax payers) and the local authority (i.e. local rate payers). By 1979 around 6.5 million dwellings had been built by local authorities (representing around a third of all the nation's dwellings at that time). However, by the end of the 1960s, the cost of funding council housing (and other areas of social policy) was becoming problematic, and changes in the subsidy system brought about a reduction in the role played by council housing. The Conservatives' Housing Finance Act 1972 instigated a major change in the way in which the sector was funded. In response to criticisms that tenants were being subsidised unnecessarily, the previous building subsidies, which provided a contribution towards the cost of each new dwelling, were withdrawn and replaced with one based on a formula calculated on the local authority's notional income and expenditure. Although the impact of this subsidy system was delayed by the election of a Labour government in 1974, the principle, that a rent would be fixed for the property and that tenants could claim a personal subsidy (see later) in order to help meet that cost, remains to this day.

Although the state's contribution to the nation's housing stock by way of council housing is probably the most visible element of its direct intervention there are a number of other examples such as compulsory purchase powers, which have enabled it to undertake substantial slum clearance and redevelopment or urban renewal schemes, and the postwar state-led New Towns programme.

As mentioned above, one of the state's earliest housing interventions was concerned with the standard of fitness of both individual and groups of dwellings. As early as the 1860s various parts of the state structure were given power to determine which dwellings were allowed to remain and to take action in removing those that it considered unfit. Although early state action was minimal and can be regarded as forming part of the negative 'regulatory' approach, by the 1930s the system of slum clearance had developed so as to require the replacement of those dwellings removed. Local councils throughout Great Britain created large estates during the 1930s, 1950s and 1960s to house the families displaced by town centre slum clearance schemes. Whilst the rehousing schemes of the 1930s and early 1950s were often based on replacing town centre terraced housing with new traditional housing located on large suburban estates, by the end of the 1950s substantial emphasis was being placed on the use of 'non-traditional' housing built on a variety of sites using industrialised building techniques.

Most examples of state intervention in housing supply are to do with supplementing or regulating the market. Between 1945 and 1951, however, faced with the need not only to build the new welfare state but also to rebuild the nation's dwellings, towns and economy after the war, the incoming Labour government chose to go further and take control of most private development to ensure that their plans could be met (see Harloe 1995: 283). This period saw the birth of state planning, the New Towns programme and, for a short while, the over-riding of individual rights in the 'national interest'.

Alongside rationing of food and other household products the government introduced the rationing of land and building licences so as to ensure that the dwellings it was producing were not delayed because of competition for labour, land or materials. Not only were these restrictions intended to protect the state's construction from delays but also to avoid the inflationary problems that had beset house building after the First World War, which were caused by the huge competition for scarce resources and the open-ended subsidy provided to local authorities at that time. This time the state had first choice of almost everything and the private builder was allowed to use scarce resources only when the local authority did not require them.

The New Towns programme is a good example of the state taking control, at national and local levels, in order to identify needs and meet them in a planned and controlled way. The programme aimed to provide additional accommodation in specific locations as part of a planned redistribution of both industry and population. In response to the reports of Barlow, Uthwatt, Scott and, later, Reith, the government introduced the New Towns Act in 1946, enabling it to establish and fund a total of twenty-eight Development Corporations, in various parts of the country, to acquire land and construct new communities. Many of these (for example, Crawley, Hemel Hempstead, Harlow, and later Basildon, Welwyn, Bracknell, Hatfield and Stevenage) were to alleviate the continuing expansion of London, which was to be enclosed by a 'Green Belt', and to offer a new place for Londoners to live and work. Subsequently, others such as Corby, Glenrothes, Peterlee, Cwmbran, Skelmersdale and Milton Keynes, were created in other parts of the country to provide alternatives to the existing cities. In the initial stages the transfer of industry to the New Towns was achieved by preventing the establishment of new, or the expansion of old, industries in the existing cities and the provision of incentives to encourage their transfer to the newer towns. By the 1980s almost all of the original Development Corporations had been wound up and their assets transferred to local councils, housing associations and/or private bodies. Currently, however, these settlements provide approximately half a million homes for around 2 million people.

Notwithstanding such policy successes, policies of direct intervention or overall state control have never enjoyed high levels of public or political support. This is because, although they seek either to mitigate failures in local or national housing and economic markets or to stimulate new private sector activity, they place the state's role in direct conflict with the free operation of markets and involve considerable public expenditure, thus imposing a considerable burden on the taxpayer and restrictions on individual freedom.

Demand side intervention

So far we have examined the role that the state can play in influencing the quantity and quality of housing provision and have identified a number of policies adopted by the state during the last century and a half. Perhaps less dramatically, the state has also played a significant role in shaping the demand for housing during the same period and has continued to regulate the activities of individual occupiers through planning and building regulation legislation similar to that affecting housing providers. Although there have been few, if any, interventions explicitly designed to increase or reduce the overall demand for housing, the state has, increasingly over the latter part of the twentieth century, sought to influence demand for certain types of housing – specifically targeting home-ownership.

Ironically, policy interventions that are *not* explicitly concerned with housing demand can have a more dramatic impact on that demand. For example, in seeking to control the economy and to fix levels of taxation and public spending, the state's activities may impact on the amount of money available to individuals and families that they might then spend on their accommodation. Furthermore, government financial policies can have a strong influence on the level of rents charged and the price demanded for house purchase as well as on the maintenance costs of the occupiers.

The growth of owner-occupation to its present majority status in the UK has relied heavily on the government's economic and tax policies during the twentieth century, though it was not until the middle of that century that some of these policies were deliberately manipulated to promote home-ownership and/or to assist existing owners (see next section). Nevertheless, successive governments since the last war have consistently promoted home-ownership and the sheer size of the sector now means that no government can afford to ignore the demands of homeowners. Consequently, many of the state's interventions into the market have been not only to bring about change in line with the governing party's objectives but also to meet the requirements of the majority of electors. This has often taken the form of ensuring that funds are available, at a price that can be afforded, to allow people to purchase their own homes. This indicates a government acting either to protect its citizens or to stimulate them to act in a specific way.

(1) Low level intervention – consumerist policies and regulation

In responding to demand for accommodation, the state can seek to influence supply, as already discussed, but it can also directly influence demand for specific forms of housing in a variety of ways. Gibb *et al.* (1991) suggest that there are eight key determinants of housing demand in respect of home-ownership. These are: the price of owner-occupied housing; disposable household income; credit/mortgage availability; interest rate on mortgage repayments; household formation and other relevant demographic factors such as household composition, age and so on; location relative to work/travel to work costs; the price of close substitutes (such as private or public renting); and tastes and preferences for different forms of housing, location and so on (Gibb *et al.* 1991: 28). Two other possible determinants are: the rate at which house prices change, which can encourage or discourage new entrants to the market; and the quality of the alternatives to home ownership, which can push people towards owner-occupation or attract them away from it.

Whilst the state's influence on such things as household formation and tastes and preferences may be relatively tenuous, governments have sought to control, direct and influence all of the other determinants – often to promote home-ownership over and above other tenures. Family and taxation policies (such as child benefit, allowances for young people, etc.), and the language used by governments, may also influence household composition and tenure preferences, particularly as policies that encourage the demand for home-ownership also encourage the inflation of house values.

Since the 1940s, an increasing number of financial policies have been adopted that have sought to encourage or assist demand for home-ownership, on the assumption that home-ownership is 'most satisfying to the individual and the most beneficial to the nation' (MHLG 1953), and that it is best to allow individuals to spend their money as they wish. Some tax policies may be directed towards housing, and are dealt with in the next sub-section, whilst others may have another primary purpose but also have an overall impact on the individual's housing choices.

Just as tax and other policies can influence demand, so can state regulation of building standards, design, location and/or pricing. For example, if higher standards are required in one tenure than in another, the former tenure may become more attractive. Historically, this may have happened in the case of council housing, as a result of the higher design standards of Tudor Walters (1920s and 1930s), Dudley (1940s and 1950s) and Parker Morris (1960s and 1970s). However, government saw the use of such standards as a model for the private sector to follow rather than as a means to increase demand for council accommodation.

A number of interventions have impacted on the relative decline in popularity of council housing and the corresponding increase in the desirability of alternatives. The drive to increase rents, for example, coupled with the reduction and redirection of spending on council housing, have reduced its attractiveness to the general public and encouraged existing tenants to seek alternatives. Governments have manipulated the regulations that permit spending on social housing, resulting in institutional discrimination against council housing itself. This has resulted in huge transfers of council housing to private individuals (mainly through right to buy), private companies and housing associations.

Another way in which the state has influenced demand is by granting citizens certain rights such as contained within the various citizens' charters that emanated from the Major governments of the 1990s. The earliest example is that of the 'Tenants' Charter', originally proposed by the 1970s Labour government and introduced, with a number of amendments, by the Thatcher government as part of the Housing Act 1980. However, there are other examples of citizens' rights in a housing context. Some of the state's earliest interventions imply the acquisition of rights by some, if not all, citizens. The National Assistance Act 1948, for example, although it gave no rights to housing as such, placed obligations on the state to ensure that 'dependent people' were cared for. The Housing (Homeless Persons) Act 1977 did grant rights to accommodation, but only in certain specified circumstances (see Smith, this volume). Other important rights include the right to an improvement grant (see below) and the right to buy.

(2) Middle level intervention – tax allowances and grants for purchasers

Whilst exhortation may influence people to consider certain actions, and regulation may confer certain rights and/or may curtail others, direct state action, such as offering financial incentives, can have a significant impact on behaviour. As has been said, most attempts to influence demand have been designed, not to influence overall demand for housing, but to promote demand for one tenure rather than another. In general, home-ownership has been the beneficiary of more such policy interventions than have other tenures.

For a complex array of reasons home ownership became more attractive during the twentieth century and, by the mid-1960s, had become the majority tenure. As the majority of homeowners are only able to gain access to this tenure by borrowing money, the cost and availability of mortgages has been a considerable concern for the state and the control of mortgage interest rates has been an important part of any government's policy. For many years the state sought to influence the mortgage market by working in conjunction with mortgage lenders to keep funds available at agreed levels and by differential tax rates that favoured investment in housing over and above other areas.

Perhaps the most influential example is that of home owners being able to set the interest on their mortgage against tax so that they could reduce their tax bill by borrowing money to buy a home. This policy dates back to when income tax was introduced over 200 years ago, with mortgage interest tax relief being restricted to the tiny minority of the population who actually had mortgages. It was only in the latter part of the twentieth century, however, that this benefit became financially and politically important, with almost every government planning their policies around its preservation or even expansion. At its peak in 1990–1991 the cost of the benefit amounted to £7.7 billion in foregone tax. To put this figure into context, during the same year the state's total outlay on housing benefit to all tenants was slightly more than £5 billion (see Wilcox 2000: 204–213). Rising demand for home-ownership, coupled with house price and interest rate inflation, fuelled the cost of this benefit and, finally, during the 1980s steps were taken to curb its cost to the state. Initially, relief was restricted to the basic rate of tax (then 25 pence in the pound) and to a fixed amount of mortgage (the first £30,000) but, after several years during which relief became a diminishing proportion of the total mortgage, it was finally withdrawn at the end of the 1990s.

The impact of mortgage interest tax relief on the growth of home ownership and house prices was substantial. In addition, continuing talk by government ministers and White Papers, about home-ownership fulfilling a 'basic and natural desire' and about the 'creation of a property owning democracy', has emphasised the lack of attractiveness of alternative tenures. The continuing residualisation of the council sector as a safety net for those who cannot afford anything better, coupled with the insecurity and cost of private renting – all products of government policies – have succeeded in conveying the message that home-ownership is the tenure of choice.

A further intervention that strongly influenced the level of home-ownership in the UK was the introduction, in the 1980 Housing Act, of the right to buy, which gave virtually all council tenants and many housing association tenants the right to purchase their rented home from their landlord. This right was supported by rights to substantial discounts and mortgages. Subsequent legislation increased the levels of discount but removed the absolute right to a mortgage.

Discounts now commence at 32 per cent, for tenants with at least two years' qualifying tenancy (not necessarily in their present home), and rise to 60 per cent for those with at least 30 years' qualifying tenancies. There is a much higher rate of discount for tenants buying flats (starting at 44 per cent and rising, after 15 years, to 70 per cent). Murie (1998: 90) notes that, for purchasers, 'the experience of purchase under the Right to Buy has generally been a good one.' The majority of purchasers have bought the better houses in the most popular areas and their financial commitment has been much less than that of other first-time buyers (see Nationwide Anglia Building Society 1990), whilst the rent paid by their neighbours has outstripped their own mortgage repayments. Since 1980 around two million council dwellings throughout the UK have been sold to their former tenants, many of whom continue to live in the same home (DTLR 2002: 32 noted that, in England, 1.1 million households were still living in properties they had purchased under the right to buy).

This policy had a marked effect on public sector finances. The income from council house sales provided £2.2 billion (ODPM factsheet – http://www.odpm.gov. uk/stellent/groups/odpm_housing/documents/page/odpm_house_601844.hcsp) to be set against public expenditure, and represents the largest ever privatisation return. This has enabled the state to finance other projects without having to raise taxes. Initially, councils were allowed, even encouraged, to re-invest the capital receipts that they accumulated from the sale of dwellings, but the rules concerning the use of such receipts were steadily tightened during the 1980s. This resulted in almost no new building to replace the lost stock but, in some areas, these funds were applied to the rehabilitation of the remaining stock. In many areas the income from council house sales has been used to repay debts incurred in the building of council houses and, subsequently, other local authority borrowings, thus reducing the burden on council tenants and council tax payers.

(3) High level intervention – financial aid packages

Whilst many of the state's financial interventions have been directed towards encouraging the supply of housing, the market may also be manipulated by ensuring that those who are seeking to acquire (or trying to retain) appropriate accommodation have sufficient finance to enable them to do so. There have been many examples of such interventions and whilst some, such as housing benefit, have resulted from a pro-active approach specifically designed to achieve certain outcomes (see below), other policies, for example those relating to the homeowner's tax liabilities, have been far more reactive.

It is clear that the expansion of home-ownership in the UK has been as a result of a complex series of inter-related issues – the overall availability of housing; the degree of attractiveness of each tenure; the comparative cost of acquiring and maintaining property in each tenure; the availability and cost of finance etc. The way in which these factors interact can be, and has been, influenced by state action. As discussed above, the state has made numerous attempts to influence the supply of housing, many of which have been specific to a single tenure, for example, owner-occupation or council housing. However, a variety of forms of tax relief and direct financial contributions have also been used to achieve the government's housing plans. In the 1960s the state made clear its support for home-ownership, first, by abolishing the Schedule A tax, which meant that home owners would no longer have their tax assessment calculated as if they received a rent for their home; and second, by the introduction of the 'option mortgage' scheme to make home-ownership more accessible to poorer households. Whilst the former was designed to ease the costs of home-ownership for the majority of taxpayers, the latter was introduced to ensure home-ownership was within the financial reach of even those whose tax liability was minimal. It did this by allowing people the option of either claiming tax relief or paying a reduced mortgage instalment.

At the time that these policies were introduced, home-ownership had become the largest single tenure, and the main political parties had begun to vie with one another to win the home owner vote. This therefore marked an end to government policies designed simply to boost the number of dwellings, and their replacement by policies that sought to promote one form of tenure over another. Arguably, the 1960s signalled the end of 'housing policies' and the beginning of 'tenure policies', in that policy began to be directed towards changing the relationship between tenures rather than influencing the overall supply or standard of property.

Other forms of assistance to property owners have included a variety of grants, available since 1949, to encourage them to improve, convert or modernise their properties. This chapter has described how the state first intervened in the nation's housing by setting compulsory standards and clearing the worst housing but, as the Deeplish Study (MHLG 1966) found, improving houses could be considerably cheaper than demolishing and replacing them. Between 1959 and 1989, several grants became a statutory entitlement for many owners, enabling some of them to considerably improve the value of their asset before selling and capitalising on this publicly funded improvement. From 1964, local authorities were also encouraged to designate specific areas for renewal under their overall control and to direct grants and improvement work into those areas. This marked a change in government emphasis, away from building or demolishing housing towards preserving and rehabilitating it. Governments justified this change of emphasis by claiming that sufficient new housing had been provided to eliminate the postwar housing shortage. At the same time, however, home improvement offered a much cheaper option for the state than the alternative of large-scale slum clearance and redevelopment.

The improvement grant system was not without its critics, in that its operation depended on the state contributing to the cost of improving the homes of private owners who could, subsequently, benefit from its improved resale value (even though, in some circumstances, the state could require the repayment of the grant if the dwelling was sold on soon after work had been completed). Whilst supporters of the system pointed to the substantial number of dwellings, peaking at around 300,000 per annum in 1983 and 1984, that were improved using one of the range of grants, critics questioned how many of these dwellings would have been improved without state aid and how many would have deteriorated, requiring action by the state. Furthermore, there is considerable evidence that the grant-aided improvement system contributed substantially to the process of gentrification:

> From what evidence is available the grant system has largely benefited the higher income strata of the working population. To some extent this has happened through 'mediated' gentrification … But, overwhelmingly it has come about by these strata improving their existing homes or buying deficient or dilapidated dwellings and then rehabilitating them.
>
> (Merrett 1979: 117–118)

In 1989 the grant system was changed and became 'means tested', and more recently changed again, to its discretionary, pre-1959 status, so that grants are now only available to poorer householders and at the discretion of the local authority.

Whilst the improvement grant system largely benefited the increasing number of owner-occupiers, the final intervention to be examined in this chapter was introduced specifically to provide assistance to tenants. The facility for local authorities to make rent rebates available to tenants was originally introduced in 1935 but its implementation was haphazard, with many councils choosing not to do so. The major reason for their reluctance was simply that it was easier not to – central government provided a general, unitary subsidy, to meet the costs of all new building, and the rest of the cost could be met by drawing a subsidy from the local rates and by 'pooling' all of the rents of the authority's stock. Given the enormous demand for council housing in the 1930s, 1940s and 1950s, housing officers could select tenants not just on the basis of 'need' but also, in the case of allocations of the new and more expensive housing, on the basis of the prospective tenant's social and economic situation. Consequently, rebates would be payable only to a small minority of tenants whilst the majority would have to pay a larger rent in order to fund these rebates.

So, on the one hand, those who received a rebate would resent the implication of a regular means test in order to gain their rebate while, on the other hand, the rest of the tenants would resent having to pay more in order to subsidise the minority of 'scroungers' (see Malpass 1990: 44ff.; Merrett 1979: 58). Some local authorities did, eventually, introduce some form of differential rents, often by adding 'lodger charges' to a basic rent or by simple staged reductions based on the dwelling's occupancy rather than the disposable income of the household. In 1972, however, the government forced the introduction of rebates by requiring all council house rents to be raised to reflect the 'fair rents' charged in the private and housing association sectors and by producing a model rent rebate system with which every council had to comply (although it could, at its discretion, improve the rebate by up to 10 per cent of the model at its own expense) and which would be largely funded by the Exchequer. This policy marked a shift in the funding of housing from 'subsidising bricks and mortar' to 'subsidising people'; from 'object' to 'personal' subsidies. The subsequent expansion of the rebate system to all parts of the rented sector helped to cushion poorer tenants from rent increases and facilitated various attempts to stimulate the private rented sector. The removal of rent controls for new tenancies in 1988 has, in many cases, been funded via the housing benefit system, allowing landlords to increase rents in the full knowledge that these increases will be met by housing benefit payments made directly to them by the local authority.

The housing benefit system is now widely criticised, on the one hand, because of its spiralling costs[1] and claims of wide-scale fraud and, on the other hand, for its complexity and contribution to the problems of the 'poverty trap'. The latter criticism arises from its 'taper', which means that the tenant loses benefit at almost the same rate as their household income increases, whilst some tenants can actually lose more than a pound for every extra pound they earn.

Currently, nearly two-thirds of council tenants, around half of private tenants, and nearly 70 per cent of housing association tenants receive a contribution to their rent. Explanations for this phenomenon vary. It is claimed by some people, for example, that the scheme is too generous, discouraging people from seeking employment and encouraging them to over-consume accommodation; or that the de-regulation of the rented sector has resulted in rising levels of rent meaning that the housing benefit system simply subsidises the landlord; or that increasing residualisation of the rented sector (be it private or council housing) has resulted in a greater proportion of tenants being on low incomes.

As we have seen, the state has done a lot for the individual: by its intervention it has stimulated and/or facilitated the building of many new homes, it has set standards that determine how and where new homes can be constructed and it has ensured that resources are available to allow private builders to build and private individuals to purchase homes. The state has played a substantial part in maintaining the quality of the nation's dwellings and has made money available to help individuals to pay their mortgage or rent. Therefore, the simple answer to the title question 'What has the state ever done for us?' is 'A lot even if we don't immediately recognise it!'

Why has the state been involved?

Whilst the housing policies pursued by the state during the last two centuries have been well documented we have to rely on official statements, such as Green and

White Papers, for an explanation of the reasoning that lay behind particular initiatives. Events in the post-Iraq war period have, however, reinforced the view that governments may not always make information available in such a way as to provide an even-handed review of all of the evidence and that it is reasonable to assume that governments will always explain and justify their policies in such a way as to present themselves in the best possible light. Consequently, we are left to speculate on the actual rationale for each initiative and have to rely on a variety of sources to assist us in our understanding of these initiatives. This section examines some of the possible explanations for government activity in the housing field.

Broadly speaking, policy interventions can be classified as *re-active*, in that they are introduced as a response to some evident problem (for example, ill health, overcrowding, housing shortages etc.), or *pro-active*, designed to advance or achieve the policy objectives of a ruling party. They can also, as with mortgage interest tax relief, be simply a residue of long-standing rules and practices of government departments. This classification, however, falls short of being an adequate explanation of state intervention in housing. This last part of the chapter, therefore, attempts to review a number of explanations of government decision-making as an aid to determining the rationale behind the intervention and its form. This is not to suggest that any particular policy can be attributed to a single explanation but to recognise that there is a range of factors that influence governments in making their decisions.

The rational planning model explanation

For most of the twentieth century the dominant explanation for the role of the state in housing policy and other welfare activities was that it was a rational response by a relatively neutral state to problems perceived by the electorate, social reformers, or experts in government. This *rational planning model* is essentially one in which the state attempts to remedy a perceived problem. Pickvance (1982) has suggested that the model comprises three stages: the problem is identified; the best solution is formulated; and then the necessary policy is implemented to remedy the problem. Thus this model sees the state as being responsive to society's needs as a whole (e.g. crime, disease, illiteracy, poor housing) rather than to the needs of a particular section of society.

Melling (1980: 12) takes this a step further by indicating that housing policy evolves as a result of '… the gradual recognition of pressing housing needs by a large section of the population, as voiced in various housing "movements"', whilst Stafford (1978: 10) suggests that governments 'appraise problems and devise appropriate strategies to achieve clearly prescribed objectives'.

These comments suggest a rather mechanical process in which the state, acting on behalf of the majority of its citizens, responds to some obvious problem for the 'common good'. In reality, the process of policy intervention is rarely so clear cut, the outcome often being determined by the decision-makers' perception of the nature of the original problem and its causes as well as their preferred outcome and preferred vehicle to deliver that outcome. Donnison and Ungerson (1982: 64) indicate similar policy initiatives across Europe, each of which involved the state seeking to influence the supply of housing but for very different reasons.

Thus housing policy may form part of a much larger approach to both social and economic policy and may not even be implemented specifically for housing purposes. Just as governments may seek to stimulate the housing market in order to ensure a supply of new housing, intervention may also be justified for much wider economic (or political) reasons. A Keynesian approach may seek to stimulate investment in new housing because of the 'spin offs' that may boost the wider economic situation but 'housing' may also be the 'sacrifice' that is necessary to facilitate the achievement of other priorities such as controlling or reducing public spending.

A common motive for intervention on the rational planning model is to correct some form of 'market failure', either by promoting the supply of homes, when and where the market fails to do so, or by providing people with the resources to access housing, when their income is too low to afford the market prices. This intervention solves a 'problem' in enabling citizens to gain access to and/or retain the use of decent housing. Typically, however, it is little more than a 'safety net' to ensure that some basic standard is achieved by all.

The initial involvement of the state in the provision of dwellings via council housing policies from 1919 onwards may be seen as an example of such an attempt to address a market failure. In this case, however, the level of intervention went further in seeking to provide 'homes for heroes', indicating that wider political problems were being addressed through the policy. Another example would be the introduction of rent rebates for private housing in 1972, which could be represented as a solution to the problem of accessing affordable rented accommodation, but could also be interpreted as an attempt to 'save' the private rental market because, if tenants can afford to pay more, landlords can charge higher rents.

Whilst early interventions were mainly concerned with seeking to ensure a supply of decent homes for the general population and could perhaps be characterised as fitting the rational planning model, in more recent times the situation has become more complex. Writing in the early 1990s, Cole and Furbey suggested that the rational planning approach was now rather dated:

> The last two decades, however, have seen a growing disillusionment with this rationalist model of the state as a neutral instrument for meeting the essentially agreed functional needs of a changing society. In part, the critique of this conventional view was prompted by the events and changed economic circumstances after 1973. The growth of state expenditure permitted in the 'long boom' of the post-war years sustained a growth in welfare services

which could be financed without any social group experiencing a real decline in material living standards. With the onset of recession, however, the welfare state came under fierce attack by a resurgent New Right and cuts in services implemented, notwithstanding the persistence of the problems which the welfare provisions were supposed to ameliorate.

(Cole and Furbey 1994: 11)

A further criticism of the rational planning model is that it assumes there is general agreement on what constitutes the problem. It is likely, for example, that most people would agree that 'homelessness' constitutes a problem and 'something should be done about it'. The preferred solution to the problem, however, will vary according to each person's view. If the problem is seen as one of people having nowhere to live, then the solution is to provide them with somewhere. If, however, the problem is seen as one that affects society as a whole, then a more holistic approach is needed, directed at preventing the situation occurring. Again, if homelessness is seen simply as a nuisance that is offensive to the majority, the solution may be to criminalise it in order to drive the homeless from the streets.

We are, therefore, forced to look at other explanations for policy interventions, not just to explain their occurrence but also the form of their occurrence. This is particularly so since the 1970s as successive UK governments have sought not so much to respond to problems that have been recognised by the population as to bring about change in order to meet the government's own objectives. This may have come about partly as a result of the major problems of housing quantity and quality having been resolved but it also indicates the ideological influences that shape the way in which the decision-makers both interpret data and perceive the role of the state.

Explanations in terms of policymakers' ideologies

A second type of explanation for the way in which the state intervenes recognises that not everybody contributes directly to the decision-making process and that certain people act as leaders charged with the responsibility for acting on behalf of others (whom they may be supposed to represent). Decisions are, therefore, strongly influenced by the decision-makers' own values and beliefs, particularly on how society is organised and what constitutes social justice. Perspectives vary on such issues as: the balance between individual freedom and state intervention; support for a free market economy as opposed to a command economy; an enthusiasm for a decentralised or centralised system of decision-making and administration; and promoting social equality or upholding 'traditional family values' (Blakemore 1998: 17).

Governments may formulate social and housing policy as a means of achieving their own ideological goals, and they may perceive problems, and formulate solutions, on the basis of their own value systems. Thus 'left' governments may pursue housing policies as part of a wider programme that seeks to achieve equality of opportunity by redistributing income. For them, relatively high public spending may be an acceptable price to pay in order to achieve high standards of public provision and quality of life. In contrast, 'right' governments place an emphasis on the freedom of the market, individual responsibility and personal choice, and limited state intervention (primarily, to maintain social order and the rule of law), with public spending being kept to a minimum so that individuals retain control over their own spending. A 'right' government would be likely to view 'left' interventionist policies as being the work of a 'nanny state', which would penalise those who worked hard to be self sufficient. A 'left' government, in contrast, would justify state intervention as necessary to avoid market anarchy and to counter the harmful effects of capitalist exploitation.

However, the state may act not only in pursuit of its ideological objectives but also for more pragmatic reasons. Dunleavy (1981), for example, suggests that, in developing their policies on high-rise housing provision, governments were influenced by powerful interest groups such as the construction industry and architectural professionals. Similarly, it has been suggested that it was only for reasons of political expediency and not ideology that housing was chosen to bear the brunt of the public expenditure cuts of the early 1980s (Malpass 1986: 233) (see the rational voter explanation below).

Economic explanations

Governments of whatever political persuasion have usually sought to assist or direct the economic development of the country and, with the rapid advancement of home-ownership during the twentieth century, housing has become an extremely significant feature of the state's management of the economy. The production and acquisition of housing involves considerable expenditure, frequently financed via borrowing, whilst also serving to create jobs and a demand for services both tangible (like energy utilities and goods) and less tangible (like mortgages, loans and insurances).

With the continuing expansion of home-ownership the state needs to consider the impact on the economy of rising house values and the consequent increased borrowing potential for general spending and investment (see the discussion in Sprigings and Somerville, this volume). The current value of owner-occupied stock in the UK is in excess of £3 trillion (Halifax Group PLC, 29/3/2004, based on figures provided by ODPM), at least two-thirds of which is 'debt-free', so it is clear that any government must consider the implications of individuals borrowing against the equity of their property in order to release millions of pounds of extra spending. In 2000 such borrowing used £11.4 billion to fund around 2 per cent of all consumer spending.

Not only must governments consider the impact of housing on the economy but they must also be aware of how the general economic environment affects the housing system. Kemp makes the point that the levels of inflation since the 1960s substantially affected the attractiveness of home-ownership compared with private renting. As a result of inflation eroding the real value of mortgage repayments, people were willing to incur large initial debts on the assumption that inflation would rapidly reduce the actual repayment cost as a proportion of their spending. Furthermore:

> The failure of British economic policy to contain inflation was thus a contributory factor in accelerating the decline of private renting, by making it more attractive to buy than to rent … the high rates of inflation prevalent during the 1970s had the effect of sharply reducing the rental yield on accommodation let on regulated tenancies with a fair rent.
>
> (Kemp 1997: 76)

So, regardless of their ideological position, governments need to constantly consider the relationship between housing and the economy.

The rational voter explanation

Since Adam Smith much has been made of the way in which self-interest in a competitive market promotes activity, and such views lead to a theory of public choice and the behaviour of the rational voter (see Downs 1957 and Hirschman 1970). Such explanations, that voters are primarily stimulated by self-interest, help us understand why political parties operate in the way that they do. Governments are motivated not only by their ideology but also by their interpretation of the voters' interests. In order to govern they must, first, be elected and, subsequently, must retain and reflect the support of a substantial minority of citizens. Consequently, they have to devise and present policies that are attractive to the electorate (see, for example, Dunleavy 1991). Whether behaving reactively or proactively, therefore, all political parties tend to veer towards the 'middle ground' in order to maximise their electoral support, with the ideological preferences of politicians being constrained by the need for electoral approval.

The rational voter theory can explain starkly contrasting government policies. On the one hand, for example, the proactive policies of the 1950s and 1960s, in which the two major political parties competed with each other in setting targets for new house-building, clearly demonstrate how, by promising action, politicians may seek to win popular support and, consequently, election. On the other hand, the inaction of governments in the 1960s, 1970s and early 1980s on the issue of mortgage interest tax relief[2] points to an unwillingness on the part of both main political parties to act against the self-interest of the growing majority of the electorate whose income would be adversely affected. Instead, in order to reduce public expenditure, the minority, council house tenants, were required to fund the tax savings through reduced subsidies and steadily increasing rents whilst still having to pay taxes.

Conclusion

This chapter has described how, during the twentieth century, housing policy priorities shifted from the overall supply of housing to the quality of housing, to the cost of accommodation and, finally, the tenure of people's homes. Whilst there may have been general agreement that sufficient decent accommodation should be available to everyone at a price within their means, there has been a constantly shifting emphasis, and associated disagreement, on *how* this might be achieved and *who* will actually produce this. The preferred delivery vehicle has shifted from being the private sector, to local authorities, to housing associations and back again to private developers.

In terms of explanations for housing policy development, although rational planning, ideological perspectives, economic considerations and electoral support all play a part, it can be concluded that the rationale for different policy initiatives is rarely entirely clear, and may involve different combinations of these explanatory factors. As Donnison and Ungerson (1982) ask: was the introduction of the UK's nineteenth-century Public Health Acts (a reaction to the perceived problems of disease and ill health) designed: to improve the living standards of those who lived in the expanding urban areas (rational planning); to ensure that capitalism had a supply of healthy and fit workers for longer (economic); or to inhibit the development of contagious diseases, which might, if unchecked, spread to damage either the bourgeoisie or their elected representatives (electoral)? Was the postwar 'planning' movement, in which the state sought to limit or control the use of land whilst embarking on an expensive New Towns' programme: an attempt to preserve the environment (rational planning); a means to ensure that decent housing was available to all (ideological and electoral); an attempt to control and revitalise the building industry (ideological and economic); a way of expanding the role of the state (ideological); a means to 'kickstart' the economy (economic); an attempt to equalise the availability of industry and employment (rational planning); or a strategy to ensure labour was readily available to serve both the needs of capital and provide the services needed by the bourgeoisie (economic)?

A good example of a policy that derived from a combination of ideological and electoral considerations was the right to buy. It was designed both to win votes and to pursue the Conservative party's ideological goals of 'allowing people to share in the wealth of the nation' and enabling tenants to 'join a property-owning democracy'. It neither added to the stock of dwellings nor improved the quality of housing but simply enabled the transfer of publicly owned dwellings into private ownership. Whatever the merits or otherwise of the neo-liberal ideology driving the policy (for further discussion, see Sprigings, this volume), many have argued that its electoral appeal was a more important factor. This policy epitomises the 'rational voter' explanation in that, by dangling the 'carrot' of home-ownership before the 6 million or so council tenants of the time, the Conservatives brought about a significant shift in voting behaviour in the 1979 election campaign.

Although the rationale for state intervention in the housing field, and the vehicle subsequently chosen to carry out the policy, may be the subject of considerable debate, the development of modern capitalist societies has made the role of the state much more complex than when it first intervened less than two centuries ago. As Forrest and Lee indicate, housing policy:

> ... is now no longer about whether housing investment leads to growth; it is more about how housing policy should be integrated with economic policy objectives and how an optimal level of public housing should be attained ... it is now widely recognized that resources for housing finance from the state are dwindling fast ... Housing policy, both East and West, is now commonly pursued as a conscious attempt by the state to boost private consumption and economic growth.
>
> (Forrest and Lee 2003: 267)

Notes

1 By the end of the twentieth century around 4.3 million tenants cost the state over £11 billion in support to meet the rent charged by either their local council or any other form of landlord (Department for Work and Pensions 2001).

2 Mortgage interest tax relief cannot be explained in terms of the other three types of explanation. It is not an example of rational planning, being simply an unintended effect of the way in which income tax was introduced. It is incompatible with both 'left' and 'right' ideologies: with the former, because it exacerbates income inequality; and with the latter, because it constitutes an interference in the operation of a free housing market. And it has no clear economic rationale, e.g. it causes house price inflation.

References

Blakemore, K. (1998) *Social Policy: An Introduction*, Buckingham: Open University Press.

Burden, T., Cooper, C. and Petrie, S. (2000) *'Modernising' Social Policy: Unravelling New Labour's Welfare Reforms*, Aldershot: Ashgate.

Burnett, J. (1980) *A Social History of Housing 1815–1970*, London: Methuen.

Clapham, D., Kemp, P. and Smith, S.J. (1990) *Housing and Social Policy*, London: Macmillan.

Cole, I. and Furbey, R. (1994) *The Eclipse of Council Housing*, London: Routledge.

Cope, H. (1999) *Housing Associations*, 2nd edn, London: Macmillan.

Department of Transport, Local Government and the Regions (DTLR) (2002) *Housing in England 2000/2001*, London: DTLR.

Department of Work and Pensions (DWP) (2001) *Other Statistics: Housing Benefit*. Online. Available http://www.dfwp.gov.uk/asd/asd4/Table8.xls (accessed 1 July 2004).

Doling, J. (1997) *Comparative Housing Policy*, London: Macmillan.

Donnison, D. and Ungerson, C. (1982) *Housing Policy*, Harmondsworth: Penguin Books.

Downs, A. (1957) *An Economic Theory of Democracy*, New York: Harper & Row.

Dunleavy, P. (1981) *The Politics of Mass Housing in Britain 1945–1975*, Oxford: Clarendon Press.

—— (1991) *Democracy, Bureaucracy and Public Choice*, Hemel Hempstead: Harvester Wheatsheaf.

Forrest, R. and Lee, J. (2003) *Housing and Social Change: East–West Perspectives*, London: Routledge.

Gibb, K., Munro, M. and Satsangi, M. (1991) *Housing Finance in the UK: An Introduction*, London: Macmillan.

Harloe, M. (1995) *The People's Home? Social Rented Housing in Europe and America*, Oxford: Blackwell.

Hill, M. (1983) *Understanding Social Policy*, Oxford: Blackwell.

Hirschman, A. (1970) *Exit, Voice and Loyalty*, Cambridge, MA: Harvard University Press.

Kemp, P. (1997) 'Ideology, public policy and private rental housing since the war', in P. Williams (ed.) *Directions in Housing Policy*, London: Paul Chapman Publishing.

Lansley, S. (1979) *Housing and Public Policy*, London: Croom Helm.

Ministry of Housing and Local Government (MHLG) (1953) *Houses: The Next Step*, Cmnd 8996, London: HMSO.

—— (1966) *The Deeplish Study*, London: HMSO.

Malpass, P. (ed.) (1986) *The Housing Crisis*, London: Croom Helm.

—— (1990) *Reshaping Housing Policy: Subsidies, Rents and Residualisation*, London: Routledge.

—— (2000) *Housing Associations and Housing Policy*, London: Macmillan.

Malpass, P. and Murie, A. (1999) *Housing Policy and Practice*, 5th edn, London: Macmillan.

Melling, J. (ed.) (1980) *Housing, Social Policy and the State*, London: Croom Helm.

Merrett, S. (1979) *State Housing in Britain*, London: Routledge and Kegan Paul.

Murie, A. (1998) 'Secure and contented citizens? Home-ownership in Britain', in A. Marsh and D. Mullins (eds) *Housing and Public Policy*, Buckingham: Open University Press.

Nationwide Anglia Building Society (1990) *Lending to Council House Tenants*, London: Nationwide.

Pickvance, C. (1982) 'The state and collective consumption', *Urban Change and Conflict*, Milton Keynes: The Open University Press.

Spink, B. (1998) 'Housing management 1800 to 2000 – a practice in search of a policy', in C. Cooper and M. Hawtin (eds) *Resident Involvement and Community Action: Theory to Practice*, Coventry: Chartered Institute of Housing.

Stafford, D.C. (1978) *The Economics of Housing Policy*, London: Croom Helm.

Wilcox, S. (2000) *Housing Finance Review*, York: Joseph Rowntree Foundation.

3 Housing policy and social justice

The case of anti-social behaviour

Nigel Sprigings

Introduction

This chapter will consider some approaches to social justice in the context of a particular aspect of housing policy in England, namely the treatment of anti-social behaviour as a growing social problem. Although English examples will be used, the wider moral and political theory issues discussed should be relevant to other countries in the UK and Europe. The chapter will present outlines of influential political ideologies. It will illustrate and criticise differing approaches to social justice using a government proposal to respond to the apparently growing problem of anti-social behaviour by the reduction in housing benefit paid to a perpetrator. This would make them unable to pay rent which would lead to an eviction for rent arrears which is procedurally more simple than proving a case of anti-social behaviour.

Finding an appropriate way of evaluating policy initiatives can be difficult when policy makers are focused (as government currently is) on 'what works'. The questions about who something may 'work' for or what 'works' might mean can be overlooked. By seeing a social policy problem in these purely administrative terms it is also easy to lose sight of what matters. Do apparently simple administrative solutions to problems contain within them the seeds of something that may be far more damaging to social life overall than the threat presented by the specific problem? Judgements on this are likely to be influenced by one's overall political beliefs but it could also be that one's political beliefs may be altered by thinking through the consequences and implications of an apparently attractive policy proposal – in this case, a proposal to combat anti-social behaviour.

Anti-social behaviour (ASB) is a particularly challenging topic area to address in this context. It has been subject to a variety of policy interventions recently (Introductory Tenancies and Anti-Social Behaviour Orders, for example), which attempt to tackle it through administrative, civil and criminal punishment interventions. It is hard to define. We will see that it covers a very wide range of behaviours yet is also highly emotive as it is clearly, in its more serious forms, corrosive of quality of life for individuals and neighbourhoods. Even in its minor forms (e.g. ball games) it can cause distress to individuals who have to endure unwelcome noise often from gatherings of young people who may be perceived as intimidating.

This chapter will demonstrate that there are wider implications to be considered than simply the effectiveness of a response and asks whether other factors, such as forms of equality (especially equality of citizenship) should also inform our policy responses. The decisions made at national and organisational levels have important impacts on our rights as citizens. As will be shown, these rights can be enjoyed only when agencies act to protect them so even decisions within an organisation (on allocations policy, or benefits advice for example) impact on the practical rights that its customers may enjoy as equal citizens. Social justice is implicit in the activities of social landlords and other agencies acting for the public good rather than simply for profit.

Social policy is designed to resolve or ameliorate problems in the social world and as such it is rooted in practice. By bringing the more theoretical issue of social justice to bear on a social problem that has been (perhaps erroneously) linked to housing tenure the chapter addresses disputed ethical matters and their relevance for the evaluation and implementation of policy initiatives. It will also challenge the false dichotomy that is now widely established that if you do not favour swift, punitive and potentially disproportionate responses to ASB then you are arguing that no response is needed and that sections of society should simply be abandoned to their fate while others run wild. In a complex social world this has to be a false dichotomy.

Trying to address a very specific issue such as ASB involves addressing topics such as are included in the 'rights and responsibilities' debate – for example, the basis and changing nature of citizenship and the effectiveness of punishment strategies in increasing public protection. These are political issues so we need to be clear who will win or lose in the particular outcomes of these political struggles. The question underpinning the purpose of the chapter is: what political views of social justice would support or oppose the administrative punishment (with its undermining of rights of appeal etc.) outlined below? Answering this question should allow us to judge which of the views most deserves our support in the way they propose to treat people.

The chapter will outline the forms of tenure to be included in the discussion and then discuss the growth of, and the activities that constitute, anti-social behaviour. It will next examine the belief that such behaviour exists primarily in the social housing sector, a belief that partly explains why attempts to tackle it have also been concentrated in this sector. The chapter will then introduce some of the political philosophies that form the basis for different approaches to social justice and, finally, will apply these to one of the more recent proposals for tackling anti-social behaviour (henceforth referred to as 'the proposal').

The proposal is to cut housing benefit for perpetrators of anti-social behaviour. It was put forward by the Department for Work and Pensions, with widespread political support, in a consultation paper requesting responses by 12th August 2003 (DWP 2003). It has been temporarily shelved because 'The Government wants to [give other powers more time] and see what really works before introducing a housing benefit sanction' (DWP letter 27/01/04). The main objections received during the consultation period were doubts about whether or not the sanction would be 'workable or effective' (DWP 27/01/04). The main concern seems to have been that social landlords could simply end up carrying more rent arrears.

The proposal contained two options. Option 1 ('Sanctions triggered by Court action') involved the additional punishment of a cut in housing benefit after a court of law had decided, on the basis of evidence presented to it, that some other order of the court (an Anti-Social Behaviour Order or ASBO, injunction, suspended possession order or criminal conviction, for example) was merited. The court would then issue a 'declaration of anti-social behaviour' that would trigger the housing benefit sanction (it was unclear whether the sanction would be mandatory). This process allowed the accused person

- a hearing of the prosecution evidence and a chance to present their own evidence in defence,
- an independent judgment on the case (the court having no vested interest), and
- routes for appeal through the courts and tribunal.

This was not the government's preferred option. Their preference was for Option 2 ('an administrative sanction'), which simply empowered an officer of the council to demand the imposition of the housing benefit sanction on the basis of their judgement on the evidence, with no requirements for the quality of evidence and no method for testing it. The officer could be the officer responsible for pursuing ASB within that authority's area (the 'anti-social behaviour coordinator' is suggested in the consultation document) so any decision would not be fully independent as the officer and the local authority may see punishment as being in their interests. Thus Option 2 gave complete power to the officer who would 'identify and determine' cases. It also reduced the possible value of appeal because a new appeals tribunal would have to be established, and the local authority would probably run this as the government would be unlikely to want to run a separate tribunal service for this purpose. The proposal is also vague about later reinstatement of housing benefit, stating: 'If the anti-social behaviour ceases completely for a significant period, *consideration might* be given to reinstating benefit' (my emphasis).

Because Option 1 had elements of protection from abuse of the sanction built into it the chapter will not consider it any further. Option 2, however, as the preferred option, warrants more detailed consideration. It is not the intention of this chapter to argue that ASB should not be punished, merely to suggest that we examine closely proposals (even on such emotive issues) where the punishment can all but remove the ability of the accused to defend themselves. Such 'solutions' to social problems may, as we shall see, add to other problems such as social exclusion because the actual context of ASB is far more complex than the simple solution proposed in Option 2 would suggest. This proposal has been temporarily shelved but it remains a document that is very revealing of government thinking on issues of justice, social justice, equality, rights and responsibilities, effective deterrence and so on.

The intention of the analysis in this chapter is to arrive at a position where a judgement can be made about the social justice of such a proposal rather than its administrative difficulties (which was the reason the proposal was shelved temporarily).

Tenure

This brief section of the discussion will consider tenure. There are three main tenures in England; owner-occupation, social renting and private renting. There are subdivisions within each tenure but each has distinct characteristics and carries with it different rights and responsibilities. In 1914, 90 per cent of UK housing was privately rented. Housing policy since then has produced rapid growth in owner-occupation (consistently throughout the period since 1914) and, intermittently, social housing. The proportions are now (approximately), ownership 70 per cent, social renting 20 per cent and private renting 10 per cent.

Owner-occupation has subdivisions of leasehold and freehold, outright ownership, purchasing with mortgage, and shared ownership for example. Burdens of ownership include maintenance of the dwelling while benefits include capital gains from increasing value. Within this tenure something that would be both an advantage and a disadvantage is ability to choose location and property based on income. Those with a lot of income have a lot of choice and vice versa. Choice is important as location gives access to other social goods such as transport, jobs, education and environmental quality. Some owners with declining property values have reducing choices while others can move 'up the property ladder'.

Social tenants have subdivisions including housing associations and local authority landlords and between assured and secure tenancies. Burdens of tenancy include rent payment, lack of control over maintaining quality, being subject to contract conditions restricting behaviour, access being based on needs assessment, and being located in areas where wider social policy interventions may impact disproportionately (for example, community care policies). Benefits include a state supported non-profit landlord and stock built to a minimum quality standard with social objectives including support to tenants, and obligations to consult tenants on aspects of management. Traditionally rents have been below 'market rents' and secure tenants have the right to buy their house at a discount.

Private tenants are subdivided most clearly by market position with high quality, high rent property at the top end and low quality, low rent property at the other extreme although the last decade has seen some growth in mid value renting. Landlords could be institutional/commercial landlords or individuals renting a spare house. The benefits of private renting are ease of access and therefore mobility and possibly greater choice, rent protection in some instances, and usually low levels of landlord interference as long as rent is paid. Disadvantages include insecurity of tenure in some instances, time limited tenancies, and inexperienced management in a potentially high profit sector with no possibility of capital gain for anyone other than the landlord.

Anti-social behaviour

There is a perception that anti-social behaviour is a growing problem. The term is, of course, vague. Anything that is ultimately damaging to society as a whole could be deemed anti-social. So everything from murder (which increases fear as well as causing direct harm) to tax avoidance (legally withholding the means to provide essential social services such as health care or roads, for example) could be counted as anti-social under such a broad definition. However it is unlikely that either extreme would be included in any list drawn up by politicians or members of the public under the heading of anti-social behaviour although many lists do include, as we will see, a range of activities from the criminal to the irritant. Frank Field MP, whose views will be discussed later, is very clear on the need to uphold a distinction between criminal and non-criminal forms of ASB (Field 2003).

The vagueness of the term means it could be taken to include any activity by other people that we (as some self-defining group) do not like. In fact the Chartered Institute of Housing (the professional body for housing managers) has a definition from a 1995 Good Practice Guide along these very lines: '[anti-social behaviour is] behaviour that opposes society's norms and accepted standards of behaviour' (CIH 1995).

Such imprecise definitions can lead housing management practitioners to develop, and act upon, their own wide definitions such as 'anything unacceptable to neighbours' (quoted in Allen and Sprigings 1999: 60). Clearly any offending activity under this definition would depend as much on the neighbour as on the activity. The author once dealt with a complaint that consisted of the complainant being able to hear neighbours switching lights on and off and furthermore, that 'they were doing it deliberately'.

Within the social housing sector, housing managers have dealt with a range of problems that they regard as anti-social to such an extent that they would like to, or in some cases have a duty to, intervene. These include at the more serious end of the scale, activities such as harassment, racial harassment, intimidation/threats, abusive/insulting behaviour, domestic violence, alcohol/solvent abuse, damage to property/vandalism, and use of premises for illegal activity such as drug dealing or prostitution (Allen and Sprigings 1999). These would all appear to be criminal activities or breaches of civil law or clearly bound up with illegal activities. The inclusion of those activities in any list is unlikely to provoke much dissent but responses from appropriate authorities may depend upon the age of the perpetrator and the consequent ability (or inability) to prosecute. It is also debatable whether landlords should be expected to deal with criminal activity.

There are other regularly included activities that are more contentious such as littering, dogs barking, youths playing in the street, communal area misuse, poor condition of the garden and various levels of noise including loud music but also arguing, and doors banging (Allen and Sprigings 1999). The Policy Action Team Report on Anti-Social Behaviour (PAT 8, 2000: 15–17) included among the potentially minor incidents dogs barking, unkempt gardens, being drunk in public, graffiti, and playing ball games. Agencies with the power to intervene (such as social landlords, who have powers to evict tenants for causing nuisance/disturbance to neighbours) therefore have to make judgements to which consideration of social justice is central. For example, how many balls used or how many games played or individuals from the household need be involved, before behaviour warrants a response that may include the eviction of a whole family? Courts would always consider the need for it to be *reasonable* to grant a possession order evicting a family wherever they have the discretion to do so. Such discretion has been reduced in recent years for social sector tenants (Introductory Tenancies, Ground 8 for possession for housing associations for example) and the proposal to be discussed in detail in this chapter would, as shown above, undermine tenants' ability to defend themselves against accusations that could lead to eviction.

The range of activities that may constitute anti-social behaviour is only one aspect of the problem for policy makers. The other is the amount of anti-social behaviour that actually occurs. The alleged increase in anti-social behaviour has become a prominent concern for social housing managers in recent years. The perceived extent of such behaviour is indicated in quotations from two participants in a recent Housing Corporation funded Innovation and Good Practice project (Allen and Sprigings 1999): 'Anti-social behaviour is the biggest problem facing housing associations. There has been a noticeable growth in incidents of ASB over recent years'. And 'Research shows that up to 20 per cent of a housing officer's time is spent dealing with nuisance behaviour'.

It was also claimed that half of staff time in one office was taken up with ASB. However, not all social landlords are affected similarly, with another participant in the project saying ASB was 'well down the list of priorities' for their organisation. Without questioning the seriousness of some of the issues social landlords have to deal with the variety of perceptions gives cause to wonder whether the issue has not become something of a 'moral panic' (Cohen 1972) fuelled by media stories about 'neighbours from hell'. Recent research has found that

> Due to deficiencies in landlords' recording and monitoring systems, it was impossible to measure the scale of anti-social behaviour or to establish whether the problem was increasing or decreasing.
>
> A third of local authorities (34 per cent) and over half of registered social landlords (54 per cent) failed to keep any records of the number of complaints received, and only a quarter of registered social landlords were able to provide detailed information on action taken to deal with individual cases.
>
> (Hunter *et al.* 2000: 2)

A recent briefing from the Local Government Association cites their community safety research (LGA 2001) asking local authorities to:

> select from [a given] list of 18 issues, which three were the most important to their authority currently. Most likely to appear in the top three issues were anti-social behaviour (selected by 53 per cent of authorities), youth crime (37 per cent), domestic burglary (36 per cent) and vehicle crime (26 per cent).
>
> (LGA 2002)

This seems an extraordinary level of occurrence for ASB until we remember that ball games may be included by authorities as an anti-social problem due to the nature of their recording systems and the intensive management of some housing stock by the authorities themselves.

The extent of the problem remains as unclear as its potential severity is clear to all. The Policy Action Team Report on anti-social behaviour (PAT 8, 2000) opened with the statement that 'Anti-social behaviour is a widespread problem' but the opening paragraph concludes with a comment that '[T]he lack of hard facts compounds the problem' (PAT 8, 2000: 7). They say that three quarters of social landlords regard it as a 'medium to large' problem with some recording up to 285 complaints per 1,000 tenancies per year. They note police records showing increases in disorder offences and environmental health officers' records showing a 56 per cent increase in complaints about neighbours between 1993 and 1997. But they also emphasise the lack of information (PAT 8, 2000: 8) and the difficulty of interpreting records given the lack of a standard definition. Increased recording also does not necessarily equate to increased incidence.

The National Society for Clean Air and Environmental Protection has recently reported a 52 per cent increase over the past year in complaints about noise nuisance (a common form of ASB). This comes from across all tenures. Interestingly, the head of pollution control for Southwark Council 'finds a doorstep conversation is enough to achieve resolutions in a large proportion of the 11,000 complaints about neighbourhood noise his team receives each year' (*Observer* 23/05/04). Doorstep conversations are not part of the Option 2 proposal. It may be that there is an assumption that these will already have taken place but that assumption is likely to be erroneous. Social landlords are increasingly punitive in their approach to breaches of tenancy so the negotiations that may take place in the private sector (where straightforward punishment is less easy) are less likely to occur.

One thing that is clear in most of the literature attempting to assess the extent of the problem is the reliance on data and case studies from social landlords (local authorities and Registered Social Landlords). This can give the impression that the problem is exclusively, or almost exclusively, a social sector problem. The danger here, as will be shown in the case study discussion, is that responses become concentrated on that sector and therefore help to stigmatise the sector by treating its tenants unequally compared to other members of society. Interestingly, PAT 8 (2000) presents some international comparisons of ASB responses and definitions. In France no action can be punished unless it constitutes a crime (which is defined equally across tenures). This issue of equality of treatment is one the chapter will return to in some detail.

Is there, though, any truth in the notion that anti-social behaviour is exclusively a social sector problem? The reality is that many of the activities defined as constituting ASB are not confined to the social sector. Certainly the criminal behaviours referred to above are not tenure specific. Even initially minor issues, however, such as disputes over gardens, occur in all tenures. The *Guardian* (25/6/ 03) reports the Hedgeline website including 'an illuminating, if thoroughly depressing, photogallery of disgruntled homeowners posing ... in front of quite enormous boundaries [and claiming to be] aware of 10,000 neighbourhood disputes over hedges'. The story in the *Guardian* was written following three deaths in Lincolnshire over two separate hedge disputes (one in Lincoln and another in Louth).

The incidents above are clearly not confined to the social housing sector but there is evidence that criminal activities affect the population unequally, with the already poor being more likely to be victims than the well off, and social sector tenants are over represented in the category of low-income households. Murie, for example, cites the 1988 British Crime Survey data as showing

> that households in council tenure faced over twice the risk of burglary as those in owner-occupation – 92 burglaries or attempted burglaries per thousand households (weighted data) compared with 44 in owner-occupation. The greater crime risk faced by council tenants was largely associated with neighbourhoods that were predominantly of council tenure. [...] The British Crime Survey showed that households in council tenure, living in areas of majority council tenure and with the highest levels of poverty, faced a risk of

burglary around five times greater than tenants who live in areas where council housing is not the majority and where tenants are better off.

Murie 1998: 23)

The same 1988 British Crime Survey, however, illustrates the complexity of the relationships between crime and poverty. Wiles and Pease (2001: 224) cite analysis of the Survey (sourced to Trickett *et al.* 1995) showing that, in relation to violence, 'it is the better off households within the worst areas which are most prone to victimisation'. They also use other sources to show that young households, single parent households and people living in areas with what they term 'high levels of physical disorder', are more than twice as likely to suffer burglary compared with the national average (Wiles and Pease 2001: 232 using Budd 1999). All this data refers to victims not perpetrators.

These statistics and analyses, of course, relate to actual criminal activity, for which there are criminal penalties. This lumping together of activities under the anti-social behaviour heading serves little analytical purpose when the issue of anti-social behaviour as a whole is, as we have seen, much wider than this. The British Crime Survey does not log ball game offences.

Is there, then, any evidence that social sector tenants are more likely to commit, or suffer, the more common but less criminal activities associated with anti-social behaviour? A recent 'audit' carried out at the government's behest is interesting in this context. Organised by the Anti-Social Behaviour Unit of the Office of the Deputy Prime Minister (ODPM), a one-day cross-sector audit of anti-social behaviour and nuisance reports revealed that the social sector accounted for just under 13 per cent of the 66,107 cases of anti-social behaviour recorded on 10 September 2003 by over 1,500 organisations. This is relevant to our discussion of the extent of the problem within the social sector because the social housing sector accounts for just over 20 per cent of the housing stock in England and Wales (the area of the UK involved in the incident count) (Revell and Leather 2000). This would seem to indicate that the sector actually experiences *less* nuisance and anti-social activity than the minimally managed private rented and owner-occupied sectors and other public spaces such as town centres. The most common reported problem for councils was littering (*Inside Housing* 17/10/03: 4). Again some of these complaints will not be tenure specific and occur in non-housing public spaces.

However, this spread of anti-social behaviour across all tenures is not reflected in the powers to tackle the behaviour and the new proposal would only affect people claiming housing benefit, around 80 per cent of whom are social sector tenants (Wilcox 2002). Tenants of the social sector are disproportionately subject to other control powers to address their littering and ball games. This may be because social landlords have lobby groups such as the professional body (the Chartered Institute of Housing) or the Social Landlords Crime and Nuisance Group to argue the case with government for continually extending the landlords' powers. Government has responded positively to these requests and a variety of punitive powers have been introduced or extended over the past fifteen years. In contrast, the private rented sector landlords (through the National Federation of Residential Landlords and the Small Landlords Association) have rejected proposals to make them more responsible for the behaviour of their tenants. *Property People* magazine reports the Small Landlords Association chair as saying:

> It is not for landlords to usurp the role of the forces of law and order in the battle against anti-social activities. The government cannot shift its respon-sibilities in this area onto us. [...] This does not mean that we as a sector turn our backs on these problems. It is rather that we recognise *the impracticality* of implementing what the government appears to propose, not least because of the *legal minefield that would be created if landlords were to take on the role of policing their tenants' behaviour*. [emphasis added]
>
> (*Property People* 31.7.03: 4)

This quotation neatly encapsulates several of the issues of rights and respon-sibilities that feature heavily in communitarian ideology and to which the chapter shall return. Across all sectors, though, there is a range of significant powers. These include powers held by local authorities under specific pieces of legislation (Noise Act 1996, Public Order Act 1986, Race Relations Act 1976, Local Government Act 1972, for example) and the police have powers to deal with any criminal behaviour. It is also possible for individuals to seek injunctions against others who engage in activities that cause nuisance and this power is available across all tenures.

The effectiveness of the above legislation is hard to assess as much of it is rarely used. Even the more recently introduced Anti-Social Behaviour Order (ASBO) powers, although legally applying to all residents of a local authority area, are often applied more intensively to social housing tenants. This can happen because the teams responsible for implementing ASBOs are based in the housing management section of the authority or because social housing is more intensively managed than other tenures and therefore action can be better co-ordinated. It is also likely that tenants are more used to contacting their landlord about such complaints. Thus the organisational imperative is driven by the needs of the local authority's own housing stock and tenants rather than the community as a whole.

Existing social landlord powers to tackle anti-social behaviour

Powers of eviction and injunction have long been available to landlords for breaches of tenancy conditions (which would normally require tenants not to cause disturbance to neighbours) or other nuisances but these would require evidence to be presented and considered by a court. Such action would also involve some of the 'doorstep conversations' referred to above if they were being conducted thoroughly. Some of the newer powers reduce the requirements for evidence to facilitate punishment.

For example, Introductory Tenancies, which make it much easier to evict tenants in the first twelve months of a tenancy, were introduced as a response to ASB in order to speed up possession in the face of landlords' complaints about slow court procedures. Tenants cannot really defend such cases as the courts' powers are curtailed in law. Research by Shelter found the powers were used mainly for simple rent arrears cases. This would be an example of a landlord organisation using an administrative tool primarily for a purpose for which it was not intended. They have made a judgement that this use is 'just' in suiting the business (not necessarily the social) objectives of the organisation.

Also the scope of normal possession powers was increased in the Housing Act 1996 to include actions *likely* to cause a nuisance; previously the occurrence of an *actual* nuisance had to be proved in order to secure an eviction. This small distinction clearly widens the scope for legal action by a landlord.

This is not an exhaustive list of powers but is illustrative and shows how occupants of the social housing sector are subject to greater control than occupants of the other sectors. The potential to be subjected to a more extensive range of punishments for the same action/offence simply because you cannot choose another form of tenure is surely one of the ways in which, in Lister's phrase, 'poverty is corrosive of citizenship' (Lister 1990). Losing the rights to defend yourself against accusations, to have the case judged by an independent person and to have scope for effective appeal would seem to be some of the corrosive elements of the proposal, which targets people in a way that is possible only because of their poverty.

Before examining the case study in detail, however, the chapter will consider political ideologies and the bases they offer for judgements about social justice.

Social justice and political ideologies

Social justice, as Amartya Sen (1992) points out, is a common feature of political ideology and is commonly thought of in terms of some kind of equality: '[E]very normative theory of social arrangement that has at all stood the test of time seems to demand equality of *something* – something that is regarded as particularly important in that theory' (Sen 1992: 12).

So the question Sen asks is 'equality of what?' Before considering some of the normative theories he refers to, we can look at some of the possible answers to this question. In our case study of ASB, for example, it is reasonable to assume that the majority of people want a more or less equal level of peace and quiet in which to enjoy their home. We would like to be equally free of the fear of crime. However, if we were accused of committing an act that could lead to our prosecution or eviction we would also expect to be treated as if innocent until complainants and prosecutors could convince an independent body, such as a court of law, of our guilt. We would expect to be able to defend ourselves against accusations that may have been unfairly made. We would therefore expect equal treatment in that we would expect everybody to have these opportunities of fair trial and defence. This is fundamental to our sense of justice in relation to which the 'equality of what' can be defined.

A common thread throughout is, as Badiou says, that '… injustice is clear, justice is obscure' (Badiou 1999 in 2003: 69). Or, in Ricoeur's words, 'our sense of injustice is ordinarily more reliable than is our sense of justice' (Ricoeur 2000: 54). Injustices strike us all the time but we are rarely clear about how exactly they should be resolved. In wealthy cities people sleeping on the street seems unjust; our sympathies are aroused because something seems unfair (Ricoeur 2000) and we often want to respond as individuals to that perceived, or sensed, injustice. We may do this by giving an amount of money directly to the person or to a relevant charity, for example. Unless we are very generous the amount we give is unlikely to resolve the problem for any specific individual. Giving to the charity acknowledges that some form of collective action will be required to correct the social injustice that we sense in the person's homelessness. State intervention through housing and other social policies is another recognised form of collective intervention.

But if social policy is to intervene in the form of state action a wide range of decision questions arise immediately. What would constitute adequate housing provision for that individual and how would we define adequate? Would 'adequacy' be our desired standard for housing provision and, if so, for what proportion of the population as a whole and when should someone expect a higher standard? What redistribution of wealth would be fair to allow the state to pay for this provision? How might redistribution hamper other people's ability to house themselves as they choose? How would we define 'fairness' in this context and whose interests would be paramount, the givers or the receivers? Once the state is supporting housing provision through our taxes, how do we make sure we allocate it to the person most in need of it and how would 'needs' be defined? Who should provide the housing? What if housing is not the key problem? How much should/ could/would we expect the individual to contribute to their own housing before we (as the citizens of the state authorising the provision) would want to see it withdrawn again and the individual put back on the street? How would we go about agreeing this radical reversal of fortune for someone?

So injustice is often clear while its opposite is not, and the attempt to agree on appropriate methods to achieve a more just society is the stuff of politics. The New Labour government in power since 1997 has maintained that 'what matters is what works'. Sometimes such a simplistic approach loses sight of what matters and fails to recognise that, faced with the same problem, different things matter to different people or groups of people but a starting point has to be that all of them are citizens with some kind of equal status granted by the law of the land. Citizenship will be central to this discussion of social justice as citizens have rights that subjects do not. Citizenship 'implies a sense of inclusion into the wider community' and is 'incompatible with domination' (Faulks 2000).

Faulks also claims that:

> Since all citizenship rights involve the distribution of resources, and because obligations are exercised within a societal context, any discussion of citizenship is also a consideration of power. If society fails to provide the necessary resources to sustain rights […] rights become a sham.
>
> (Faulks 2000: 6)

While many generalised outcome equalities may be impossible to achieve (equal wealth, health etc.) the final thread running through this chapter is that impact on *equality of citizenship* should be an essential touchstone in assessing the justice, or otherwise, of any policy measure. Marshall provides an inclusive definition of citizenship which he says is 'a status bestowed on those who are full members of a community. All who possess the status are equal with respect to the rights and duties with which the status is endowed' (Marshall 1963: 87). As we have seen above, the intent of this 'preferred' option in the proposal is to reduce some of this equality of rights. Again, this is not an argument that perpetrators of ASB should not be punished, but that the process leading up to their punishment should give them the same right to a fair hearing etc. as any other citizen accused of wrongdoing, which may elicit punishment in the form of reduced liberty or a fine.

Citizenship may even be the one factor that matters equally to each of the political ideologies discussed here, thus constituting a sound basis for debate and decision-making.

The political ideologies

In order to make the discussion manageable in a chapter of this size political ideologies have to be characterised (hopefully not caricatured). While this will miss some of the subtleties of particular positions it also avoids the many subdivisions of each position and the extensive space where different positions overlap. The ideologies used are shown in Table 3.1.

The *neo-liberal* position sees a minimal state largely engaged in protecting individuals' rights to property (Nozick 1974; Machan 2003). In the UK it is mainly associated with aspects of the Thatcher government and its efforts to 'roll back the state' by reducing state ownership and welfare. Markets are to be trusted in

Table 3.1 Political ideologies

Title	Orientation
Neo-liberal (libertarian in some literature, e.g. Nozick, Machan)	Right
Liberal Democratic (with Rawls as the major justice theorist)	Centre
Socialist (usually within a democratic tradition, e.g. Cohen)	Left
Communitarian (with representatives from all three orientations)	Any of the above

their ability to distribute goods efficiently as long as all individuals are able to enter into contractual commitments that the state will uphold if necessary. Thus markets support neo-liberal views of liberty.

So, in this neo-liberal society you may have the means to buy or rent accommodation and can enter the market. For Machan equality means 'that we are all equally in charge of our lives' and have equal liberty to 'obtain and keep valuable stuff' (Machan 2003). Within this framework free markets ensure efficient distribution of goods to those who manage their lives best and create the greatest opportunity for themselves to 'obtain' stuff. Yet even Adam Smith, the supposed inventor of the 'invisible hand' justification for free markets, felt that a very visible hand was required for some public goods such as education (see Smith 1997; Rothschild 2001: 95–100).

Neo-liberal ideology, as we can see from the experience of Victorian Britain, actually leads us to the *start* of state housing policy and market intervention (not necessarily public housing) rather than to its end. The case study discussion will try to apply this position (no targeted intervention, but only enforceable contracts applied equally) to the more specific issue of anti-social behaviour.

Liberal democratic or *social democratic* ideologies would approach social justice as interventions attempting to ameliorate inequalities rather than eradicate them. This moves to the left of the neo-liberal position in recognising that markets generate inequality and that the state has a role in moderating the inequalities that arise from unrestrained economic processes. Liberal democratic/social democratic approaches to social justice *will* involve the consideration of power Faulks referred to, with intervention to create greater equality of citizenship. From the neo-liberal point of view, affairs of state should be secondary to market forces, while for social democrats market forces should conform to the requirements of state-determined redistributive justice.

It seems likely that any liberal democratic/social democratic theory of justice will be founded upon the notion of rational beings submitting their proposals to the 'rule of argumentation' (Ricoeur 2000: 57) among equals. The equality here is a political equality where freedoms and duties arise because the polity has granted equal citizenship incorporating those freedoms and duties regardless of each individual's economic status.

Socialist ideology approaches social justice in a more 'materialist' way. For example, the statement 'from each according to his means, to each according to his needs', advocated by Marx and Engels in 1875, clearly requires the meeting of material needs as a minimum (non-material needs being more difficult to transfer from one person to another). The implication is strong that needs will vary from person to person. What is harder to accommodate structurally or administratively is that our needs change as society changes.

The decision problems raised in the introduction to this section still remain (how to respond to the homeless person?). As Cohen points out, social institutions are involved in 'the distribution of benefits and burdens to individuals' (Cohen 2000: 130) and injustice may be more dependent on the distribution of burdens. As Vincent says:

> Socialism has been predominantly associated with achieving the goal of equality in society. The outcomes of human endeavours should not give rise to inequality [that constitutes injustice]. Socialism has also advocated the idea that equality can be a condition or opportunity for the development of human beings, what is now sometimes referred to as a 'starting-gate' equality. Without a basic minimum of educational, health and welfare conditions as a point of departure, individuals cannot develop their potentialities and powers.
>
> (Vincent 1995: 103)

All the above implies equality of citizenship in terms of entitlements to these 'starting gate' provisions that society will create.

Communitarianism is influential on New Labour thinking (Phillips 1994), which is why it is being considered here. However, there are communitarians of the left, right and centre (see Miller 2000). Communitarians have significantly driven the 'rights and responsibilities' debate (the distribution of benefits and burdens) in recent years, as they seek to expand the role of individual responsibility (it is rarely associated with increased rights) in community-based policy initiatives. In particular, the communitarian Labour politician and former Minister, Frank Field, has written extensively on the problem of anti-social behaviour. His arguments will be presented as an introduction to the government proposal on cutting housing benefit entitlement for anti-social tenants.

Although, as Little states, 'there is a lack of coherence within the group labelled as communitarians' (Little, 2002: 19), there are common features of their critique of liberalism/individualism:

The communitarian critique of liberalism has tried to shift the focus of political philosophy away from individual rights and towards a consideration of the 'common good'. However, in some instances this has been a rather conservative enterprise, in so far as it endorses models of 'community' based around traditionalist concepts of the family or religion.

(Martin 1999: 168 in Ashe *et al.*)

In assuming a norm of community behaviour the communitarians run the risk of being authoritarian, backward looking and regressive (Little 2002). This can be said without denying the potential for positive community engagement (see Somerville, this volume). The danger, though, is the romantic assumption of a past golden age of tightly knit, self-supporting and self-policing communities. Despite their poverty, it is imagined that these communities did not endure the disruptive behaviour that often currently blights the lives of residents in run-down neighbourhoods.

It is easy to forget the vivid descriptions of these past communities that exist in neglected literature. For example, White (1986), in his exploration of Campbell Bunk between the wars, finds descriptions of a place with 'broken windows', 'litter' and food waste in the street. Also 'thieves and prostitutes congregate' along with 'Pugilists, Card Sharpers, Counter Jumpers, Purse Snatchers, street singers, and Gamblers of all kinds ...' (White 1986: 25, quoting public health committee minutes). This is not, we assume, what politicians imagine when they want to recreate community and it is difficult to begin to address the problem of how many Counter Jumpers a 'balanced' or 'sustainable' community may contain. What remains unclear in much of the communitarian literature, Frank Field included, is the importance they give to citizenship rights as opposed to citizenship respons-ibilities inequitably applied. The case study may make their position clearer as it is a policy proposal based on their philosophical position.

New Labour communitarianism – the views of Frank Field

In putting forward arguments for the overall reform of welfare, Frank Field argued that 'the underclass, at its strongest point, is fed by unemployment, the abuse of welfare, crime and drugs' (Field 1996: 18). Because of this tendency to contribute to '[undermining] the whole fabric of our character [and thus] helping to erode the wider moral order of society' (Field 1996: 20), means-tested welfare should be abolished. It should be replaced with a system that, among other things, would 'openly reward good behaviour and it should be used to enhance those roles which the country values' (Field 1996: 9). This sounds very similar to the US commun-itarian, Etzioni (1993), and his call for upholding 'values that all Americans share' without stating what these are or what happens to those who do not share them with him.

At the heart of Field's argument is the principle that 'One of welfare's roles is to reward and to punish' (Field 1996: 111). This point is elaborated in his book specifically addressed at anti-social behaviour (Field 2003). He begins with the Victorian era as a high point of shared social values where society 'transmitted' its values. The values of this era with its 'peaceable kingdom' (Field 2003: 24) where 'virtuous behaviour' was an 'unquestioned norm' (Field 2003: 112) should be transferable to modern times. There is no mention of poverty, cholera, work-houses, Poor Law, overcrowding, job insecurity, dangerous workplaces/practices and other common ingredients of that social era, nor of White's 'Counter Jumpers' mentioned above. Victorian evangelism and growing civil society created a 'natural ecology' (Field 2003: 78) that began to be lost when the failure to maintain the empire led to a breakdown of respect for authority (Field 2003: 51). He also discusses the prevalence of a 'now' society that he seems to think affects the poor but not the stock market. So how should we recreate this eroded natural ecology, he asks.

Field's analysis leads him to advocate a range of recovery measures such as the police acting as surrogate parents, schoolteachers also acting as parents, and welfare being used as a (disciplinarian) teacher. All the while in these proposals he seems to be assuming (Field 2003: 98) that the only 'offensive' people in society live on benefits, which can be used punitively as the basis for a new contract of citizenship.

He asks the question 'What kind of people do we want our citizens to be?' We could equally ask what kind of citizens we want our people to be. Some of us, it seems, deserve to be less than equal citizens, or perhaps even less than citizens. This is the authoritarian tendency of communitarianism and Field believes that the government proposals on cutting housing benefit did not go far enough as they only proposed a partial cut. But now is the time to look at these proposals in detail and to see how they match up to the principles of justice in the political ideologies outlined.

Case study and discussion

The government's proposal on cutting housing benefit

The chapter will now consider in more detail the government's proposal that housing benefit payments to anti-social tenants should be cut. The effect of this proposal would be to force the tenants into rent arrears thus making eviction easier (and in some cases mandatory). In discussing the level of the cut, Annex B p.5 noted that there is a 'risk that the tenant will not pay the sanction and that it is at too low a level for the landlord to secure an eviction'. It is worth noting that the 'risk' being identified here is that the eviction may *not* be facilitated by the sanction and the landlord will simply carry increased arrears. Homelessness as a result of the sanction taking effect is the objective that may not be met.

The principles underpinning the proposal are those of

- deterrence
- responsibilities of individuals
- facilitating punishment (but for what breaches of acceptable behaviour is not clear from the proposals).

Deterrence

It is assumed throughout the consultation paper that any easily actionable sanction will act as a deterrent to anti-social behaviour (ASB). This seems an extraordinary assumption to begin with. Over the past decade, as we have seen, social landlords have reported growing concerns about the extent of ASB. They have used this concern to lobby successfully for increased powers. Anecdotally, they claim that despite all these deterrent powers the problem is increasing.

Their own claims, therefore, would argue that increasing deterrence through enlarged capacity for punishment does not work. Furthermore, several of the ASB examples given on page two of the consultation document are criminal offences (actual violence, damage to property). The DWP presents no evidence to justify the belief that, in the case of criminal activity, a partial loss of HB is a greater deterrent than criminal prosecution.

Responsibility

The consultation paper makes much of the responsibility of individuals in relation to the rights of others. But in the overall rights and responsibilities debate, little is made of the existing right of landlords to act in cases of ASB through the tenancy agreement and other legislative powers, nor of their responsibility to use these powers to protect the tenant's right to 'quiet enjoyment'. Tenants' rights and landlords' responsibilities are therefore inextricably linked. If ASB is on the increase it may be because landlords (and/or the police in the case of criminal activity) are failing in their responsibilities.

Facilitating punishment

As has been stated, Option 2 was the government's preferred option as it required no case to be proven to an independent judge at all. Without court involvement it is difficult to see how this procedure would not be open to abuse. It would be almost impossible to produce evidence 'guidelines' as a lot of ASB arises out of disputes with neighbours or other specific case issues that may be unique. The officer would therefore be the sole arbiter and would only need to consider the possibility of an internal appeals system as a moderator of their decisions. It is not difficult to imagine situations where households are accelerated to eviction for rent arrears they cannot avoid (after HB reduction) on the basis of complaints that would never, of themselves, have warranted eviction or that may even be fabricated (earlier ASBO guidance warns of this possibility).

There can be little doubt that more criminals would be prosecuted and sentenced if the police were responsible for these stages of the criminal justice process as well as detection, arrest and evidence gathering. There are very good reasons why the administration of criminal justice in the UK has not adopted this procedure and there is no need to elaborate on the reasons here. We have, so far, rejected any calls for the abolition of the courts made on the grounds that they are independent of the prosecutor and thus pose obstacles to facilitating punishment.

Option 2, as we have seen, gives the accused no rights to any form of hearing before punishment is enacted. The second-class citizenship status would thus have become embedded in statute and practice. One of Ricoeur's bases for 'competent' judgement is 'the intervention of qualified, competent, independent persons who we say are "charged with judging"' (Ricoeur 2000: 128). 'Independent persons' are nowhere visible in Option 2.

The proposal raised other questions about the treatment of individuals now government have accepted that low income social sector tenants can be treated as having no basic right to equal citizenship. Housing benefit (HB) restrictions can lead directly to eviction. Once eviction is speeded up it was proposed that the tenant take their HB sanction with them into their homelessness. How would a household with an HB sanction find alternative accommodation with or without the local authority's help and assistance? What landlord is going to house a tenant who cannot pay rent? We must not forget that HB is means tested. Without HB tenants on low incomes do not have the means to pay.

The proposal did not state how long an HB sanction would last. Assuming that a sanction results in eviction and no other accommodation is available because of the transferability of the sanction, how long would the members of the household all have to behave as model citizens while sleeping rough in order to have their HB restored? How would they be advised of the restoration if they were without fixed abode?

Section 17.4 stated that those 'who ... condone anti-social acts' will also be subject to sanction. Of what might 'condoning' consist? Could a tenant have HB sanctions imposed for refusing to give a complaint statement because they did not believe the actions warranted a complaint when the 'determining officer' believed a complaint should have been made? Could tolerance be punished while intolerance is encouraged?

The consultation paper dealt confusingly with the issues of hardship and vulnerability. Given that many landlords (Hunter *et al.* 2000; Allen and Sprigings 1999) have found that vulnerable people (mental health problems etc.) are often perpetrators of ASB the issue of sanctioning them needs to be resolved much more clearly than vague references to 'reduced sanctions'. What part does appropriate support play in this equation? An early ASBO application was unsuccessful because appropriate (and legally required) assessments had not been completed. Under Option 2 this omission would not be picked up as the ASB co-ordinator (possibly responsible for ASBO prosecution and HB sanctions) would have made the decision without being subject to any 'independent' scrutiny.

The social justice of the government's proposals

Although the proposal has been temporarily shelved (see above) it is to form part of the Labour Party's 'Big Conversation' in the run up to the next election (*Property People* 4/12/03). It also remains significant for our understanding of Third Way priorities in that it can be seriously considered by government and promoted by a former Minister. Discussion in the housing press concentrated on the administrative difficulties (social landlords carrying larger arrears etc.). Potential problems with the justice of the proposal have been avoided although Andrew Heywood of the CML has said 'It appears unjust to single out a particular group in this way' [targeting tenants on HB] (Heywood 2003).

How would the different political ideologies view the proposal in terms of their approaches to social justice? Dealing with ASB is essential as it is damaging to individuals or groups, especially in its extreme forms. But it is unlikely that equality of peace and quiet or non-interference can ever be delivered. We may all have a clear view of examples of nuisance that it would be unjust to expect someone to suffer from neighbours, but a 'fair' amount of disturbance (from children, or someone with behavioural problems for example) is hard to specify. This topic area thus highlights the problems of judgements in the real world where injustice is clear but justice may be less so.

ASB is also a good example of a problem where realistic satisfactory *outcomes* are impossible to specify but this does not mean that perpetrators cannot be engaged with through satisfactory *processes*. All the ideologies would support tackling it somehow but, if we take citizenship as the basis of our processual judgement, how would the proposal fare?

Neo-liberals have as a fundamental principle of their approach the equal status of citizens under a minimal framework of law. Without such equality of status there is no basis for them to negotiate the contracts for rights or entitlements that the state would protect. In tackling ASB (which would be a personal infringement of another's right to non-interference) they would act equally against all people and groups with arrangements such as courts to weigh evidence and make judgments. The proposal does not pass their test as it targets a particular group for action and does not offer equal protection from ASB to all citizens.

Liberal/social democratic or utilitarian approaches similarly have little difficulty with the notion of treating individuals unequally in terms of outcomes but would seek the greatest good for the greatest number, which, it could be argued, the proposal does. However, there is no definite evidence available that allows such a calculation to be made. There is insufficient evidence on the extent and nature of ASB across tenures as well as little evidence on the efficacy of other solutions including the more efficient use of existing powers (which already affect social sector tenants disproportionately).

Being treated equally as a citizen remains fundamental here even though there need not be material equality. To quote Rawls:

> The basis for self-respect in a just society is not then one's income share but the publicly affirmed distribution of fundamental rights and liberties. And this distribution being equal, everyone has a similar and secure status when they meet to conduct the common affairs of the wider society. [Acknowledging less than equal liberty] ... would also have the effect of publicly establishing their inferiority as defined by the basic structure of society . ... In a well-ordered society then self-respect is secured by the public affirmation of the status of equal citizenship for all ...
>
> (Rawls 1999: 477–8)

Equality of citizenship, in this view, is one of the social goods the state 'distributes' and protects. If the processes of social institutions lead to outcomes that are unequal in distributing citizenship (such as lack of a fair hearing before punishment, or those sitting in judgement not being impartial), then these processes should be changed or not introduced. On this issue there would seem to be little difference from the neo-liberal position.

Socialist justice as described would also baulk at the proposal to cut housing benefit because it contains no potential for equality of outcome (i.e. equal freedom from ASB for all citizens). A more acceptable route might be to consider the evidence (assumed in drafting the proposal) that tenants are more likely to commit ASB. If no such evidence were found, then powers crossing all tenures could be drafted that would deter or punish all offenders equally. If it were found that tenants commit more ASB, however, socialists would want to target activities at the underlying causes of this inequality of distribution – perhaps by improving education or social conditions (being tough on the causes of crime) so that the problem could be judged, and resolutions sought, from a more equitable base. Targeting disadvantaged groups and reducing their scope to realise their potential as equal citizens would not be an acceptable solution.

Communitarians may be the only group who would have sympathy with the proposal. Their emphasis on traditional stable communities allows them to see both location mobility and social mobility as disruptive to community. Once movement is restricted by social pressures and responsibilities (as envisaged by Young and Lemos 1997), the very different social basis of different places allows them to treat the people in those places differently by creating additional responsibilities through administrative frameworks that place responsibility at a community level.

If there were to be community level decision making within a national legal framework, then communities would need to establish some sort of principles for applying punishments. Communitarians may be unhappy about distant 'administrators' making decisions (see Etzioni 1993: 144) but they also acknowledge the potential for communities to be authoritarian or puritan. At this point they fall back onto a wider framework of protected rights. Etzioni, for example, looks to the rights of equality enshrined in the American Constitution (Etzioni 1993: 49ff). Without such protections it would be inevitable that powerful community members would seek to impose sanctions on the unpopular community members without clear justification that would be obvious to an impartial outsider. An extreme illustration of this is the case of a man acquitted of indecent assault charges subsequently being killed in his home by arsonists. A neighbour explained the crime by saying they were 'a close knit community' (Channel 4 News 10/2/01; also reported briefly in the *Independent on Sunday* 11/2/01).

The credibility of different political philosophies depends, in part, on their applicability to real social situations. The community base for the rights and responsibilities debate seems to play fast and loose with the principle of equal citizenship at national level. As communitarianism is influential under New Labour (the DWP consultation paper uses communitarian terminology extensively), its wider implications need to be given due consideration. For example, Field, as a right (as opposed to left) communitarian would argue that perpetrators of anti-social behaviour have forfeited their right to equal citizenship or equal treatment. They do not *deserve* these rights.

Even if this argument is accepted, it is surely unfair that the government's favoured proposal does not require that the reason for this forfeiture of rights be proved to an independent person. The sanction could simply be imposed because someone was accused of ASB and the administering officer supported the accusers. Because communitarians occupy the left, right and centre of the political spectrum it is difficult to attribute a specific view to them. However, the weakness of community as an authority for judgement (which is its strength in other respects) is its common lack of impartiality. Yet impartiality is what most accused people seek from justice, while what accusers seek, and seek powerfully as a community, is punishment. The distant administrators Etzioni derides are the very people who may be needed to achieve socially just solutions in such circumstances.

Conclusion

The conclusion is that ethical judgements are relevant in all policy interventions and practice, but may depend on deeply held beliefs. For example, someone who believes that all the individuals constituting the adult population of England are equal citizens may have been surprised to learn how unequal housing policy makes some of England's citizens and how this acceptance of fundamental inequality has become embedded to such an extent that policy makers can devise a proposal such as the one discussed in detail here, and think it reasonable.

What has been helpful here in assessing a proposal designed to tackle a social problem is applying the notion of equality of citizenship to the realities of the social situation. This allows us to consider both values and problems of implementation. In this instance all the political ideologies (except possibly communitarians of the right) would acknowledge equality of citizenship by rejecting an unjust proposal. Starting from the assumption that certain groups of citizens (those in receipt and those not in receipt of housing benefit) can be subjected to unequal levels of punishment would strike most people as unjust. Removing the rights of some people to a fair (impartial judgement by 'independent persons') hearing on the basis of income demeans us all potentially. Who knows when we may have to prove that our household income is over some notional figure, say £50,000/year, in order to *deserve* a fair trial when we are accused of wrongdoing?

Of course you may believe from the outset that all adults in England are *not* equal citizens and are not entitled to a fair trial or to defend themselves against accusations, and you may have a variety of reasons for believing this. Even so, there is still the issue of where to draw the line and how it should be decided where the line is drawn. Many activities are categorised by housing managers as constituting 'anti-social behaviour', for example. These, as has been shown, include some quite minor incidents when taken on their own, such as dogs barking, unkempt gardens, slamming doors, being drunk in public, graffiti, and playing ball games. A full list of examples would also cover activities generally regarded as being more serious such as racial harassment and domestic violence (all examples taken from PAT 8, 2000: 15–17). The question is: what can be done to ensure a just outcome for all, across all tenures, where anti-social behaviour occurs? It seems unlikely to me that a fair outcome will be achieved where the accused has the basic right to defence removed.

Housing policy is of interest partly because it is focused on one of the areas of greatest social inequality and injustice. Housing is a 'site' for social justice considerations, both as process and outcome. Injustice may be more obvious than justice. Some obvious injustices would include:

- substandard housing
- segregated housing
- housing that reduces life chances (health, opportunity, wealth)
- housing that has a second-class tenure creating excluded citizens (social housing)
- housing that reduces quality of life through poor environment, ASB etc.

All of the above will have obvious outcomes but the processes that may correct them will be less obvious, for example:

- fair allocations policies
- efficient dealing with ASB to ensure 'quiet enjoyment'
- effective regulation of standards.

While it is probably impossible to judge the 'equality' of conditions or circumstances, the case study shows how impacts in terms of equality of citizenship for the parties or groups with an interest can be quite straightforward to assess. This will clearly lead to conflicts but, as was said at the start, social justice is the stuff of politics, which requires the resolution of conflict.

Stuart Hampshire (1999) goes so far as to claim that justice is conflict. Certainly, without very different views, there is little cause for debate. Rather than assuming consensus, New Labour could increase the achievement of social justice by considering some radical positions that equalize citizenship instead of undermining it as some of their recent proposals seem to do. There is certainly a temptation, with the marketisation of social services, for the delivery organisations to be driven by objectives that are not their original or stated purpose. How many housing associations claiming to meet housing needs now actively exclude the most needy people on the basis of creating sustainable communities, for example? Or how many are so driven by short-term rental income objectives that they forget the needs of the customers they are evicting (see Sprigings 2002 for a detailed case)?

So social justice is something that involves everyone working in housing practice and everyone involved in making the policies, national, local or organisational, that direct the activities of practitioners. As soon as it becomes easier to evict innocent people along with guilty people we are all diminished, as we are complicit in the creation of unnecessary homelessness and distress.

For this reason all social policy changes should be measured against the likely impact on *all* individuals affected by the change and not simply those we would like to be affected. Some people may want perpetrators of ASB to be unable to defend themselves in court but legislation that brings this about means that *none of us* will be able to defend ourselves in court. It should be the evidence that determines our guilt, not the charge. By using equality of citizenship as a basis for judging the merits of social policy proposals, we have seen, through the case study, how several of the common political philosophies would reject the proposal.

That it may be difficult for social landlords to respond to the conflict between the right to quiet enjoyment and the right to fair trial is not in doubt. But it is only by grappling with this difficulty that landlords will fulfil their responsibilities. We know that poverty leads to social exclusion. We only exacerbate that exclusion by removing protection from eviction for poor citizens. And as we saw in the section above on deterrence, increasing the vulnerability of the poor to punishment shows no sign of being effective, anyway. As Faulks says, 'would removing the remaining stake that an individual has in society really compel them to good citizenship?' (Faulks 2000: 81) Protecting citizenship rights is fundamental to countering social exclusion and should be central to the policies driving all social policy.

References

Allen, C. and Sprigings, N. (1999) *Managing Risk Together*, Manchester: GMPS/Housing Corporation.

Ashe, F., Finlayson, A., Lloyd, M., MacKenzie, I., Martin, J. and O'Neill, S. (1999) *Contemporary Political and Social Theory: An Introduction*, Buckingham: Open University Press.

Badiou, A. (1999) 'Philosophy and politics', *Radical Philosophy*, 96: 29–32; reprinted in *Infinite Thought* (2003), London: Continuum.

Chartered Institute of Housing (1995) *Neighbour Nuisance: Ending the Nightmare*, Coventry: Chartered Institute of Housing.

Cohen, G.A. (2000) *If You're an Egalitarian, How Come You're So Rich?* Cambridge, MA: Harvard University Press.

Cohen, S. (1972) *Folk Devils and Moral Panics*, London: Paladin.

DWP (2003) *Housing Benefit Sanctions and Anti-Social Behaviour: A Consultation Paper*, London: Department of Work and Pensions.

—— (27/01/04) Letter to consultation paper respondents and Minister's statement, London: Department of Work and Pensions.

Etzioni, A. (1993) *The Spirit of Community: The Reinvention of American Society*, New York: Touchstone.

Faulks, K. (2000) *Citizenship*, London: Routledge.

Field, F. (1996) *Stakeholder Welfare*, London: Institute for Economic Affairs.

—— (2003) *Neighbours From Hell: The Politics of Behaviour*, London: Politicos Publishing.

Finer, C.J. and Nellis, M. (eds) (1998) *Crime and Social Exclusion*, Oxford: Blackwell.

Guardian 25/06/03 'The hedge war', London: Guardian Newspapers.

Hampshire, S. (1999) *Justice is Conflict*, London: Duckworth.

Heywood, A. (2003) 'This is not the way', *Property People*, 393, 17 July: 7.

Hunter, C., Nixon, J. and Shayer, S. (2000) *Neighbour Nuisance, Social Landlords and the Law*, Coventry: Chartered Institute of Housing/Joseph Rowntree Foundation.

LGA (2001) *Partners Against Crime: A Survey of Local Authority Approaches to Community Safety*, Research Report 24, London: Local Government Association.

—— (2002) *Tackling Anti-Social Behaviour: Information and Case Studies about Local Authority Work*, Research Briefing 16, London: Local Government Association.

Lister, R. (1990) *The Exclusive Society: Citizenship and the Poor*, London: CPAG.

Little, A. (2002) *The Politics of Community: Theory and Practice*, Edinburgh: Edinburgh University Press.

Machan, T. (2003) 'Libertarianism in one easy lesson: an open debate', *The Philosophers' Magazine*, Issue 21, 1st Quarter.

Marshall, T.H. (1963) *Sociology at the Crossroads and Other Essays*, London: Heinemann.

Martin, J. (1999) 'The social and the political', in F. Ashe, A. Finlayson, M. Lloyd, I. MacKenzie, J. Martin and S. O'Neill (eds) *Contemporary Social and Political Theory*, Buckingham: Open University Press.

Marx, K. (1875) 'Critique of the Gotha Programme', reprinted in D. MacLellan (ed.) (2000) *Karl Marx: Selected Writings*, 2nd edn: 615, Oxford: Oxford University Press.

Miller, D. (2000) *Citizenship and National Identity*, Cambridge: Polity Press.

Murie, A. (1998) 'Linking housing changes to crime', in C.J. Finer and M. Nellis (eds) *Crime and Social Exclusion*, Oxford: Blackwell.

Nozick, R. (1974) *Anarchy, State and Utopia*, Oxford: Blackwell

Observer (23/05/04) 'Protests rise over noisy neighbours', London: Guardian Newspapers.

PAT 8 (2000) *Anti-Social Behaviour*, Report of Policy Action Team 8, London: Home Office/HMSO.

Phillips, M. (1994) 'The father of Tony Blair's big idea', *Observer*, 24/7/94, Manchester.

Property People (17/07/03) 'This is not the way', London: Property People Publications.

Rawls, J. (1971, revised edn 1999) *A Theory of Justice*, Oxford: Oxford University Press.

Revell, K. and Leather, P. (2000) *The State of UK Housing: A Fact File on Housing Conditions and Housing Renewal Policies in the UK*, Bristol: Policy Press/Joseph Rowntree Foundation.

Ricoeur, P. (2000) *The Just*, Chicago: Chicago University Press.

Rothschild, E. (2001) *Economic Sentiments: Adam Smith, Condorcet, and the Enlightenment*, Cambridge, MA: Harvard University Press.

Sen, A. (1992) *Inequality Re-examined*, Oxford: Oxford University Press.

Smith, A. (1997) *The Wealth of Nations*, London: Penguin.

Sprigings, N. (2002) 'Delivering public services under the new public management: the case of public housing', *Public Money and Management*, 22, 4: 11–19.

Trickett, A., Osborne, D.R. and Ellingworth, D. (1995) 'Property crime victimisation: the roles of individual and area influences', *International Review of Victimology*, 3: 273–95.

Vincent, A. (1995) *Modern Political Ideologies*, Oxford: Blackwell.

White, J. (1986) *The Worst Street in North London: Campbell Bunk, Islington, Between the Wars*, London: Routledge & Kegan Paul.

Wilcox, S. (2002) *UK Housing Review 2002/3*, York: Joseph Rowntree Foundation/Chartered Institute of Housing/Council of Mortgage Lenders.

Wiles, P. and Pease, K. (2001) 'Distributive justice and crime', in R. Matthews and J. Pitts (eds) *Crime, Disorder and Community Safety*, London: Routledge.

Young, M. and Lemos, G. (1997) *The Communities We Have Lost and Can Regain*, London: Lemos and Crane.

4   Places, 'folk devils' and social policy

Charlie Cooper

Introduction

This chapter is concerned with the significance of 'place' for social policy. More specifically, it examines the way popular perceptions of place – fostered mainly by the media, politicians and academics, reflecting middle-class concerns – have influenced social policy interventions in Britain. The argument presented is that policy reactions to these perceptions of places, and the people who live in them, have not only failed to address the causes of difficult neighbourhood circumstances but also exacerbated the marginalisation and suffering of disadvantaged groups. Drawing on Stanley Cohen's classic study of 'deviant' groups ('folk devils') and society's reaction to them ('moral panics'), this chapter will illustrate how ideological constructions of 'dangerous' places and their 'dangerous' residents have underpinned social policies that have systematically sustained socio-spatial differentiation and disadvantage. It is argued that these symbolic constructions largely reflect the broader logics at work in western society – namely, the perpetuation of capitalism and the interests of the established order through disciplinary power and control. The chapter concludes with an assessment of the possibilities for a transformative community politics out of which more equitable social and spatial arrangements might emerge.

'Folk devils' and 'moral panics'

Cohen's seminal text *Folk Devils and Moral Panics*, first published in 1972, drew largely on two concepts – 'labelling theory' and 'deviancy amplification'. Howard Becker introduced the concept of 'labelling' in his book *Outsiders*. He argues that people become labelled 'outsiders' by breaking rules or norms defined by others more 'powerful'. As a consequence, 'social groups create deviance by making the rules whose infraction creates deviance, and by applying those rules to particular people and labelling them as outsiders' (Becker 1966: 9). Labelling is not natural, but constructed as 'moral meaning' by the powerful to legitimate exerting social control over those labelled. The notion of 'deviancy amplification' was originally introduced by Leslie Wilkins (1964), who argued that 'deviants' were liable to be subjected to distorted and exaggerated representations by the 'moral majority' (the media and politicians for instance), resulting in deviancy amplification. This creates new problems, such as some people living up to the distorted image constructed. There is, therefore, a 'deviant' act (largely petty and sporadic) subject to exaggeration, leading to the construction of an image that others can identify with and thereby making it more likely that the 'deviance' will be constructed in a more durable form.

Cohen applied these two concepts in his PhD study on Mods and Rockers in the 1960s, which identified the production of 'folk devils' and moral panics. 'Folk devils' are 'deviants' whose styles and ways of behaving run counter to 'acceptable' middle-class values. Cohen argues that such fashions are often a reaction to thwarted ambitions caused by the middle classes responsible for discrimination and the denial of opportunity.

> Rejecting the 'emotional containment of affluence' ... , increasing numbers of young people celebrated diversity and personal liberation, experimenting with alternative lifestyles.
>
> (Valier 2002: 82–3)

The existence of diverse and different lifestyles is therefore seen as a rational response to the lack of access to middle-class defined aspirations. In turn, the middle-class machinery – the media, politicians, expert commentators – seeks to discredit these lifestyles by demonising them as a threat to decency and order, thereby producing a 'moral panic'. The social construction of 'deviant' groups acts as a metaphor for all that has gone wrong in society. They are blamed for society's failings – crime, poverty, unemployment, homelessness, violence and so forth. This negative discourse allows dominant power holders to avoid taking responsibility for the structural problems of society that produce crime, poverty, unemployment, homelessness, violence and so forth. Rather than address these structural factors – which would require measures to redistribute power and wealth – it is more convenient to construct 'folk devils' to blame, simplify their cause (decline in discipline and moral standards), stir up public indignation or moral panics (calls for tougher action), and respond with harsh social and public policies (Muncie 1999). As Cohen warned:

> More moral panics will be generated and other, as yet nameless, folk devils will be created. This is not because such developments have an inexorable inner logic, but because our society as present structured will continue to generate problems for some of its members – like working-class adolescents – and then condemn whatever solution these groups find.
>
> (Cohen 2002: 172)

The concern with 'deviant' and 'threatening' behaviour has a long tradition. The identification of certain ways of behaving as a social problem was evident in social investigations and commentaries from the first half of the nineteenth century, generated by a growing apprehension amongst the new industrial middle class about the labouring classes. This fear has focused on the impact of place on both the people living there (their stunted moral development and disgusting behaviour) and society at large (in terms of crime, health and social breakdown). This concern has expressed itself through 'moral panics' that label places and socially construct their people as 'deviant folk devils' in opposition to 'mainstream' values. These panics have helped to serve the interests of the dominant capitalist classes whilst legitimating a series of punitive social policy responses towards 'others' and, in many cases, 'criminalising' behaviour deemed 'anti-social'. Indeed, as Bauman argues, capitalism survives through the ability of the dominant classes to satisfy their needs by suppressing another (larger) class in this way. Freud contributed to this ordering of modern society by suggesting that the 'masses are lazy and unintelligent' and in need of 'a certain degree of coercion' (cited in Bauman 2001: 25–6). They had to be squeezed into the new routines required by industrial manufacturing. People once proud of their work – farmers, craft workers and artisans – had to be forced to accept the indignity and drudgery of the factory floor. They had to be uprooted from self-sufficient, rural 'communities' (*Gemeinschaft*) and relocated to 'modern society' (*Gesellschaft*), an unfamiliar, futile and meaningless setting (Tönnies 1955).

> It was at that all-too-human dislike of futility and meaninglessness that the charge of laziness, raised against men, women and children torn away from their home environment and subjected to a rhythm they neither set nor understood, was in fact targeted.
>
> (Bauman 2001: 29)

Labelling the masses as lazy legitimised their regulation. As John Stuart Mill observed:

> The lot of the poor, in all things which affect them collectively, should be regulated for them, not by them … . It is the duty of the higher classes to think for them, and to take responsibility for their lot … [in order that] they may resign themselves … to a truthful insouciance, and repose under the shadow of their protectors … . The rich should be *in loco parentis* to the poor, guiding and restraining them like children.
>
> (Cited in Bauman 2001: 31)

The economic system of early modern capitalism was often represented as a living body that must be kept in good health. Any threat to this body must be operated on swiftly. Henry Mayhew, for instance, believed that the health of the economic body was threatened by parasites in the social body – the unproductive 'vagabonds' who prey 'upon the earnings of the more industrious portions of the community' (Mayhew 1861/1967: 90). As Foucault observed, central to disciplinary power under capitalism is the production of 'docile bodies', ventures in creating bodies that could be 'subjected, used, transformed and improved' (Foucault 1977: 136). In achieving this, the masses required close supervision and control, achieved through the Benthamite principle of 'panopticon' – discipline by means of continual surveillance. Bentham believed this could be achieved through an architectural model, but it eventually evolved in a more generalisable (and cost effective) form – through discourse (Foucault 1977), labelling and the production of 'moral panics'. These discursive practices serve to preserve the social order through stigmatising 'the Other', constructing them as 'deviant' and thereby legitimising authoritarian and punitive forms of social control.

In his third edition of *Folk Devils and Moral Panics*, Cohen highlights seven clusters of social identity – young working-class violent males; school violence (bullies and shootouts); drug 'abuse'; child abuse; media sex and violence; welfare cheats and single mothers; refugees and asylum seekers 'flooding' the country and 'swamping' our services – each of whom have been the subject of: concern (as a potential or imagined threat); hostility (moral outrage); consensus (widespread agreement) that something should be done; exaggerated claims (in terms of the risk posed); and volatility (the panic erupts and dissipates suddenly). He suggests that the discrete and volatile moral panics evident since the Second World War have 'been replaced by a generalized moral stance' against 'marginal groups and cultural deviance' (Cohen 2002: xxix).

The next section of this chapter applies Cohen's thesis to people *and* places. It will illustrate how a generalised moral stance against 'dangerous' places and the people who live there has existed throughout modern times, and that this position has contributed to the maintenance of socio-spatial differentiation and disadvantage, and the reinforcement of the established social order.

'Dangerous' places and 'dangerous' people

Places have held significance for academics, policy-makers and politicians alike throughout modern times, primarily reflecting the curiosities and concerns of the middle class about the 'dangerous' people who live there. Since industrialisation and urbanisation in Britain, moral panics about people and places have served to differentiate between the 'respectable' and the 'disrespectable', creating 'landscapes of exclusion' (Sibley 1995: 14). Similar panics, continuing to serve exclusionary processes, can be identified today.

In the immediate post-industrial period, moral panic took the form of the 'diseased other':

Disease metaphors were characteristic of nineteenth-century scientific discourse ... . The fear of infection leads to the erection of the barricades to resist the spread of diseased, polluted others ... . Contagious diseases like cholera or venereal disease were 'working-class diseases' which threatened the bourgeoisie and threatened to invade bourgeois space.

(Sibley 1995: 24–5)

Epidemics spread throughout the new industrial towns, largely due to a lack of adequate sanitation. These provoked a number of social inquiries, including Dr James Phillips Kay's classic 1832 study of the homes of Manchester cotton workers:

The houses, in such situations, are uncleanly, ill-provided with furniture; an air of discomfort, if not of squalid and loathsome wretchedness pervades them; they are often dilapidated, badly drained, damp; and the habits of their tenants are gross – they are ill-fed, ill-clothed and uneconomical – at once spendthrifts and destitute – denying themselves the comforts of life in order that they may wallow in the unrestrained licence of animal appetite.

(Cited in Burnett 1986: 55)

Chadwick, who published his report on the sanitary conditions of the labouring classes in 1842, believed that these conditions posed a threat not only to economic prosperity, but also to the moral order. They depressed the human spirit to such an extent as to tempt people to 'drown care in intoxicating liquors' (Chadwick 1842, cited in Lund 1996: 23). Peter Gaskell, writing in 1833, described the homes of the labouring classes in the manufacturing districts of Manchester as presenting 'many of the traces of savage life ... too truly an index of the vicious and depraved lives of their inmates' (cited in Burnett 1986: 55). His purpose was to stimulate corrective intervention. The early reports on housing reform in the 1840s drew attention to the social costs of squalor in terms of 'intemperance, immorality and criminality' (Burnett 1986: 93). Similar moral panics emerged in Charles Booth's description of Whitechapel, east London, in 1902: 'There is a large class who must be regarded as outcasts ... and who must be regarded, in the mass, as hopeless subjects of reform' (Booth 1902, cited in Sibley 1995: 56). The Irish were particularly vilified for their association with that 'disgusting domestic companion, the pig' (Peter Gaskell 1833, cited in Burnett 1986: 58).

With the development of transport and, subsequently, suburbanisation, the middle classes were able to increasingly distance themselves spatially and socially. With this, the perception of the working class as a moral danger became more exaggerated:

As socio-spatial segregation became yet more pronounced, the distance between the affluent and the poor ensured the persistence of stereotyped conceptions of the other. Social and spatial distancing contributed to the labelling of areas of poverty as deviant and threatening, a lack of knowledge being reflected in myths about working-class living conditions and behaviour.

(Sibley 1995: 55)

The poor were conceptualised as 'idle, thieving bastards' (Grayson 1997: 15), 'improvident', 'reckless', 'intemperate' and with 'an habitual avidity for sensual gratification' (Sibley 1995: 56); their places were described as 'slums', 'cesspits', 'rookeries' and 'fever nests' (Lund 1996: 22). For Englander, these attitudes reflected a traditional middle-class preoccupation with 'the pathological, a fascination for the curious' (cited in Grayson 1997: 15). The working class became 'objects' to be classified (under the workhouse test) as 'deserving' or 'undeserving' and subsequently transformed:

Standing between adapted workers and undeserving poor are those who may be saved or civilised. Repressive policies deal with outcasts who are to be if possible eliminated, driven into workhouses or ousted through immigration. Reform policies ... are chiefly targeted towards those who might be reshaped so as to comply with the norms of a swiftly changing industrial capitalism.

(Topalov 1985, cited in Harloe 1995: 21)

The public health discourse that came to dominate nineteenth-century social policy 'characterized one of the main ways to reform: cleansing' (Topalov 1985, cited in Harloe 1995: 22):

Nineteenth-century schemes to reshape the city could thus be seen as a process of purification, designed to exclude groups variously identified as polluting – the poor in general, the residual working class, racial minorities, prostitutes, and so on.

(Sibley 1995: 57)

Early public health legislation specified minimum housing standards and measures to be taken where these were breached. The Nuisances Removal Acts of 1846 and 1855 enabled authorities to deal with urgent threats to public health. The 1851 Common Lodging Houses Act gave the police powers to inspect accommodation, largely to control the 'filthy, overcrowded thieves' dens and "twopenny brothels"' (Burnett 1986: 63). The 1868 Artisans and Labourers' Dwellings Act and the 1875 Artisans and Labourers' Dwellings Improvement Act permitted local authorities to clear unfit houses and areas of unfit housing respectively. Such measures as these 'dealt with the problem of the putrid masses' (Sibley 1995: 58), but did little by way of widening housing opportunities. An alternative to removing nuisance properties was improving their management.

This included the work of Octavia Hill, who combined intensive housing management with social work. She aimed to 'help' 'slum dwellers' by 'educating' them in the virtues of prudence and abstinence. Effectively, her regime 'policed the morals and behaviour of working-class tenants' (Harloe 1995: 27). A similar regime was the 'model villages', developed by philanthropic employers 'to recreate community centred around the place of work and, conversely, to make factory employment into a "whole life" pursuit' (Bauman 2001: 35).

Moral panics towards the poor continued into the twentieth century, fuelled in part by Social Darwinism and concern for Empire. The 'feckless' were now portrayed as a threat to Britain's economic and military global position. Proposed solutions to this problem included loss of citizenship, loss of parental rights and incarceration in labour 'colonies' – measures supported by Beveridge (Harloe 1995). Writing in 1884, the Cambridge economist, Alfred Marshall, a supporter of proposals to depopulate London of its 'residuum', argued that a great many of the poor 'have a taint of vice in their history' and that of 'these immigrants a great part do no good to themselves or others by coming to London; and there would be no hardship in deterring the worst of them from coming by insisting on strict regulations as to their manner of living here' (cited in Harloe 1995: 38).

An evaluation of housing policies throughout the post-industrial period provides a good example of the way socio-spatial differentiation has been produced in Britain. In particular, when housing policies favoured the working-class heroes of the two World Wars – the skilled working classes or labour aristocracy – the estates were built to high standards, often in leafy suburbs, with generous gardens and local environments. In contrast, when housing policies targeted the unskilled working classes and 'slum dwellers' in the latter part of the inter-war years and from the late 1950s, the quality of homes were poorer – often flatted developments in inner-city or peripheral areas (Forrest and Kennett 1998).

> the *public* debate about council housing allocation has centred around questions of what might be termed 'morality'. This reflects a broader public debate about welfare entitlements, and the historic divide between those deserving of assistance and those undeserving of it .... Appropriate safeguards have always been required to ensure that the 'right' people obtain the 'right' type of accommodation.
>
> (Cowan 2001: 133 – original emphasis)

The use of filtering systems in social housing allocations has been a consistent feature of housing management practice, permitting the urban gatekeepers a potent role in the exacerbation of social and spatial disadvantage (Burden *et al.* 2000). 'Good' neighbourhoods needed to be protected from the 'riff-raff'.

Early sociological interest in the management of neighbourhoods can be found in the empirical tradition of the Chicago School – in particular, Park and Burgess'

1925 study, *The City*, on urban segregation. For Park and Burgess, socio-spatial arrangements resemble bio-ecological processes, with the 'dominant species' controlling the highest-valued spaces. As dominant groups invade the most desirable locations (through suburbanisation or gentrification) the less powerful occupy the spaces left behind. Each group, therefore, occupies their 'appropriate space' – 'the product of evolutionary processes of "the survival of the fittest"' (Savage and Warde 1993: 15). The focus of interest in the Chicago studies, however, was 'deviant' groups – gangsters, tramps, prostitutes and slum-dwellers, socially and spatially segregated from the 'mainstream' – and, more specifically, their 'pathological behaviour'. The concern was with the way such social formations posed threats to the social order, and how such threats might be addressed through reformist policies aimed at encouraging social cohesion and inclusion. In other words, by examining how some neighbourhoods worked while others broke down into vice and lawlessness, the Chicago School believed they could offer policy prescriptions for creating safe and efficacious places. Similar approaches can be found in community studies in postwar Britain. Roberts, citing examples from various investigations, shows how the characteristics of working-class communities subjected to these studies appeared to conform to a preconceived agenda derived from middle-class accounts:

> They are either abnormal and ignorant, have impaired ego due to role restrictions, display low cultural horizons or are 'incurious, inarticulate, almost inanimate'. Implicitly their salvation would seem to lie in adopting middle-class attitudes and behaviour.
>
> (Roberts 1999: 148)

One example Roberts cites is Zweig's 1961 study, *The Worker in an Affluent Society*, which offers evidence of the 'moral rise' of the working class by way of their declining drunkenness and rising temperance, the benefits of which 'can be seen in car and home ownership. This is seen as the working class conforming to a more middle-class attitude and way of life' (Roberts 1999: 157).

The view of working class 'moral failings' was particularly evident in the initial work of the Community Development Projects (CDPs), established in 1968 in response to a rise in urban and 'racial' tensions. In a context where the British government believed primary poverty had been eradicated by the postwar welfare state, these rising tensions were linked to the social pathology, rather than poverty, of some inner-city communities (Lewis 1966). Policy interventions were therefore designed to change the behaviour of such communities and to equip them to compete more effectively in the market place (Atkinson and Moon 1994). Drawing on lessons from the USA's 'War on Poverty' initiative, introduced under President Kennedy, area-based strategies were established that included pre-school initiatives, youth and community projects, employment-related measures and environmental improvements. There was a strong emphasis on giving deprived children the necessary skills to succeed in school and, subsequently, the world of work. Summing up this approach, Atkinson and Moon argue that it represented:

> the *culture of poverty* theory ... which assumed that the poor were in essence the cause of their own problems; the behaviour and culture, of both individuals and communities, was the root cause of urban problems. There is very little evidence that any of the programmes attempted to analyse, define or tackle systematically the problem of poverty in terms of structural inequalities.
>
> (Atkinson and Moon 1994: 37 – original emphasis)

Seabrook sees this as a sustained moral attack on working-class communities:

> There has been a sustained and untiring ideological assault on traditional working-class values, initiated and egged on by the media, with its shifting focus on threats and fears that undermine community – all the scares about mugging, or rapists or vandals; the scare about scroungers and idlers, the hysteria about aliens and migrants, the panic about child-molesters, drug addicts or alkies, glue-sniffers, hooligans, criminals, moles, Reds and wreckers – have swept regularly through the working-class districts.
>
> (Seabrook 1984: 4)

The initial CDP approach was also an attempt to deal with rising 'racial' tensions in some British towns and cities. Black people faced discrimination throughout the late 1950s and 1960s. There were street riots targeting black tenants in Nottingham and Notting Hill (1958); 'colour bar' petitions to exclude black residents from council estates; institutional racism in the form of residential qualifications for council housing; and overtly racist adverts excluding black tenants (proclaiming 'no coloureds' was legal until 1977). In response, black people organised around their own associations (Grayson 1997). In parallel, governments responded by increasing efforts to exclude the 'foreigner':

> Governments strain their ingenuity to the utmost in order to ingratiate themselves with the electors by tightening the immigration laws, restricting the rights to asylum, blackening the image of 'economic migrants' who, unlike the electors encouraged to mount their bikes in search of economic bliss, happen also to be foreigners ...
>
> (Bauman 2001: 101)

At the same time, racist press reports of so-called 'racial' urban tensions have also remained unchallenged by governments. Hall *et al.*, for example, highlighted the disproportionate media attention given to 'black muggers', resulting in a moral panic about black 'youth' as 'trouble'. They suggest that such reportage provides a screen behind which to hide broader social and economic problems (Hall *et al.* 1978). It also led to a correspondingly disproportionate amount of attention given to young black people by the criminal justice system. At the same time, at the local level, such media portrayal feeds negative attitudes held by many white people towards ethnic minorities:

> The proximity of 'ethnic strangers' triggers ethnic instincts in the locals, and the strategies that follow such instincts are aimed at the separation and ghettoization of 'alien elements', which in turn reverberate in the impulse to self-estrangement and self-enclosure of the forcefully ghettoized group.
>
> (Bauman 2001: 103)

This process has utility for powerful elites, splitting neighbourhood versus neighbourhood and lessening the possibility for 'communities' to unite against oppression: 'When the poor fight the poor, the rich have every reason to rejoice … Global order needs a lot of local disorder "to have nothing to fear"' (Bauman 2001: 104–5).

Whilst the CDPs' diagnosis of urban tensions was to shift later towards one emphasising the structural causes of urban problems, this change did not endear them to the government. As Atkinson and Moon put it, it was 'one of the greatest ironies that the Home Office found itself funding a bunch of Marxists' (Atkinson and Moon 1994: 50)! From 1975 funding for CDPs was cut and, by 1978, they were defunct.

In the 1980s the theoretical basis of social policy changed under the political domination of the neo-liberal welfare discourse. At the heart of the neo-liberal project is the desire to encourage individuals to take responsibility for their own and their family's welfare. In respect of the nature of the urban problem, this is perceived in terms of social and physical dereliction – effectively, a maladjusted population spatially concentrated in pockets of the inner city. The 'folk devils' now are the 'criminogenic', inner-city 'underclass':

> In essence, the inner city has become a criminogenic community, a place where the social forces that create predatory criminals are far more numerous and overwhelmingly stronger than the social forces that create virtuous citizens. At core, the problem is that most inner city children grow up surrounded by teenagers and adults who are themselves deviant, delinquent, or criminal. At best, these teenagers and adults misshape the characters and lives of the young in their midst. At worst, they abuse, neglect, or criminally prey upon the young.
>
> (DiIulio 1994, cited in Himmelfarb 1995: 228)

A central feature of the underclass thesis is its assault on the single-parent family, 'the most important factor associated with the "pathology of poverty" – welfare dependency, crime, drugs, illiteracy, homelessness' (Himmelfarb 1995: 233). As Muncie observes, in the 1980s in Britain:

> A resurgent radical right revived a neo-classical vision of criminality as voluntaristic – a course of action willingly chosen by wicked, calculating individuals lacking in self-control. In policy circles a burgeoning administrative criminology argued that all that could be realistically hoped for was to implement pragmatic means aimed at reducing the opportunity for crime and to manage crime through situational preventative measures. Managerial efficiency (what works at some times in some places), cost effectiveness (what works cheaply) and pragmatic risk assessment have become its defining principles.
>
> (Muncie 2000: 3)

In contrast to the single-parent underclass are 'decent' married couples, deserving of state support. This is exemplified in the 1996 Housing Act, which removed the rights of homeless single parents to permanent rehousing in favour of rewarding 'married couples who take a responsible approach to family life, so that tomorrow's generation grow up in a stable environment' (DoE 1995, cited in Jacobs and Manzi 1996: 556). At the same time, the council estate is symbolised as the place most contaminated by single-parent 'folk devils'; a place where 'any idea of parental guidance has in many homes been lost. Most of the children there live in, take for granted, a violent, jungle world' (Hoggart 1993, cited in Himmelfarb 1995: 241). By the 1980s, council estates came to symbolise the monstrous failings of the welfare state. Paul Harrison, in *Inside the Inner City*, preludes his chapter on local authority 'dump estates' with a quote from Dante's *Inferno*:

> There, sighs, laments and loud wailings resounded through the starless air ... Strange tongues, horrible cries, groans of pain, cries of anger, shrill and hoarse voices, and the sound of beatings, made a tumult, circling in the eternal darkness, like sand eddying in a whirlwind.
>
> (Cited in Harrison 1983: 225)

Harrison goes on to suggest that: 'If the inner city is like a chemistry lab full of dangerous social reagents, the dump estate is the test-tube where they are most corrosively combined' (Harrison 1983: 225). The image of council estates as 'problem places' is also one Anne Power has been at pains to emphasise. Her focus on the difficulty of managing these areas led to her prescribed rescue plan of 'tight urban management' (Power 1997: 397) rather than addressing the underlying poverty and inequality council tenants experience.

The neo-liberal project appears to have become the only credible option given 'globalisation'. In the global 'risk society' (Beck 1999), work has become fragile and unsustainable. Jobs vanish overnight. In this context, nation states can no longer have autonomy over their economies, never mind their welfare policies. More of us are facing 'insecurity of social standing, uncertainty about the future of one's livelihood and the overwhelming feeling of "no grip on the present" ' (Bauman 2001: 41). As a consequence, people are losing commitment to 'place'. Drawing on the work of Sennett, Bauman argues:

> the place where the whole of life is conducted or hoped to be conducted 'springs into life with the wave of a developer's wand, flourishes, and begins to decay all within a generation'. In such a place (and more and more people come to know such places and their bitter atmosphere the hard way) no one 'becomes a long-term witness to another person's life'. The place may be physically crowded, and yet frighten and repel the residents by its moral emptiness.
>
> (Bauman 2001: 46)

Nothing remains the same for very long, and this has important social significance. 'Gone is the certainty that "we will meet again", that we will be meeting repeatedly and for a very long time to come' (Bauman 2001: 47). Consequently, as Maurice R. Stein argued back in 1960:

> community ties become increasingly dispensable ... personal loyalties decrease their range with the successive weakening of national ties, regional ties, community ties, neighbourhood ties, family ties and finally, ties to a coherent image of one's self.
>
> (Cited in Bauman 2001: 48)

In 'postmodern', post-Fordist times, people's increasing detachment, indifference and disengagement, alongside attacks on the so-called 'dependency culture', has legitimated the withdrawal of social protection on a massive scale. Absence of commitments to 'others' is epitomised in the new 'gated' communities that are emerging, where those who can afford it 'keep their distance from the "messy intimacy" of ordinary city life' (Bauman 2001: 54). Some even wish to live in villages that exclude the young, such as Hartrigg Oaks, near York, which excludes the under 60s, or the new retirement hamlet at Firhall, near Nairn in the Scottish Highlands, which excludes the under 45s ('Escape to a kid-free village', *The Observer*, 4 May 2003: 6). Hartrigg Oaks is presented as an innovative example of a Continuing Care Retirement Community by the Joseph Rowntree Foundation, offering 'a range of benefits that can contribute to a full and active life: independent living, secure environment, care when needed and a vibrant and stimulating community' (JRF 2003a: 1). It is a place where 'numerous residents' groups have been established to pursue common interests' (JRF 2003a: 1–3), one of which is to exclude 'dangerous' others. These are effectively initiatives in escaping 'community', and the responsibility of caring for and sharing with others. They reflect what Nettleton and Burrows see as a society becoming so individualised that the:

> ... homeless on the street reflect the 'sacrificial lambs' upon the altar of the market gods; even if we wanted to intervene, we are all so insecure in our jobs it becomes almost immoral to care.
>
> (Nettleton and Burrows 1998: 154)

Perhaps one of the most cynical cases of this lack of care was the recently reported role of Barry Legg in the placement of homeless families in asbestos-riddled tower blocks in Westminster in the 1980s (*The Guardian*, 6 May 2003). Iain Duncan Smith (then leader of the Conservative Party) appointed Legg Chief Executive of the Conservative Party in February 2003.

Continuing and extending the neo-liberal moral discourse, New Labour policies since 1997 have constructed a number of new 'folk devils'. Keen to be seen to be tough on crime, the 1998 Crime and Disorder Act introduced a range of initiatives targeting 'anti-social behaviour', including specific measures aimed at 'unfit' parents (parenting orders) and their 'feral' children (child safety orders, curfew orders and the removal of truants to designated places). In order to deal with 'unruly' behaviour, the Act also introduced Anti-Social Behaviour Orders (ASBOs). ASBOs can be served on any person aged 10 years or over who has acted in an 'anti-social manner' – that is, 'a manner that caused or was likely to cause harassment, alarm or distress'. If a person does anything which he or she is prohibited from doing by an ASBO they face imprisonment or a fine. In the co-joined appeals of *Clingham v. Kensington and Chelsea LBC* and *R. v. Manchester Crown Court ex parte McCann [2002]* the House of Lords recognised that although ASBO proceedings were civil in nature, a breach of an ASBO is a criminal offence that can incur up to five years' imprisonment (Sykes 2003). Consequently, behaviour once deemed 'unacceptable' can now be criminalised. Moreover, 'Clingham also confirmed that hearsay evidence may be adduced in ASBO proceedings' (Sykes 2003: 22), reflecting a shift away from protecting the rights of those accused. In discussing the 'drawbacks' for registered social landlords seeking ASBOs, Gail Sykes remarks on the need to 'overcome the onerous obligation to consult with the Local Authority and the local Police before making an application', while 'trying to prove the offence always takes a time and effort' (Sykes 2003: 23). How inconvenient. Meanwhile, a recent survey by the *Law Society Gazette* showed that finding legal advice on housing-related issues is becoming increasingly difficult:

> Citing problems with bureaucracy and low fees, more and more solicitors and law firms are pulling out of housing work funded by the legal aid system

… This can cause real hardship and injustice for clients. In urgent cases people may not be able to get the advice they need to keep a roof over their heads.

(Baker 2003: 23–4)

On 27 March 2003, New Labour published a Bill devoted entirely to anti-social behaviour. This defines a new 'folk devil' – the 'demoted' tenant (applicable only to council tenants, or those of Housing Action Trusts, because of their 'anti-social behaviour'). Tenants of 'demoted tenancies' lose security rights, a policy Shelter condemns. In particular, Shelter is concerned this measure will, alongside separate proposals to cut the benefits of people found 'guilty' of anti-social behaviour, exacerbate the problem of homelessness (Shelter Press Release, 8 April 2003). Regardless of this, Alistair Darling, Secretary of State for Work and Pensions, justifies cutting housing and child benefits from 'disruptive' families as a means of promoting social objectives:

I believe there is no unconditional right to benefit. It's entirely consistent with our beliefs that we should give people rights and support when they need support but say in return that people behave [with] responsibility in relation to other citizens … It's not only possible, but entirely desirable that we should look at making sure the social security system and the benefits system are matched by responsibility.

(Alistair Darling, cited in the *Independent*, 16 May 2002: 10)

Darling went on to state that New Labour was looking at linking the criminal justice system with the benefits system:

It is right that we should ask ourselves if there is a role for the benefits system as part of the wider system in asserting the values we hold and asserting the kind of behaviour that we want to see.

(Alistair Darling, cited in the *Independent*, 16 May 2002: 10)

Perhaps one of the strongest campaigners on the 'politics of behaviour' is Labour MP Frank Field. In an article for *Inside Housing* magazine, Field argued:

As part of the armoury of civilised society the government must move to a position where, on their second offence, families lose their housing benefit in its entirety. Children growing up in such families are in danger and should be taken into care until the families learn how to behave.

(Field 2003: 15)

As for the 'worst offenders', Field advocates housing these on their own, 'away from decent people': 'In Birkenhead, I would have them housed under the motorway, out of harm's way where they can torment each other while learning how to behave' (Field 2003: 15).

Any readers disputing Mr Field's proposals should also be punished.

> If readers of *Inside Housing* disagree, I would be very pleased to hear from them so that I can suggest to their local authorities that such hoodlums are, wherever possible, relocated to their road and, even better still, in an adjoining house.
>
> (Field 2003: 15)

As Harrison and Davis observe: 'discourses about conditionality and social order have gained ground, suggesting growing desires to deter or punish through administrative practices of welfare provision as well as through law and order systems' (Harrison with Davis 2001: 191–2).

Stuart Hall identifies a moral crusade in the politics of New Labour and that 'discredited and obscene Victorian utilitarian distinction between "the deserving" and "the undeserving" poor' (Hall 1998: 12). While New Labour distinguish themselves from the Conservatives through their proclaimed commitment to social inclusion, it is a discourse of inclusion closer to the underclass thesis (inclusion through moral and behavioural reform, and re-engagement with paid work) than to structuralist accounts (inclusion through the redistribution of power and wealth) (Levitas 1998). Indeed, during New Labour's first six years in office, income inequality widened – caused largely by sharply rising wages at the top and a slow-down in wage and benefit increases at the bottom.

Additionally, many of Britain's second and third generation immigrants continue to face disproportionate levels of social disadvantage – higher unemployment, poorer housing conditions and greater levels of morbidity – than white Britons (Census 2001). At the same time, immigrants are re-emerging as the new 'folk devils' of the early twenty-first century. Shortly after New Labour's election victory in 1997, the then Home Secretary Jack Straw announced plans to tackle 'abusive asylum claims' while Immigration Minister Mike O'Brien stated the government was going to take a tough stand on 'economic refugees' and 'bogus asylum seekers' (Movement for Justice, 2003: 1). Subsequently, David Blunkett spoke of asylum seekers 'swamping' British schools ('The Today Programme', BBC Radio 4, 25 April, 2002). More recently, Chris Fox, president of the Association of Chief Police Officers, argued that the number of refugees entering Britain had reached 'tidal wave' proportions, bringing with it: 'a whole new type of crime, from the Nigerian fraudster, to the eastern European who deals in drugs and prostitution to the Jamaican concentration on drug dealing' ('Immigrants "behind crime wave" – police', *Observer*, 18 May 2003: 1).

Following urban riots in northern England in summer 2001, rather than address the poverty, inequality and racism that divides society, New Labour saw the way forward as 'community cohesion' – the blueprint for which was set out in the Cantle Report (Home Office 2001). The Cantle Report is effectively:

> ... the government's race manifesto. It provides a new formula, in which the separate cultural development that had been encouraged for decades is to be subsumed to the demands of 'community cohesion'. A set of core values is to put limits on multiculturalism and black people are required to develop 'a greater acceptance of the principal national institutions'.
>
> (Kundnani 2002: 3)

A new Community Cohesion Task Force was established under David Blunkett who initiated a national debate suggesting immigrants take an 'oath of allegiance' to the British state, adopt British norms and speak English in their homes. In addition, the Cantle Report advocated the fostering of mutual understanding and respect between ethnic groups through cross-cultural contact (for instance, by holding inter-faith dialogue or twinning schools) (Kundnani 2002; Appleton 2002). Both these initiatives blame ethnic minorities for the problem – their inability to integrate with the British way of life – and reflect 'the government's increasing concern with the assimilation of immigrants' (Appleton 2002: 1). This is a shift away from notions of multiculturalism. Immigrants must now assimilate into New Labour's particular brand of 'community' – homogenised and Anglo-Saxon – even though it is that same 'community' that continues to discriminate against them.

Under the neo-liberal project – first under the New Right Conservatives and then New Labour – we have experienced welfare reforms based on a politics 'which questions the value of solidarity' (Andersen 2003: ix). In today's Britain, the 'other' is consigned: 'to a prospectless misery, as the triumph of meritocratic ideology leads inexorably to its logical conclusion, that is to the dismantling of welfare provisions, that communal insurance against individual misfortune' (Bauman 2001: 59). Today, 'Troubles are supposed to be suffered and coped with alone and are singularly unfit for cumulation into a community of interests which seeks collective solutions to individual troubles' (Bauman 2001: 86).

While it could be argued that this claim does not square with New Labour's commitment to 'strong communities' as a source of social integration – supported by such initiatives as Sure Start and the New Deal for Communities – what Bauman and others appear to be suggesting is that New Labour's particular notion of community represents a return to 'the moral and social inflections of communitarianism' (Newman 2003: 148). Communitarianism, whilst critical of liberal individualism, retains a strong attachment to traditional morality.

> The main idea of communitarianism is to balance individual rights and community responsibilities. Unrestrained individualism is seen as having undermined family and community relations. The goal of communitarians is

to promote community rather than equality ... Communitarianism has become a key idea in those versions of reformism that downplay economic egalitarianism and emphasise moral improvement. The solution to social exclusion needs to include the return to traditional community values ... [A] strong community requires traditional nuclear family structures, providing strong parenting ... It also requires members of communities to accept their duties and responsibilities in the form of service to others, effectively prioritising civil duties over civil rights.

(Burden *et al*. 2000: 29–30)

For New Labour, community involvement is 'formal volunteering; helping a neighbour; taking part in a community organisation' (SEU 1998: 68) – effectively, being a dutiful, responsible citizen. This duty now includes spying on our neighbours – 'Large posters urge on us the patriotic duty to report a "benefit fraud"' (Redgrave 2003: 35). Human suffering is no longer a public concern in the sense that the state's role in protecting civil and social rights has been diluted (Berghman 1995). New Labour's social policies continue to deny redistributive claims to welfare and collective rights. However, the detrimental effect of the socio-spatial divide in Britain – as Blair concedes, 'comfortable Britain ... knows the price it pays for economic and social breakdown in the poorest parts of Britain' (cited in Pantazis and Gordon 2000: 14) – is a public concern, and must be managed and contained. In pursuance of this, and drawing on the work of 18 Policy Action Teams, New Labour set out its National Strategy Action Plan (NSAP) on neighbourhood renewal (SEU 2001). Despite evidence that previous area-based strategies have failed to address the structural causes of neighbourhood decline associated with economic, social and political disempowerment (Pantazis and Gordon 2000), the thrust of the government's Action Plan is area-based intervention. This would appear to contradict the government's own assessment in 1998 of the failings of neighbourhood regeneration initiatives since the 1960s:

despite the continuing refinement of these programmes, the condition of many of the most deprived areas has either not improved or in some cases, has actually worsened. Many of the neighbourhoods that are most deprived now have been so since Victorian times, despite the amount of public money spent on them and their appearance in one Government regeneration programme after another ... Some of the reasons have to do with the impact of structural economic changes on towns and regions.

(SEU 1998: 34)

Three years later, the team behind the Cantle Report into community cohesion stated how they were:

particularly struck by the depth of polarisation of our towns and cities. The extent to which these physical divisions were compounded by so many other aspects of our daily lives, was very evident ... Programmes devised to tackle the needs of many disadvantaged and disaffected groups ... often seemed to institutionalise the problems. The plethora of initiatives and programmes, with their baffling array of outcomes, boundaries, timescales and other conditions, seemed to ensure divisiveness and a perception of unfairness in virtually every section of the communities we visited.

(Home Office 2001: 9–10)

What *is* prominent in New Labour's NSAP is its emphasis on supervising 'social dysfunction' through encouraging access to paid work (with education and training support), user involvement in neighbourhood management and the enhancement of community networks (see SEU 2001, Chapter 3). As Sullivan observes, the focus of the plan is 'in relation to the interpersonal. This reflects the New Labour pre-occupation with citizens needing to accept their responsibilities' (Sullivan 2002: 509).

This represents continuity with previous policies that have adopted a view of urban deprivation as being caused by the flawed pathology of individuals. New Labour's renewal strategy continues to express a strong moralising discourse that constructs categories of 'people' and 'places', distinguishing the 'socially excluded' from the 'norm' – viz. 'mainstream' society:

The cultures of groups defined as socially excluded were viewed in terms of deficits (of aspiration, confidence, willingness to take risks, and so on) or a surfeit of 'troubling' characteristics (e.g. school truancy, drug addiction, anti-social behaviour).

(Newman 2003: 153)

As with previous policies, New Labour's strategy will fail to resolve difficult neighbourhood circumstances because the material, political and ideological structural constraints that divide society will remain. Indeed, New Labour's politics is one that has managed over ever widening inequalities in health, education, housing (Howarth *et al.*1999) and income (Shephard 2003). Wide income differentials have a direct bearing on the nature of social relationships, including lower levels of trust and social support, and higher levels of hostility and conflict (Wilkinson 1998). Widening gaps in social status exacerbate notions of 'difference' and access to essential resources, fragmenting society into competing groupings and encouraging more aggressive social interaction (Jordan 1996) as people attempt to ward off feelings of ineptitude and lack of power. As Wilkinson argues, the 'psychosocial welfare of the population is determined by structural factors' (Wilkinson 1998: 39). Consequently, what is needed is a multi-dimensional policy response that addresses the wider economic, political, social and interpersonal processes within which neighbourhood problems and social inequality are rooted. For Berghman, this requires attending to the labour market (economic integration), the democratic and legal system (civic integration), the welfare state system (social integration), and the family and community system (interpersonal integration) (Berghman 1995). It also requires attention to processes of exclusion structured around gender, 'race', sexuality and disability. Effectively, this calls for:

> a reshaping of democracy, enabling the possibility of challenges that move forwards ... [and] recognise the need for a continued array of feminist, anti-racist, gay and disability politics that articulates issues of recognition and redistribution.
>
> (Newman 2003: 180)

Having illustrated the way moralising discursive practices have retained a dominant role in shaping social policy throughout modern times, and the way these subsequent policy developments have helped to maintain socio-spatial differentiation and disadvantage in Britain, the final section of this chapter considers the prospects for building a different 'community' politics out of which more equitable social and spatial arrangements might emerge. There is a need to step back and examine the utility of discursive practices for maintaining dominant power relationships. If the creation of 'folk devils' through discourse has been integral to preserving inequality and disadvantage in society, then challenging this discourse must be central to any strategy of equality.

Challenging the moral discourse

Dominant notions of 'dangerous' people and 'dangerous' places seldom focus on the broader social context, presenting instead a myopic view of 'danger' which disguises everyday injustices and more serious harms – poverty and inequality; exploitation and environmental decay; state crime and corporate crime. To reverse this tendency, there needs to be a broader appreciation of 'commonsense' notions of 'danger' and 'harmful' practices. This requires wider public recognition than what is defined as 'danger' rests essentially on having the power to define:

> A conception of crime without a conception of power is meaningless. The power to render certain harmful acts visible and define them as 'crime', whilst maintaining the invisibility of others (or defining them as beyond criminal sanction) lies at the heart of the problem of working within notions of 'the problem of crime'.
>
> (Muncie 2000: 5)

Understanding mainstream notions of 'deviance' and 'danger' requires attention to the way power holders construct 'deviance' and 'danger', and the 'folk devils' in need of treatment or punishment. The key issue for social policy, therefore, is to expose the way social order is maintained through discursive practices, and how this impacts on life chances. This implies a radical departure from much mainstream social policy thinking which, as we have seen, tends to accept dominant discourses of social problems – e.g. 'the underclass', 'problem neighbourhoods', 'dump estates', 'feral youth', the 'criminogenic', 'anti-social behaviour', 'bogus' asylum seekers, and so forth – and searches for solutions to these. One recent example of this is a Home Office job advertisement for 'Head of Web Services' (*The Guardian*'s Jobs and Money Supplement, 21 June 2003: 48), which opens: 'Help tackle yob culture, cut crime and reduce drug use. All before lunch'. Another is the Joseph Rowntree Foundation, 'one of the largest social policy research and development charities in the UK' (JRF 2003b: 1), which in 2003 still 'shares the hopes of its founder that *"to seek out the underlying causes of weakness or evil"* should contribute to *"the right measures of human advancement"* which over a period of time could *"change the face of England"*' (JRF 2003c: 1 – original emphasis). Of particular significance is the increase in social policy investigations which embrace New Labour's 'evidence-based' policy research agenda, exemplified in the title of the 2003 UK Social Policy Association Conference at the University of Teesside – 'What Works? Evidence, Research and Inference in Social Policy'. Such trends have led to:

> a commitment to determine 'what works' *and* the ceaseless evaluation of what exists which, as Phil Scraton has pointed out, 'invariably means a revival of number crunching, schematic and instrumental positivism' …. Thus academics compete tirelessly for the right to work for the national and local state, producing evaluations of programmes that they themselves have urged, often only to suggest some tinkerings with those programmes – tinkerings that then become subject to the need for further evaluation.
>
> (Hillyard *et al.* 2004: 370)

Meanwhile, social inequality in Britain and other serious social harms generated by the powerful receive little attention. Policy responses to 'dangerous' people and places have invariably focused on social control through criminal justice measures, urban management and top-down 'community development'. Particularly since the 1980s, the dominant political discourse on social policy has shifted away from principles of welfare redistribution and social justice towards the criminalisation of the most vulnerable – particularly the 'wayward', the working class, single parents and their 'unruly' offspring – leading to an increase in disciplinary mechanisms (Burden *et al.* 2000). As Cohen argues: 'Social policies once regarded as abnormal – incarcerating hundreds of asylum seekers in detention centres, run as punitive transit camps by private companies for profit – are seen as being normal, rational and conventional' (Cohen 2002: xxxiv).

All this is not intended to downplay or minimise disruptive or violent behaviour, or to deny that residents want to feel something can be done to address their troublesome neighbours. It is, however, intended to present the case that such activities need to be explained within a broader framework of understanding, one that acknowledges the wider social context (social structure and societal values). For example, is 'incivility' a reflection of more deep-rooted social problems such as inequality and human despair? And is the attention given to such behaviour disproportionate in comparison to other harms – corporate killing, human rights abuses, financial fraud and so forth (Hillyard *et al.* 2004). As Cohen argues:

> The idea that social problems are socially constructed does not question their existence nor dismiss issues of causation, prevention and control. It draws attention to a meta debate about what sort of acknowledgement the problem receives and merits. The issue indeed is *proportionality*.
>
> (Cohen 2002: xxxiv – original emphasis)

Setting social problems in context would allow us to ask such questions as, is 'anti-social' behaviour a rational response to perceptions of social injustice and political marginalisation? Sardar and Davies illustrate this point with reference to Mathieu Kassovitz's 1995 film *La Haine* ('Hate') in which three young men, each a member of an ethnic minority group, 'discover the meaning of hatred' whilst living on a Parisian housing estate:

> These adolescents have no jobs, no money and, even more important, no prospects of any kind. So, they hang out much like any inner-city group of marginalised young men, drifting aimlessly through the streets and suburbs. But doing nothing has its consequences, particularly when the police have singled you out as a possible source of criminal activity ... Kassovitz ... is concerned with showing that marginalisation itself is a form of violence; that it leads to other types of violence, feeds back on itself and eventually spirals out of control. The film's protagonists are not particularly bad or violent individuals. They are simply humans trying to be human, with all their strengths and faults. But their ethnicity and appearance, their class and social background, have labelled them as inferior and violent. So that's the way they are treated by society in general, and by the police – who do not hesitate to torture the boys – in particular. And, in their turn, the boys' hatred is a compound product of their economic marginalisation, their cultural and racial treatment, and their own interpretation of their existence.
>
> (Sardar and Davies 2002: 193–4)

Social policy research needs to reconnect with more meaningful debates around democracy, social justice and emancipation (see other chapters in this volume).

This means taking a step back and questioning the dominant discourses behind and shaping current developments in policy research and policymaking. Specifically in relation to this debate on 'dangerous' people and places, there is a need to analyse, first, the way 'knowledge' and meaning are produced through discursive practices and, second, understanding the effects of these social constructions on social policy developments. A framework for such analyses can be found in Niels Åkerstrøm Andersen's recent work, *Discursive Analytical Strategies*, which offers a set of strategies drawing on Foucault's discourse analysis, Koselleck's theory of concepts, Laclau's notions on hegemony and Luhmann's systems theory (Andersen 2003). Taken together, elements of these four theorists' thinking offer a toolbox for deconstructing commonsense notions of understanding – for the purpose of this chapter, 'dangerous' people and places – and subjecting these to critical scrutiny.

First, Foucault offers a framework for contesting discursive assumptions:

> He challenges individual will and reason by showing how every utterance is an utterance within a specific discourse to which certain rules of acceptability apply … Foucault wants to show how any discourse involves excluding procedures, which not only exclude themes, arguments and speech positions from the discourse, but also produce outsiders, denounce groups of people as sick, abnormal or irrational, and grant other groups the right and legitimacy to treat these people (for example by imprisonment or therapy) … [C]riminality and illness are discursive positions, which are established with the intent to control.
>
> (Andersen 2003: 3)

Foucault's framework here provides a useful tool for unravelling moral interpretations. Who or what determines what is morally 'good' or acceptable and conversely what is 'evil' or unacceptable? And what 'knowledge' sources – ideas and ways of communicating – have been excluded from such determinations? And how are the subjects of these discourses represented – as 'acceptable' or 'unacceptable'? And what are the effects of such representations – inclusion or exclusion? And how do policies respond to these effects – supportively or punitively? And finally, who has gained most from such discursive practices? Have they led to a general social improvement, or merely served to maintain existing dominant power relationships? In other words, Foucault offers an approach to deconstructing moral judgements of people and places, and assessing who gains (as included insiders) and who loses out (as excluded outsiders).

Sibley's study on spatial exclusion adopts a similar approach. He is particularly critical of power structures in academia that establish and maintain hierarchies of knowledge to the exclusion of conflicting and threatening ideas – particularly those that come from the oppressed. He suggests, for example, that if critical concepts come from:

women or black authors in certain contexts, or from minorities whose world-view is informed by their sexuality, they may be considered dangerous because they challenge white heterosexual male domination of the western knowledge industry. If the marginalized claim the centre ground, or argue that there is no centre ground, there is at least an implicit threat to the authority of the guardians of established knowledge.

(Sibley 1995: 116)

Sibley offers the case of W.E.B. DuBois as an example of excluded discourse. He argues that DuBois 'is a major figure in black American history whose work on the city was, I think, a significant contribution to the understanding of social space' (Sibley 1995: 137–8). However, DuBois' work was overshadowed by the Chicago School and failed to gain a voice in mainstream urban geography. His book *The Philadelphia Negro*, published in 1899, offered an analysis of socio-spatial segregation that exposed processes of racism – explanations glaringly absent from Chicago sociology. His research was dismissed as 'unscientific'. Similarly, research into Chicago's housing problems by women reformers in the 1920s and 1930s was dismissed as 'social work', inferior to 'scientific sociology, an implicitly masculine form of knowledge' (cited in Sibley 1995: 168). These cases illustrate how 'race' and gender factors can influence whether one's perspective or expectations find endorsement within mainstream society.

Second, Koselleck's theory of concepts offers a terrain upon which counter positions to dominant discourses can be built. He emphasises both the contestability of concepts and their centrality to social and political action. 'Without concepts … there is no society and no political fields of action' (Andersen 2003: 34). For Koselleck, concepts are also always ambiguous (otherwise they cannot be concepts): 'concepts are always fundamentally *ambiguous* … Precisely through its ambiguity, the concept can create positions for later occupation and conquest' (Andersen 2003: 36 – original emphasis).

The ambiguity of concepts means that they can never offer a true representation of their subject. At the same time, concepts are ideas that need to be linguistically formulated. Therefore, conceptual arguments through discourse always produce counter-concepts around which alternative understandings can be formulated – effectively, a site for 'a semantic battle about the political and social; a battle about the definition, defence and occupation of conceptually composed positions' (Andersen 2003: 34). There are always possibilities, therefore, for resisting dominant discourses of 'dangerous' people and places through counter concepts that expose structural issues – such as 'race', class and gender – or alternative notions of 'harm'.

Third, in Laclau's analysis of hegemony we can see genuine possibilities for identifying where organised resistance to dominating discourses might occur. As Laclau argues:

> [H]egemony is only possible when something exists that can be hegemonised, and that this is only the case when discourse lacks final fixation, when the discursive elements hold a surplus of meaning and when the signifiers are not irreversibly linked to the signified. Consequently, hegemony signifies the never-concluded attempts to produce a fixation, to which there will always be a threat.
>
> (Andersen 2003: 55)

In other words, hegemonic consent can never be fully secured because hegemony is something that has to be constantly strived for – a 'battle of fixating' (Andersen 2003: 55). Consequently, there is always potential for counter-hegemonic projects against the dominating discourse of people and places – be they residents challenging the way they and their neighbourhoods have been constructed by power holders (Cooper and Hawtin 1997), or autonomous research working to non-prescribed agendas (Hillyard *et al.* 2004), which allow the underlying mainstream assumptions behind neighbourhood problems to be challenged.

Finally, Luhmann's systems theory offers a framework for exposing the motives of social institutions and bringing these bodies to account. His particular interest is the way the 'function systems' of modern society – the scientific system, the political system, the economic system, the education system, the judicial system, the media system, and so forth – observe and explain 'social reality'. He introduces the idea of 'observations' as 'operations' that 'do not refer to conscious subjects but to differences' (Andersen 2003: 64). In other words, an observation is defined as a specific operation or activity that involves the selection of a particular distinction. We cannot observe any social phenomenon and make judgements about its essence without first having selected a means of distinguishing. Andersen explains this with an illustration:

> We might, for example, fasten upon something artistic. 'Art' is then indicated. But art can only be indicated within the boundaries of a distinction. The opposite side could be ugliness, unsightliness, disharmony and so on, and this other side of the distinction makes a difference to the way art appears as an object to the observer. Therefore, what we observe is above all dependent on the distinction that defines the framework for what is indicated in the world at large.
>
> (Andersen 2003: 64)

Ways of seeing and naming something in the world always occur as a result of one particular choice of distinguishing and indicating. Therefore, what is named will always possess characteristics that are not indicated (a blind spot).

Such a distinction isolates the marked from the unmarked and it is therefore only possible for one side of the distinction to be indicated at a time. If both

sides are marked, the distinction is cancelled out. It is not possible simultaneously to observe an object as beautiful and ugly...

(Andersen 2003: 65)

Luhmann's systems theory is an attempt to illuminate the blind spots in
observations, and to expose the way social systems select 'the distinctions that
fundamentally decide what can appear in society and how' (Andersen 2003: 65).
Through conducting what he terms 'second-order' observations of social systems,
Luhmann suggests that it becomes possible to reveal how those systems only see
what their choice of distinguishing allows them to see – allowing social phenomena
to be understood within a broader context, beyond the limited perspective drawn
from observations based on a particular distinction or vantage point. It will require
self-restriction and precision of observation on behalf of the second-order observer.
It may involve asking such questions as, why was a particular distinction chosen
in preference to a different one and what was the implication of that choice
(Andersen 2003). In this way, social systems can be made to account for the way
they observe and subsequently construct social reality. In the case of 'dangerous'
people and places, why do explanations of neighbourhood problems emphasise
'yob culture' rather than lack of opportunity? Why have 'curfew orders for young
people ... become the starting point for the law-and-order debate, rather than the
construction of youth clubs or community centres' (Hillyard et al. 2004: 384)?

In the current context, social policy solutions to social and spatial problems are
constructed within a New Labour discourse which maintains the need to adapt to
flexible markets as an 'inescapable reality' (Rustin and Chamberlayne 2002: 10).
The consequences of this for the most vulnerable are a reduction in social assistance
and employment rights, and the increasing commodification of public services.
What should be defined as public issues – inadequate social protection (Bauman
1998), a divisive education system (Tomlinson 2001) and growing health inequalities (Acheson 1998) – have become individualised personal problems. While New
Labour has attempted to promote 'opportunity' – particularly through New Deal
and the Social Exclusion Unit – its emphasis has been on opportunity through
'employability', presented as 'something individuals must actively achieve ...
Inclusion becomes a duty rather than a right' (Levitas 1998: 128). Such a strategy,
however, is fundamentally flawed in today's flexible labour market where it is
becoming increasingly difficult to obtain a sufficient, regular income from paid
work (Burden et al. 2000). This is particularly true for women, ethnic minorities
and disabled people (Levitas 1998). If we are to build an inclusive society that
benefits everyone, we need to look towards a new social order different from the
existing under-regulated market system. This will require social and economic
policies built around the expressed needs of a broader constituency. This requires
researchers, policy makers and practitioners giving more attention to people's
own 'narratives of lived experience' in order to gain a clearer understanding of
'the complexities of the world and how we are constructed in it' (Davis Creal

1999: 4). Specifically in relation to socio-spatial differentiation, Andersen's framework, set out above, offers a toolbox for researchers and community development practitioners working with disadvantaged communities to:

- unravel and scrutinise the dominant discourse on 'dangerous' people and places to assess its validity;
- develop counter-concepts that expose the contradictions within the dominant discourse and convey alternative understandings of local issues, problems and solutions;
- identify sites of conflict between hegemonising concepts and counter-concepts;
- expose the underlying assumptions behind the activities of social institutions and offer alternative perspectives.

Working with communities in this way, researchers and community development practitioners can help to build different understandings of difficult neighbourhood situations and, potentially, constituencies of support for alternative social policy arrangements. To a degree, such an approach is evident in a cross-national comparative research project conducted by Chamberlayne *et al.* (2002) for the European Union Targeted Socio-Economic Research Programme 4 on Social Exclusion which aimed to 'investigate the experience of individuals who found themselves excluded, or at risk of exclusion, from important spheres of life in their societies' using 'sociobiographical methods' (Rustin and Chamberlayne 2002: 1–2). While the findings of this study 'amply convey the social catastrophes wreaked and threatened by neoliberalism, they also point towards increasingly positive possibilities, based on more dialogical forms of solidarity, in which individuality is enhanced by mutuality' (Rustin and Chamberlayne 2002: 12). A central element behind the success of many of the initiatives examined was political discourse, which played 'a vital levering role in social change' (Rustin and Chamberlayne 2002: 15).

> In this situation, researchers have the opportunity and responsibility to become mediators. In *Pedagogy of the Oppressed*, Freire writes of the 'true words, with which men [sic] transform the world. To exist, humanly, is to *name* the world, to change it' … '[N]aming' helps to bring about deliberate action in coordination with others. Biographical material provides for the possibility of this kind of mediation.
>
> (Rustin and Chamberlayne 2002: 15–16 – original emphasis)

Under 'postmodernism', we are told, there can be no single grand narrative or discourse about the human condition – it is the 'end of ideology', with different discourses and biographies possible (Bauman 2001). This leads to the prospect of promoting a dialogical concept of social problems and, subsequently, social policy responses. 'Policy and practice detail must be delegated to local areas and communities of interest [where the] characteristics of local discursive practices … will reflect local needs' (Burden *et al*. 2000: 60).

Social policy needs to develop within the context of a discourse of social problems that embraces broader social agendas reflecting diverse needs, articulated and defined by the individuals or groups concerned. This requires the facilitation of dialogue that recognises contextuality: 'a role that enables discursive practices to be fluid and relational by exposing and challenging the processes of exclusion and oppression … and encouraging active participation in policy-making and implementation' (Burden *et al*. 2000: 61).

Delivering this strategy will require effective community development, a different approach to community development from those largely confined to the state's or agency's agenda (social planning or improving service delivery) (Cooper and Hawtin 1997). For community development to be an effective tool in delivering more equitable outcomes it needs to enable different communities 'to comprehend the nature of the dominant discourse that "subjectifies" and oppresses' (Burden *et al*. 2000: 301) – to gain what Freire called 'critical consciousness' (Freire 1976).

> Community development is about allowing people to recognise that the existence of unequal power relationships in society is both a personal and political issue. Once this has been achieved, communities can engage more effectively in critical dialogue with power holders … . This way, different interest groups within communities can come to define their own objectives and, through engaging in collective action, work towards changing their circumstances.
>
> (Burden *et al*. 2000: 301–2)

Community development involves 'critical practice', a process of informal education that holds potential for creating a fairer and more cohesive society. Bamber and Murphy see a role for informal education in raising awareness about key concepts of power and forms of social action that connect personal experience to the political. They argue the need to uncover and question the basic assumptions upon which power holders exert their control and allow deep social injustices to remain. For Bamber and Murphy, 'critical practice is not an event, a final or ultimate moment of radical work, but a process of working towards a preferred anti-oppressive future' (Bamber and Murphy 1999: 227). The main outcome of Murard's study of 'deprived people' in 'deprived places' was 'the discovery, through the narratives, of a strong feeling of guilt associated with situations in which people experience difficulties in managing their lives by themselves' (Murard 2002: 43). This 'culture of guilt' was constructed in the context of a political and media discourse on juvenile delinquency, 'interpreted as the result of parental neglect' (Murard 2002: 43). Leonard argues the need for community development practices which support resistance to such labelling effects by 'de-pathologizing the experiences of subjects and renaming them as the effects of ... discourses and practices of social domination' (Leonard 1997: 164).

This way, community development becomes a site of democratic activity where people can 'attempt to address issues of social justice' (Bamber and Murphy 1999: 241). It may also allow greater attention to be given to more pervasive and serious harms. As Muncie suggests:

> Poverty, malnutrition, pollution, medical negligence, breaches of workplace health and safety laws, corporate corruption, state violence, genocide, human rights violations and so on all carry with them more widespread and damaging consequences than most of the behaviours and incidents that currently make up 'the problem of crime'.
>
> (Muncie 2000: 4)

Writing this in the aftermath of the 2003 Iraq war, there is a growing sense of unease in Britain about the legitimacy of a political leadership that seems to have embarked on an immoral war in breach of international law. Perhaps out of this disquiet may emerge a more reasoned conceptualisation of 'dangerous' people. If there was no threat to the west from weapons of mass destruction, which appears to be the case, a more likely 'justification' for the war might be found in the principles of the Project for the New American Century (PNAC), the neo-conservative think-tank behind the Bush government's foreign policy initiative. Established in 1997 to critique the Clinton administration, the PNAC's goal is 'to promote American global leadership' ('About PNAC', cited at PNAC 2003). This aim is based on:

> a few fundamental propositions: that American leadership is good both for America and for the world; that such leadership requires military strength, diplomatic energy and commitment to moral principle; and that too few political leaders today are making the case for global leadership.
>
> (William Kristol, Chairman, 3 June 1997, cited at PNAC 2003)

Included among the signatories to the PNAC are Dick Cheney, Donald Rumsfeld and Paul Wolfowitz, key protagonists in Bush's war on Iraq – arguably a war to promote American political and economic strategic leadership in the Gulf region. Critical practice through community development needs to engage with such global issues because they are part of the same logic of capitalism that exploits communities at the local level. As Miyoshi observes, under conditions of post-Fordism, transnational corporations, aided by the American influenced World Trade Organisation (WTO), are free to colonise any site that provides cheap labour, exposing workers universally to either structural unemployment or the insecurity of part-time, temporary low-paid work (Miyoshi 1993). Community development needs to expose these brutalising tendencies and, in so doing, facilitate the development of a coalition involving different communities of interest – residents on housing estates, poverty campaigners, environmentalists, trade unions, women's movements, anti-racist organisations, disability groups, global justice movements and so forth – to demand democratic control and accountability of the function systems of society. The urgency to link local community action with global protest movements is also the concern of Bauman:

> Because they stay mainly local, political agencies operating in urban space tend to be fatally afflicted with an insufficiency of the power to act, and particularly to act effectively and in a sovereign manner.
>
> (Bauman 2003: 100)

Consequently, the problem of socio-spatial segregation cannot be resolved by localised urban regeneration initiatives alone.

> The kind of 'security' that the urban developers offer is impotent to relieve, let alone eradicate, the existential insecurity replenished daily by the fluidity of labour markets, by the fragility of the value ascribed to past or currently pursued skills and competences, by the acknowledged vulnerability of human bonds and the assumed precariousness and revocability of commitments and partnerships.
>
> (Bauman 2003: 115–16)

Without democracy at the global as well as the local level, the unelected guardians of global neo-conservatism – the UN General Assembly, the International Monetary Fund, the World Bank, the WTO – will perpetuate a situation whereby the most vulnerable (and indeed the majority of us) are left without the means to influence decisions which impact upon social and economic well-being. George Monbiot offers a model of a new world order run by and for 'the people'. It is a vision based on both neo-Keynesian style regulation of international trade and the democratisation of global governance mainly through an elected World Parliament (Monbiot 2003). One would need to be extremely optimistic to believe Monbiot's schema is realisable, although such optimism does exist. Paul Kingsnorth, for example, believes the global protest movement: 'could turn out to be the biggest political movement of the twenty-first century: a global coalition of millions, united in resisting an out-of-control global economy, and already building alternatives to it' (Kingsnorth 2003: 1).

Community development has a central role to play in mobilising such movements of resistance. In particular, community development practitioners hold the tools to enable people to develop a broader understanding of power relationships and their destructive effects. In this way, more and more people may begin to feel what Leonard describes as that sense of 'rage' we should *all* feel at the:

> degrading conditions of existence – material, social, cultural – which are experienced by millions of people in the Third World [sic] and in 'advanced' capitalist countries. These conditions, and our understanding of them as economically and socially produced – the result of human action – are the basis of critical discourses and practices which are fuelled by a sense of moral outrage at the structures of domination and injustice which are manufactured, reproduced and disseminated under late capitalism.
>
> (Leonard 1997: 162)

Here we see possibilities for generating a different reading of the utility of 'moral panic' – something Cohen himself calls for:

> The genealogy of the term, its current usage and its folk meaning allow for one reading only: the term is not just 'value laden' but intended to be a critical tool to expose dominant interests and ideologies ... Perhaps we could purposely *recreate* the conditions that made the Mods and Rockers panic so successful ... and thereby overcome the barriers of denial, passivity and indifference that prevent a full acknowledgement of human cruelty and suffering.
>
> (Cohen 2002: xxxiii – original emphasis)

Adopting a different reading of 'moral panic', its utility could be the mobilisation of a collective moral outrage against the dominant ideological discourses that sustain social injustice and more serious harms.

Conclusion

Throughout modern history there have been various attempts to impose social control over 'marginalised' groups through the pathologisation of particular lifestyles. By dominating the discourse through which commonsense understandings of ways of being are constructed, power holders have been able to perpetuate the capitalist economic order and maintain disciplinary control – particularly with the aid of social policies aimed at managing 'deviance' and maintaining social cohesion. This tendency has continued to the present day, particularly in respect of regeneration policies aimed at creating safe and efficacious places. The discursive practices on 'dangerous' people in 'dangerous' places have endured the Chicago School, the postwar British community studies, the early CDPs of the late 1960s and the Thatcherite urban programmes of the 1980s into New Labour's renewal strategies in the early twenty-first century. Moreover, as New Labour itself acknowledged in its first term of office, past regeneration policies have failed to address the causes of neighbourhood decline associated with economic, social and political disempowerment, structured along class, 'race' and gender lines. What unites these failed initiatives is their consensus position on the nature of neighbourhood problems – the flawed pathology of individuals and 'communities' living there. As a consequence, New Labour's renewal strategy will also fail because it persists with the same moral discourse. At the same time, research within mainstream social policy is largely responding to 'problems' constructed and defined by this discourse. By social policy professionals and researchers working in the ways suggested in this chapter, perhaps we can begin to see the emergence of critical research and practices that allow a broader understanding of 'danger' to emerge and, consequently, a broader political coalition of support for more sensitive and efficacious social policies.

References

Acheson, D. (1998) *Independent Inquiry into Inequalities in Health*, London: The Stationery Office.

Andersen, N.Å. (2003) *Discursive Analytical Strategies: Understanding Foucault, Koselleck, Laclau, Luhmann*, Bristol: Policy Press.

Appleton, J. (2002) 'Testing Britishness', *Spiked Politics*, 19 September. Online. Available http:// www.spiked-online.com/Printable/00000006DA58.htm (accessed 8 October 2002).

Atkinson, R. and Moon, G. (1994) *Urban Policy in Britain – The City, the State and the Market*, London: Macmillan.

Baker, C. (2003) 'Losing the balance', *Housing*, May: 23–4.

Bamber, J. and Murphy, H. (1999), 'Youth work: the possibilities for critical practice', *Journal of Youth Studies*, 2, 2: 227–42.

Bauman, Z. (1998) *Work, Consumerism and the New Poor*, Buckingham: Open University Press.

—— (2001) *Community: Seeking Safety in an Insecure World*, Cambridge: Polity Press.

—— (2003) *Liquid Love*, Cambridge: Polity Press.

Beck, U. (1999) *World Risk Society*, Cambridge: Polity Press.

Becker, H. (1966) *Outsiders*, New York: The Free Press.

Berghman, J. (1995) 'Social exclusion in Europe: policy context and analytical framework', in G. Room (ed.) *Beyond the Threshold*, Bristol: Policy Press: 10–28.

Burden, T., Cooper, C. and Petrie, S. (2000) *'Modernising' Social Policy: Unravelling New Labour's Welfare Reforms*, Aldershot: Ashgate.

Burnett, J. (1986) *A Social History of Housing – 1815–1985*, 2nd edn, London: Methuen.

Chamberlayne, P., Rustin, M. and Wengraf, T. (eds) (2002) *Biography and Social Exclusion in Europe: Experiences and Life Journeys*, Bristol: Policy Press.

Cohen, S. (2002) *Folk Devils and Moral Panics*, 3rd edn, London: Routledge.

Cooper, C. and Hawtin, M. (eds) (1997) *Housing, Community and Conflict: Understanding Resident 'Involvement'*, Aldershot: Arena.

Cowan, D. (2001) 'From allocations to lettings: sea change or more of the same?', in D. Cowan and A. Marsh (eds) *Two Steps Forward: Housing Policy into the New Millennium*, Bristol: Policy Press: 133–54.

Davis Creal, L. (1999) 'The "disability of thinking" the "disabled" body', course paper for Ambiguous Bodies: Studies in Contemporary Sexuality, Masters Level English Course (6994.06), Professor Julia Creet, York University, Toronto, Canada. Online. Available http://www.normemma.com/artcreal.htm (accessed 21 May 2001).

Field, F. (2003) 'The treatment that they deserve', *Inside Housing*, 27 June: 14–15.

Forrest, R. and Kennett, P. (1998) 'Re-reading the city: deregulation and neighbourhood change', *Space & Polity*, 2, 1: 71–83.

Foucault, M. (1977) *Discipline and Punish: The Birth of the Prison*, Harmondsworth: Penguin.

Freire, P. (1976) *Education: The Practices of Freedom*, London: Writers and Readers Publishing Co-operative.

Grayson, J. (1997) 'Campaigning tenants: a pre-history of tenant involvement to 1979', in C. Cooper and M. Hawtin (eds) *Housing, Community and Conflict: Understanding Resident 'Involvement'*, Aldershot: Arena: 15–65.

Hall, S. (1998) 'The Great Moving Nowhere Show', *Marxism Today*, November/December: 9–14.

Hall, S., Critcher, C., Jefferson, T., Clarke, J. and Roberts, B. (1978) *Policing the Crisis*, London: Macmillan.

Harloe, M. (1995) *The People's Home? Social Rented Housing in Europe and America*, Oxford: Blackwell.

Harrison, M. with Davis, C. (2001) *Housing, Social Policy and Difference: Disability, Ethnicity, Gender and Housing*, Bristol: Policy Press.

Harrison, P. (1983) *Inside the Inner City: Life Under the Cutting Edge*, Harmondsworth: Penguin.

Hillyard, P., Sim, J., Tombs, S. and Whyte, D. (2004) 'Leaving a "stain upon the silence": contemporary criminology and the politics of dissent', *British Journal of Criminology*, 44: 369–90.

Himmelfarb, G. (1995) *The De-moralization of Society: from Victorian Virtues to Modern Values*, London: IEA Health & Welfare Unit.

Home Office (2001) *Community Cohesion: A Report of the Independent Review Team Chaired by Ted Cantle*, London: Home Office.

Howarth, C., Kenway, P., Palmer, G. and Miorelli, R. (1999) *Monitoring Poverty and Social Exclusion 1999*, York: Joseph Rowntree Foundation.

Jacobs, K. and Manzi, T. (1996) 'Discourse and policy change: the significance of language for housing research', *Housing Studies*, 11, 4: 543–60.

Jordan, B. (1996) *A Theory of Poverty and Social Exclusion*, Cambridge: Polity Press.

(JRF) Joseph Rowntree Foundation (2003a) *Hartrigg Oaks*. Online. Available http://www.jrf.org.uk/housingandcare/hartriggoaks/ (accessed 6 June 2003).

—— (2003b) *About the JRF – The Joseph Rowntree Foundation*. Online. Available http://www.jrf.org.uk/about (accessed 23 June 2003).

—— (2003c) *About the JRF – A Brief History*. Online. Available http://www.jrf.org.uk/about/history.htm (accessed 23 June 2003).

Kingsnorth, P. (2003) *One No, Many Yeses: A Journey to the Heart of the Global Resistance Movement*, New York: The Free Press.

Kundnani, A. (2002) 'The death of multiculturalism', London: Institute of Race Relations. Online. Available HTTP: http://www.irr.org.uk/cantle/ (accessed 8 October 2002).

Leonard, P. (1997) *Postmodern Welfare: Reconstructing an Emancipatory Project*, London: Sage.

Levitas, R. (1998) *The Inclusive Society? Social Exclusion and New Labour*, Basingstoke: Palgrave.

Lewis, O. (1966) 'The Culture of Poverty', *Scientific American*, 215, 16: 19–25.

Lund, B. (1996) *Housing Problems and Housing Policy*, Harlow: Longman.

Mayhew, H. (1861/1967) *London Labour and the London Poor: A Cyclopaedia of the Condition and Earnings of Those That Will Work, Those That Cannot Work, and Those That Will Not Work*, New York: A.M. Kelley.

Miyoshi, M. (1993) 'A borderless world? From colonialism to transnationalism and the decline of the nation-state', *Critical Inquiry*, 19, 4, Summer: 726–51.

Monbiot, G. (2003) *The Age of Consent: A Manifesto for a New World Order*, London: Flamingo.

Movement for Justice (2003) *Labour's New Attacks on Asylum Seekers!* Online. Available HTTP: http://www.users.globalnet.co.uk/~justice/Straw.htm (accessed 20 May 2003).

Muncie, J. (1999) *Youth and Crime – A Critical Introduction*, London: Sage.

—— (2000) 'Decriminalising Criminology', British Criminology Conference: Selected Proceedings, Volume 3. Online. Available http://www.lboro.ac.uk/departments/ss/bsc/bccsp/vol03/muncie.html&gt (accessed 28 May 2003).

Murard, N. (2002) 'Guilty victims: social exclusion in contemporary France', in P. Chamberlayne, M. Rustin and T. Wengraf (eds) *Biography and Social Exclusion in Europe: Experiences and Life Journeys*, Bristol: Policy Press: 41–60.

Nettleton, S. and Burrows, R. (1998) 'Individualisation processes and social policy: insecurity, reflexivity and risk in the restructuring of contemporary British health and housing policies', in J. Carter (ed.) *Postmodernity and the Fragmentation of Welfare*, London: Routledge: 153–67.

Newman, J. (2003) *Modernising Governance: New Labour, Policy and Society*, London: Sage.

Pantazis, C. and Gordon, D. (eds) (2000) *Tackling Inequalities: Where are We Now and What Can Be Done?*, Bristol: Policy Press.

Power, A. (1997) *Estates on the Edge: The Social Consequences of Mass Housing in Northern Europe*, London: Macmillan.

(PNAC) Project for the New American Century (2003) Online. Available http://www.newamericancentury.org/index.html (accessed 2 June 2003).

Redgrave, C. (2003) 'Idealists and informers', *Guardian Review*, 28 June: 35.

Roberts, I. (1999) 'A historical construction of the working class', in H. Beynon and P. Glavanis (eds) *Patterns of Social Inequality*, London: Longman: 147–60.

Rustin, M. and Chamberlayne, P. (2002) 'Introduction: from biography to social policy', in P. Chamberlayne, M. Rustin and T. Wengraf (eds) *Biography and Social Exclusion in Europe: Experiences and Life Journeys*, Bristol: Policy Press: 1–21.

Sardar, Z. and Davies, M.W. (2002) *Why Do People Hate America?*, Cambridge: Icon Books.

Savage, M. and Warde, A. (1993) *Urban Sociology, Capitalism and Modernity*, London: Macmillan.

Seabrook, J. (1984) *The Idea of Neighbourhood: What Local Politics Should Be About*, London: Pluto Press.

Shephard, A. (2003) *Income Inequality under the Labour Government*, Briefing Note No. 33, London: The Institute for Fiscal Studies.

Sibley, D. (1995) *Geographies of Exclusion: Society and Difference in the West*, London: Routledge.

(SEU) Social Exclusion Unit (1998) *Bringing Britain Together: A National Strategy for Neighbourhood Renewal*, Cm. 4045, London: The Stationery Office.

—— (2001) *A New Commitment to Neighbourhood Renewal: National Strategy Action Plan*, London: The Stationery Office.

Sullivan, H. (2002) 'Modernization, neighbourhood management and social inclusion', *Public Management Review*, 4, 4: 505–28.

Sykes, G. (2003) 'Anti-social behaviour orders: tackling neighbourhood nuisance', *Housing*, May: 22.

Tomlinson, S. (2001) *Education in a Post-Welfare Society*, Buckingham: Open University Press.

Tönnies, F. (1955) *Community and Association*, London: Routledge & Kegan Paul.

Valier, C. (2002) *Theories of Crime and Punishment*, Harlow: Longman.

Wilkins, L. (1964) *Social Deviance*, London: Tavistock.

Wilkinson, R. (1998) 'Why inequality is bad for you', *Marxism Today*, November/ December: 38–9.

5 Housing, class and social policy

Peter Somerville

Perspectives on social class and social mobility

In spite of rumours to the contrary, social class continues to be a major feature of 'late modernity' (Bradley and Hebson 1999; Scott 2002). The two main perspectives on social class, Marxist and Weberian, also continue to dominate the theoretical agenda. Broadly speaking, Marxists see class in terms of two aspects: first, a shared relationship to production (for example, as exploiters or exploited, oppressors or oppressed, managers or managed); and second, specific forms of social organisation (for example, trade unions, the labour movement, employers' organisations, class-based political parties). Marx called the first aspect a 'class-in-itself'. Under this aspect, class positions are determined by the way in which production is organised in society. For example, under conditions of capitalist production, we have positions of wage-labourers, on the one hand, and positions of capitalists and corporate managers, on the other. The second aspect Marx called a 'class-for-itself'. This aspect refers to the existence of self-conscious working-class and ruling-class organisations, which operate both within and beyond the workplace, affecting the whole of a society.

This chapter adopts a perspective that is broadly more sympathetic to Marxism, insofar as it regards the ending of class divisions as a desirable goal, and emphasises the centrality of class struggle in realising that goal.

Weberians see class not in terms of relationship to production but as an outcome of (market-based) distribution. People can be said to belong to the same (production) class if they enjoy similar conditions of work, have similar job status, and occupy similar positions in the labour market. Most Weberians see class in terms of a more or less finely graded hierarchy of position clusters or strata, and the study of class in this sense is called social stratification. Under conditions of capitalist markets, Weberians generally recognise the existence of 'working class' positions (occupied by manual workers), 'middle class' ones (occupied by capitalists, managers and professional workers), and 'intermediate' ones (occupied by routine and junior non-manual workers). Unlike Marxists, Weberians tend to see the class system not as a structure of domination but rather as a structure of opportunity, not as something to be transformed but as something to be used for one's own benefit.

Marxists and Weberians have radically different conceptions of social mobility. Weberians view social mobility in terms of the movement of individuals up and down the class hierarchy, while Marxists see it in terms of the movement of groups of people towards their collective empowerment (for domination or liberation). Both Marxists and Weberians are interested in maximising equality of opportunity, but Weberians tend to see this in terms of enabling individuals to rise, for example, from the 'working class' to the 'middle class', while Marxists argue for the abolition of class society altogether. These two conceptions of social mobility are, of course, fundamentally irreconcilable.

Saunders (1990, 1995, 1996, 1997) provides a good example of a Weberian perspective on class. For Saunders, the existing class hierarchy is taken as a given, and the only important theoretical and political issue is that of the fairness of the distribution across that hierarchy. In other words, social justice in relation to class is entirely a matter of the positioning of individuals at the right levels in the hierarchy. Saunders (1996) provides a spirited argument in favour of both the existence and justice of a hierarchy based on merit (individual ability plus effort), although disabled people (among others) will no doubt object strongly to Saunders' view that differences in 'natural ability' (ibid.: 83) can justify class inequality. Saunders (1997) shows that the best predictor of upward mobility is 'ability' (measured in terms of performance in ability tests), while the best predictor of downward mobility is lack of 'ability'. Middle-class children appear to have more 'ability' than working-class children, although this could be due to socialisation (learned ability) rather than genetics (innate ability).

Saunders recognises one of the key problems for a meritocracy, first identified by Young (1958), namely the discontent of those branded as 'failures' by the system, but he argues, naively, that 'this need not be catastrophic ... provided the competition is known to have been fair' (Saunders 1997: 90). Actually, what Saunders sees as a technical 'problem of legitimation' (ibid.: 80) is what class struggle is all about, according to Marxists. For why should people of 'lower ability' (however defined) accept the fairness of a system that socialises them into failure when it is in principle possible for that system to be changed so as to make it less of a contest and more of a co-operative enterprise? Nor is this objection confined only to Marxists. Marshall *et al.* (1997: 177), for example, make a similar point when they argue, in relation to differential aspirations to success, that: 'It is hard to appeal to differential aspirations to justify unequal outcomes if those aspirations are themselves best analysed as responses to differences in people's conditions of action'. The essential argument is the counter-intuitive one that all meritocratic justifications of inequality are spurious.

Saunders' view that class destinations are determined primarily on the basis of individual merit is not accepted by other sociologists, not even by other Weberians. Breen and Goldthorpe (1999), for example, reanalysed the National Child Development Study dataset that Saunders used and concluded that the effect of class origins was much stronger than that of ability and effort. This conclusion is also supported by findings from other major datasets such as British Election Surveys (Heath and Payne 2000), the General Household Survey (Goldthorpe and Mills 2000, cited in Aldridge 2001) and the International Social Justice Panel (see Marshall *et al.* 1997). In a review of the literature, Aldridge (2001) identifies the following causes of this:

- physical, psychological and behavioural effects of child poverty, e.g. impaired brain development, low self-esteem, behavioural difficulties;
- lack of access by working-class parents to financial, social and cultural capital;
- greater risks incurred by working class parents in investing in their children's advancement, e.g. in education;
- 'opportunity hoarding' by middle-class parents, e.g. through professionalisation of middle-class occupations and through moving to areas with better state schools.[1]

These findings imply that 'ability' itself may be, to some extent, a product of social class, so that Saunders' position becomes incoherent (see later discussion). For how can class inequality be justified in terms of differences in 'ability' when these very differences are themselves produced by class inequality (this is similar to the argument above in terms of differences in aspirations)?

Since equality of opportunity is generally regarded as desirable, Aldridge suggests a number of policy options that the government could consider for increasing social mobility (that is, weakening the correlation between class origin and class destination). Interestingly, none of these options involve housing, so we need not concern ourselves with the details here.[2] In general, the policies that Aldridge specifies are those that will improve or worsen the position of certain individuals relative to others, e.g. to assist upward mobility or facilitate downward mobility. There is something strange, however, about advocating only policies of this kind. The work of Erikson and Goldthorpe (1992) on international comparisons of social mobility, for example, suggests, as Aldridge himself recognises, that relative mobility is positively related to class/income equality, yet Aldridge does not mention any policy option directly involving a reduction in the (income) gap between the classes. The point I want to make is that Aldridge's policy options would not necessarily make a significant difference to the overall performance of the working class or middle class. The fact that a working-class child moves to a middle-class position or a middle-class child moves correspondingly to a working-class position does not change the basic class hierarchy as a structure of positions. As Marshall *et al.* (1997: 16) put it: 'However fair the processes by which people arrive at places in the structure of unequal positions, it remains a further question whether the extent of the inequality of that structure can itself be justified'.

While being cautious about the desirability of a full-blown meritocracy, therefore (because of its inherent instability and loser resentment, among other things), Aldridge adheres implicitly to a Weberian position, whereby the class hierarchy is a given, and the only problem is how to achieve a fair distribution within it. Indeed, Aldridge's main difference from Saunders is that he sees a major role for the state in promoting economic prosperity, social cohesion and social inclusion. In short, while Saunders' Weberianism is straightforwardly meritocratic, Aldridge's has a 'Third Way' spin.

A key absence from the accounts of Saunders and his fellow 'social stratifica-tionists' is any discussion of power. Typically, they view social classes as collec-tions of people in certain social positions, without any particular implications about the relations of domination and subordination involved. Adonis and Pollard (1998) have pointed out that such neo-Weberian class analysis ignores the 'superclass' elite of the rich and powerful (estimated at 1 per cent of the total population – Savage 2000), which is increasingly dominant in global affairs. Others have criticised it for its neglect of the so-called 'underclass' of socially excluded people (see, for example, Mann 1992), although the existence of such an 'underclass' is disputed (Gershuny 1994). These critics are signalling dissatisfaction with a perspective that fails to recognise the existence of a political dimension to class, in the sense of a class that rules or a class that is oppressed.

Savage (2000) identifies a general problem with neo-Weberian class analysis in that, because it takes the existing class hierarchy as a given, it is unable to provide a convincing account of class formation and change. Savage specifically criticises Goldthorpe's definition of class formation: 'Rather than class formation being itself a dynamic process, involving a particular way of linking pasts, present and futures, it is posited [in Goldthorpe's approach] as being based on a static attachment to fixed positions' (Savage 2000: 83–4). He argues that mobility does not simply occur into a pre-existing class but itself actively forms and transforms class relations. For example, where the number of middle-class occupations expands, working-class children will be recruited to them, and are likely to be deemed 'brighter' than those who are not, but their 'brightness' can be interpreted as a sign of their upwardly mobile career trajectory. Through their individual actions over time, these working-class children are changing the nature of the class system. Middle-class formation in particular, therefore, is far from leading to a stable set of class positions.

In general, Savage emphasises the *individualised* character of class relations, which follows from seeing class formation as related to the identification of individual trajectories rather than as an attachment to fixed positions (Savage 2000: 95). He takes issue with writers such as Beck and Giddens who argue as if individuals can disembed themselves from class relations and act free from all social constraints (see also Reeve, this volume). He points out how the construction of individual identities is infused with ideas of class distinction. Following Bourdieu, he argues that class is 'encoded in people's sense of self-worth and in their attitudes to and awareness of others – in how they carry themselves as individuals' (ibid.: 107). Specifically, people's sense of self-identity is linked to a claim of 'ordinariness' or 'normality', which operates as a double reaction against both the privileged above them and the 'morally suspect' below them (ibid.: 115). By this means, class identity is simultaneously concealed and reinforced. The middle classes claim to be in a 'classless middle', between the exclusive and the working class, while the working classes claim to be ordinary working people, distinct from both the workshy at the bottom and the idle rich at the top. People do not think it important to define themselves explicitly in class terms, but only to be 'ordinary'. Still, they use the language of class to label threatening 'others', who might not be 'ordinary' like themselves (Savage 2000: 116).

Savage goes on to identify the key features of working-class and middle-class cultures, and attempts to show how much of contemporary social change can be explained by reference to changes in these cultures. In Britain at least, a working-class culture of independence, cultural distance from management and masculinity, with deep historical roots, was expressed in institutions such as apprenticeship, whereby boys became both men and skilled workers, and hence members of the working class (Savage 2000: 127–8). Middle-class culture developed originally in reaction to such a culture, as a by-product of attempts to gain more effective organisational control over the labour process. Hence, dating from the 1850s, the notion of a middle-class 'career' developed: 'In place of the autonomy of the skilled manual trades, which measured itself in terms of its refusal to become incorporated into an organisational hierarchy, the idea of the career involved a mode of individuality which defined self-development through taking on the responsibility of hierarchy' (Savage 2000: 130). This involved a clear class distinction within organisations between 'staff' and 'workers', the gradual decline of the cultural value of 'manly independence', and the concurrent reconstruction of manual labour as subordinate and dependent labour (Savage 2000: 134). Savage identifies no less than eight features of this move from working class (male) independence to dependence (Savage 2000: 134–9):

- the breaking of the direct route from schooling to manual occupational culture through apprenticeship or peer training;
- the racialisation of manual work as a consequence of black and minority ethnic immigration;
- the threat of mass unemployment making workers more reluctant to challenge their employer's authority;
- manual workers' increasing expectations, for a variety of reasons, of 'internal progression' within a company;

- faster changes in skills required by employers, making apprenticeships for life outmoded;
- substantial increase of young women in professional and managerial jobs, breaking down the traditional gender 'contract';
- trade unionism ceasing to be a core part of manual work cultures;
- rise of 'servicing' employment, problematising the relevance of older models of manual worker autonomy.

In more recent years, Savage notes that the middle-class idea of a career has been reconstructed as a 'project of the self', with individuals viewing organisations instrumentally as resources for self-development (Savage 2000: 140), weakening status divisions between workers and 'staff', and declining importance for career advancement of ascriptive markers such as social background, gender and age (Savage 2000: 141). Paradoxically, however, organisations where employees feel their personal development can best be enhanced tend to be the ones to whom they show the greatest loyalty.

Savage shows how a class-focused account of social change has advantages over accounts in terms of historical stages or 'epochs'. He criticises Giddens, Harvey, Castells and others, on the grounds that 'they locate the springs of change away from the proximate worlds of everyday life and over-stress the systemic logic of social change' (Savage 2000: 151). His central claim is that 'understanding social change lies in the restructuring of social class relations, rather than in the grand narratives of "globalisation", "individualisation" and so forth' (Savage 2000: 151; see also Reeve, this volume). Specifically, he stresses the importance of the traditional association of dominant notions of individuality and citizenship with the working class, and argues that: 'It is the collapse of this association ... that is fundamental to understanding contemporary social and cultural change' (Savage 2000: 153). Essentially, working-class work has been reconstructed as 'servile' work, which no longer confers mastery or autonomy on its incumbent. An important feature of this reconstruction is the elimination of old-style trade unions, whose organisation depended on the recognition of the dignity and autonomy of individual workers (Savage 2000: 154). At the same time, the middle class, which historically emerged in Britain as precisely a servile class, being dependent upon, and morally committed to, their employer in return for secure employment and incremental rewards, has been fundamentally recast in terms of entrepreneurial independence and individuality (Savage 2000: 155–6).

Savage's analysis has major implications for our understanding of public services, and therefore for social policy generally. The professionalisation of areas of public sector work, in health, education, social work, housing, planning, environmental health, and so on, has consisted of attempts to recreate the autonomy of action and control over work output that used to be enjoyed by skilled manual workers. The stance of the public sector unions at the turn of the twentieth century echoes that of the private sector artisans at the turn of the nineteenth. Now, as then, organisational centrality is fundamental for class formation, with those culturally central to organisations being best able to take advantage of restructuring, for rapid promotion or additional rewards of property (Savage 2000: 158). Just as the old working class 'freely' served the needs of British capital and empire, so the new middle class 'freely' serves the British state and global capitalism. The implications of Savage's analysis for housing and housing policy in particular will be discussed in the next section.

Class and housing tenure

Housing can be seen as a specific focus of class relations or as a specific 'stake' in an ongoing struggle between social classes. Within housing studies, the debate between Marxists and Weberians has been reflected in a long-running split between those who see housing as a site of wider class relations and struggles and those who see housing relations and struggles as independent of these wider concerns. The terminology used in this debate has, on occasions, been rather confusing, with reference to concepts such as 'housing classes', 'consumption sector cleavages', and so forth. The basic question, however, concerns the extent to which housing can be understood in Marxist or Weberian class terms, and the implications of these different understandings (and the limitations of those understandings) for social policy. In this section, I shall concentrate on the specific issue of housing tenure.

Housing tenures can be understood as 'relatively stable and historically enduring ways of distributing housing products to housing consumers' (Somerville and Knowles 1991: 123). Typically, they are constituted by law and involve characteristic forms of control relations and exchange relations. Table 5.1 presents some examples of tenures according to this typology.

A key issue here is that of ownership rights, which create a clear distinction between homeowners, on the one hand, and tenants on the other. Two other issues, however, are also important. One is the nature of the exchange of the product. In

Table 5.1 Housing tenures

Housing tenure	Control relations	Exchange relations
Outright owner-occupation	None	Commodified
Owner-occupation with mortgage	Mortgagor/mortgagee	Commodified
Public sector tenancy	Landlord/tenant	Decommodified
Private sector tenancy	Landlord/tenant	Commodified
Co-operative ownership	Borrower/lender?	Largely decommodified

the case of owner-occupation and private sector renting, this is determined by what price (for sale or rent) the product can fetch in the market – the tenancy of the home, or the home itself, is treated as a commodity. In the case of public sector renting, however, rents are fixed by non-market means, and tenancies are allocated largely through administrative methods, for example, on the basis of need. The second issue is that of loan finance: typically, owner-occupiers borrow from a bank or building society in order to buy their homes, and use the home itself as collateral. Table 5.1 provides only a sample of tenures, and others do exist – for example, Singapore has a form of owner-occupation in which the price is determined by market forces but flats are allocated through an administrative system (controlled by the Housing Development Board); and Forrest and Murie (1995) point to forms of owner-occupation in other countries that do not involve market exchange at all but rely instead on reciprocal exchange and gift relationships among family, friends and neighbours.

The question is how these different tenures relate to social classes. In Somerville and Knowles (1991), it was pointed out that owner-occupation is a source of wealth accumulation for some better-off households, who then pass this wealth on to their children, while poorer owner-occupiers generally gain little advantage from the tenure, have little choice or opportunity to improve their position (Forrest and Murie 1989) and, in low demand areas, may actually lose out financially and otherwise (Bramley *et al.* 2000). This finding suggests that owner-occupation as a tenure tends to reinforce existing class divisions, acting as a means whereby middle-class households can 'hoard' their opportunities and transfer them to the next generations, while working-class households run greater risks of indebtedness, negative equity, and relative decline in property values. Essentially, the middle-class households are in a better position to carve out their own chosen 'housing careers', with their home lives and housing histories forming an additional arena in which their 'project of the self' is developed and played out – a construction that is actually made possible by, and reinforces, the progress of their careers in the arena of paid work.

The relevance of Savage's class analysis can readily be seen in the context of the history of housing in the twentieth century. The old class division between middle-class owner-occupiers and working-class council tenants, which actually dates from the interwar period (Daunton 1987), corresponded to an image of owner-occupation as a form of indebtedness, which would ensure compliance to the system, whereas council housing was seen as a form of democratically-controlled collective liberation from poor housing conditions. Thus, the servility of the old middle class and the democratic autonomy of the old working class were broadly reflected in the post-1919 constructions of new housing tenures. With the continuing expansion of owner-occupation, however, and the changes in class discussed above, tenure became less salient as a marker of the class divide. Just as working-class children have been increasingly recruited to middle-class occupations, so they have also increasingly purchased their own homes. However, it is not only these 'new middle classes' who have entered into owner-occupation for the first time. Those who have continued in working-class jobs have also accessed home owner-ship in large numbers. There is some evidence, however, that, for many of these households, this has been possible only because of the presence of two earners in the household (see, for example, Munro and Smith 1989). Working-class single earners are likely to find themselves in a more precarious position. At least for this minority of owner-occupiers, the tenure continues to be a source of individual indebtedness and conformity.

In principle, public sector renting should be less inequitable than owner-occupation, because allocation is not left to the vagaries of the market. Priority is supposed to be given to those in housing need and openings for opportunity hoard-ing are strictly limited. In its early days, however, council house rents were relatively high (compared with those in the private sector, which were controlled after 1915), and only the better-off, skilled working class were able to afford them. This situation reflected the image of the 'respectable' working-class male 'head of household' who paid his own way and looked after his property and family. However, with the continuing expansion of owner-occupation, the rise in private rents relative to public rents, the introduction of statutory rent rebate schemes, and a number of other factors, public renting became residualised, its occupiers were increasingly seen as 'flawed consumers' (Bauman 1998), and the tenure itself came to be viewed as a source of class disadvantage.

The working class became increasingly split between those seeking individual upward mobility through owner-occupation (among other things) and those committed to collective solidarity through their common status as tenants (among other things) – a split that neatly reflects the difference between Weberian and Marxist perspectives. Arguably, the right to buy was a key policy in shifting sections of the working class away from public renting and towards owner-occupation, representing a victory for those favouring the class status quo and a weakening of working-class co-operation. This policy was in fact the flagship of the Thatcher government's privatisation programme, so there is little difficulty in interpreting it as a milestone in the class struggle in housing. The effect of this policy, along with residualisation processes more generally, has been that, instead of being seen as a progressive form of tenure for the working class, public sector housing is now increasingly viewed as a barrier to the emancipation of that class.

So it looks as if housing can be regarded as an example of what Savage (2000: 148) has called 'the dissolution of the working class as a salient cultural identifier'. Working-class households cannot achieve emancipation through public sector housing, yet many cannot afford to liberate themselves through owner-occupation either. The best that can be hoped for is that some, but not all, working-class households can succeed in being upwardly mobile, leaving the unfortunate rest to fester in an amorphous 'underclass'. In these circumstances, the only benefit that social policy can bring would appear to be an alleviation of the distress felt by the latter (more likely, however, is an emphasis on the social control of this disparate and inchoate group – see, for example, Cooper, this volume). In Savage's terms, it can be argued that the proud independence of working-class-run council housing has been replaced by means-tested and stigmatised benefit dependency.[3]

But is such fatalism really justified? We should be wary of it, because one possibility is that it reflects Saunders' thesis that we already live in a meritocratic society (or at least a society that is moving inexorably towards a meritocracy), and therefore a large degree of 'failure' must be accepted as inevitable. As already mentioned above, this view is based on a Weberian perspective of social class, and the tenures of owner-occupation and public renting are here functioning as surrogates for Weberian classes (as positions in a class/status hierarchy). The historically contingent character of the tenure hierarchy in Britain is presented as the 'natural' state of affairs, and the possibility of transforming that hierarchy is ruled out *a priori*. If we adopt a standpoint from outside the housing system, however, it is possible to see that working-class failure in housing, as in everything else, is not inevitable. Emancipation through public sector housing or owner-occupation may not in itself be a practicable project, but this does not mean that emancipation is unrealisable in any form – for example, other tenures are possible, such as co-operatively owned and managed housing (see later discussion).

Another possibility is that it simply reflects Savage's finding of the increasing subordination and dependency of the working class in late capitalist society. Savage, however, is at pains to stress the fluid, divided and ambivalent character of the middle class, making the social control of the working class a particularly difficult and continually contested project. Although the three axes of middle-class formation (property, organisation and culture) are interconnected, the middle class does not form a coherent collectivity any more than does the working class: it is divided between 'core' and 'liminal' sections just as the working class is, with the core being recruited directly into culturally central organisational positions following education. In this context, there would appear to be considerable scope for subaltern groups to offer effective resistance.

Class and housing struggles

Historically, one of the best-known examples of housing struggle is the 1915 Glasgow rent strike. Although this has often been represented as a struggle over (housing) 'consumption' rather than a class struggle (Melling 1983; Castells 1983; Saunders 1981), Damer (2000) argues that it was very much a struggle between classes, because the 'consumption' element (concerned with rent levels) was not divorced from the wider struggle between propertyless workers and propertied capitalists/landlords. He points out that the strike was grounded in a socialist, working-class culture unique to Glasgow, and 'was led by a talented cadre, the majority of whom were members of the Independent Labour Party (ILP), *the* working-class party in Glasgow at the time … If that does not constitute a working-class struggle, it is hard to see what would' (Damer 2000: 73). Saunders' attempt to show otherwise can therefore be understood as a neo-Weberian tactic designed to make such 'urban struggles' appear doomed to failure. This is one of many revisionist projects that aim to reconcile the working class to the 'natural order' of capitalism.

As with the 1915 Glasgow rent strike, so with the Clydebank rent strike of the 1920s (Damer 2000), Poplarism in the 1920s (Johnson 2000), postwar squatting campaigns (Anning *et al.* 1980; Reeve, this volume), and the campaign against building for sale in Glasgow in 1951 (Johnstone 2000). These were all based on housing issues but were essentially class struggles aimed at the defence and advancement of the working class. Damer points to the success of the Clydebank rent strike in maintaining rent control at national level and in producing MPs such as John Wheatley who was responsible for the 1924 Housing Act. In addition:

> In class terms, the other major gain of the Clydebank Rent Strike was to shift both the material and ideological terrain on which the battle over the cost of the social reproduction of the working class was fought. It was not just that rent control of small houses was continued. It was not just that a series of Housing Acts began to alleviate the scandalous housing conditions of large sections of the working class. It was that through their own struggles over the literal costs of their own lives, the local working class conceived of a new deal for itself in housing terms, and became conscious of a future in which the norm would not be an overcrowded and unhealthy slum, but a house with sufficient bedrooms, with a bathroom, with running water, and with a garden – at a fair rent, subsidized by the state. In other words, this struggle had an impact on social welfare and housing *policy*.
>
> (Damer 2000: 93–4)

This quote clearly reveals how working-class struggle in housing is not hopeless and can have significant long-term positive effects. Nevertheless, it is somewhat dispiriting to note how few successful class-based housing struggles there appear to have been in recent years. This could, of course, be a consequence of the social changes noted by Savage (2000), namely the long-term political decline of the working class, reflected in such processes as the residualisation of council housing. In crude terms, maybe the 'death of the social' (Rose 1996) has been accompanied by the 'death of housing policy', the result being that specifically housing struggles have given way to struggles over 'community' (Hoggett 1997). This comment, however, requires some explanation.

When we look for examples of class-based housing struggles today, at least in Britain, what we find are things like the Daylight Robbery Campaign and Defend

Council Housing (see, for example, Weeks 2002). Such forms of collective action can be regarded as specific expressions of a council tenants' movement, which has a particular history of its own (Grayson 1997). This history records a number of major campaigns, such as the rent strikes from 1968 to 1973, but little in terms of real political success. Actually, this history is a good example of what Piven and Cloward (1977) called a 'poor people's movement', where occasional periods of turbulence are followed by processes of state retrenchment and incorporation. Arguably, as the number of council tenants diminishes, the influence of the movement is likely to become ever weaker.

The time seems long overdue, therefore, for representatives of the council tenants' movement to make common cause with other public sector tenants, and also with working-class private tenants and owner-occupiers, in a cross-tenure struggle for greater control over their lives and their neighbourhoods. Given the historical weakness of the tenants' movement, it seems politically unproductive for working-class activists to focus all their attention on protecting and defending council housing as a tenure. Rather, they should be concerned with the interests of the *tenants*, which go way beyond allegiance to a single tenure, and even beyond housing issues altogether. Such activists might be better advised to engage more directly with the new agenda of 'community struggle', and on grounds of their own choosing. They are no doubt right to criticise the government for its attempts to distort tenant preferences towards stock transfer rather than stock retention through substantial financial inducements (Weeks 2002), but to be correct on such an issue is not necessarily to be effective. There are political dangers for working-class emancipation in defending what amounts to a flawed tenure rather than in looking for ways in which tenures in general can be reformed. What needs to happen in the longer term is for the current 'top-down' attempt to 'govern through community' (Rose 1996) to be transformed into a 'bottom-up' movement towards governance by the community. From this point of view, transfer of housing from local authorities to housing associations, for example, can be regarded as an opportunity (for democratisation and increased working-class control), to be used to best advantage, rather than as a form of 'privatisation', to be implacably opposed.

A good (non-housing) example of how such a 'bottom-up' movement might begin to work is that of the anti-poll tax movement. This movement has been represented as a community-based new social movement (Hoggett and Burns 1991), but in fact it is a classic example of a working-class protest movement, with the grass-roots organisations 'from below' being clearly identifiable as working-class community organisations (Lavalette and Mooney 2000c).[4] In many cases, therefore, what may appear to be 'community struggle' or 'urban struggle', and is actively portrayed by government as a 'community issue', is more accurately conceptualised as community-based class struggle. As Lavalette and Mooney pointedly conclude:

> The problem with those who argue for social movement over class-based protest lies in their narrow and somewhat ahistorical and deterministic approach and interpretation of working-class struggle and working-class political organisation. Their overriding emphasis on 'community' – as something which remains distinct from working-class protest – is both symptomatic and a reflection of this kind of approach.
>
> (Lavalette and Mooney 2000c: 226)

The success of the anti-poll tax movement shows that the widespread pessimism about community-based class struggles is largely unfounded (this point is taken up further in the conclusion to this book). Following Lavalette and Mooney's argument, it should be possible to find contemporary examples of class struggles with a housing focus that have been represented as 'community struggles' only. The Confederation of Cooperative Housing, for example, is a social movement organisation, representing a number of community-controlled organisations across England and Wales, which campaigns for housing to be collectively controlled by those who live in it. This campaign holds out the promise of achieving for the working class what few local authorities or housing associations have ever delivered, namely, freedom to decide collectively what to do with their housing. Arguably, this is an essential step in the emancipation of the working class, and the co-operative movement has thrown up an increasing number of successful initiatives of this nature (Somerville 2003). In terms of tenure, co-operative housing represents a genuine and practicable alternative both to traditional owner-occupation and to what Cole and Furbey (1994) have called 'municipal landlordism'.

We can now see that the fatalism expressed in the previous section was a consequence of seeing housing options in terms of a stark choice between, on the one hand, owner-occupation and, on the other, renting from a landlord, and this analysis omitted to consider the possibility of co-operatively controlled housing as an alternative form of tenure. Strangely, Marxists have tended to miss the significance of the co-operative movement as an improvement on both capitalism and traditional representative democracy, and so have failed to suggest realistic options for working-class emancipation. Instead, the field has been left open to anarchists such as Colin Ward (1976).

The relative importance of class

There remains the question of how class is related to other forms of social division. This question can be addressed in a number of ways, for example, by investigating the life chances correlated with class positions compared with those for gender or race, or the strength of class identities compared with ethnic or sexual identities, or the social and political salience of class-based forms of organisation compared with those based on other types of cleavage.

With regard to life chances, it is well established by research that class is more strongly related than other factors to a range of life chance outcomes, including educational attainment (Blossfeld and Shavit 1992; Heath and Clifford 1996), mortality and morbidity (Acheson 1999), etc. Some, but by no means all, of the class inequalities in outcomes can even be explained on the basis of rational choices made by parents in different classes (Goldthorpe 1996; and see Marshall *et al.* 1997 for a more extensive discussion of the causation of inequality of access to class positions). In these conditions, tenure can act as a surrogate for class. For example: 'Tenure is significantly related to poverty. Children in local authority housing are three times more likely to be deprived than those in owner-occupied homes. For those in the private rented sector, the odds of being deprived are twice as high' (Gordon *et al.* 2000). These relationships are far stronger than those for ethnic group or gender. The Family Expenditure Survey (ONS 2000) finds that households headed by people in professional occupations spend more than twice as much per week as those in unskilled manual occupations, and that among middle-class households the highest proportion of spending is on leisure goods, while among working-class households the largest element of expenditure is on food and non-alcoholic drink. Such statistics suggest the existence of a huge gulf between the social classes in how they live their daily lives.

The main problem with this approach to assessing the significance of class, however, is the difficulty of disentangling the effects of class from those of other factors. The mutual embedding of class and other categories such as 'ability', age, ethnicity, and gender is so great that the question of the *relative* importance of class borders on the meaningless. As Savage (2000: 95) puts it: 'in fact, class does not stand like a puppet-master above the stage, pulling the strings of the dolls from on high: rather, it works through the medium of individualised processes', including the individual's choice of housing tenure (which is seen as a choice that is not merely constrained by class relations, but is embedded in them). Savage sees class disadvantage as inextricably linked with sexual and racial disadvantage, for example. Women and many members of ethnic minorities continue to be under-represented in advantaged positions 'because the individualised traits desired in managerial positions continue to be premised on the cultures and lifestyles of white men' (Savage 2000: 158). Even in a perfectly open system of recruitment to management posts, women and members of ethnic minorities have to prove that they are 'better' than the 'ordinary' in order to be selected – a conclusion that is supported by other research (for example, Somerville *et al.* 2000; and see chapters by Smith and by Harrison in this volume), and can probably be applied with equal validity to other groups that 'deviate' from societal norms, such as disabled people (see Milner, this volume), and/or are seen as less 'deserving' generally (see Cooper, this volume).

With regard to social and political organisation, the main issue here perhaps concerns how the labour movement is related to so-called 'new social movements'.

Numerous writers have suggested that changes in the structuring of capitalism have eroded the potential for working-class organisation (Lash and Urry 1987; Beck 1992; Crook *et al.* 1992; Pakulski and Waters 1996) and that an increasing range of social movements cannot be adequately analysed on the basis of class relations. Eder (1993), however, argues for a broader conception of class politics, encompassing contradictory ways of reacting to crises in late modernity (these crises themselves being the product of a blocked class politics in the narrower sense). This broader conception of class politics allows for the possibility of wide-ranging alliances (for example, between socialists, feminists, Greens, anti-racists, disability activists and others), which can be developed into effective oppositional movements. Such an argument suggests that it is not a matter of which form of cleavage (class, gender, race, disability, sexuality, etc.) is most prominent (this is, in any case, not a relevant issue for Greens), but of how those who are subordinated by the different cleavages can act together in concert in multiple public spheres, if not actually in a unified political movement (see Fotopoulos 2000, for further development of this idea of class divisions based on different forms of power inequality). Housing can function as one such public sphere, as is considered below.

Class, housing and regeneration policy

Housing policy is closely linked with state welfare policy (for example, on health, social services, etc.) and with policies on economic development, crime and area regeneration. A final issue to examine, therefore, is how housing in this wider policy context is related to class and class divisions. In this section, I concentrate on regeneration policy (see Pierson and Worley, this volume, for further elaboration of this theme).

Regeneration policy is generally directed at what are commonly called 'poverty neighbourhoods' (Friedrichs 1997), which are in fact poor working-class residential areas. The thrust of such policy has been broadly interpreted in two main ways: either as a genuine attempt on the part of a benevolent state to lift the poor and deprived out of their abject conditions; or as a means to strengthen the subordination of the working class through locally appropriate forms of responsibilisation and self-disciplining (Rose's 'government through community'), resulting in the political incorporation of the 'deserving' and the exclusion of the 'undeserving'. Whilst acknowledging that evidence can be found to support both of these interpretations, a third possibility is that regeneration policy, like all state policy, represents a site of class struggle (in Eder's wider sense) whose outcomes are uncertain and unpredictable. The state does not act in a straightforwardly benevolent or malevolent manner – for example, it can be simultaneously both supportive and destructive of working-class grassroots movements by providing them with funding and advice while undermining their autonomy of action through regimes of regulation.

The government's National Strategy for Neighbourhood Renewal (SEU 2001) can be used to illustrate the point. The 'benevolent state' interpretation is supported by the policy of concentrating on the poorest eighty-eight neighbourhoods and the introduction of 'floor targets' for the performance of public services in housing, health, education, and crime prevention/reduction. The New Deal for Communities programme in particular contains a long-term commitment to deliver real change (over a ten-year period), with communities at the heart of it. Critics of the Neighbourhood Renewal Strategy, however, point to the absence from it of any provision for local communities to develop their own forms of concerted action and decision-making power (see, for example, Maclennan 2000). Clearly, if the Strategy is not designed to empower working-class communities to take control of their own lives, then the renewal outcomes from this Strategy are likely only to ensure their continued subordination, thus confirming the incorporation/exclusion thesis.

However, what a strategy is designed to do and what actually happens are two different things. There is disagreement among commentators as to the effectiveness of the government's overall approach to regulation. This approach has been described as 'tight-loose-tight' (SEU 2000): 'tight' at the level of setting targets, 'loose' in terms of how those targets are to be met, and 'tight' with regard to auditing of performance. The element of 'looseness' here allows space for a wide variety of forms of action at a neighbourhood level, which could in theory include progressive working-class action. Some critics argue that this is only a new strategy of social control. Davies (2001: 217), for example, concludes that: 'The state has *increased* its capacity to steer. It may be relinquishing *direct* control but, in doing so, it is purchasing wider *effective* control'. Allen and Cars (2001), however, question whether this strategy is likely to be effective, in the sense of achieving workable and sustainable local governance. It could, instead, reinforce social exclusion, frustrate 'joined-up' working, and stimulate community resentment and unrest. In other words, implementation failure could generate concerted working-class community action, whose outcomes are not possible to predict with any confidence. The practical effectiveness or ineffectiveness of government policy on neighbourhood renewal, therefore, turns out to be a key issue for the future of working-class community struggle.

The Neighbourhood Renewal Strategy fails, in any case, to take account of the implications of achieving its targets, for example, in terms of the possible changing class composition of different neighbourhoods. In a review of the literature on gentrification, for example, Atkinson (2002) shows that neighbourhood renewal in a city tends to attract middle-class households from other parts of the same city and to displace or diffuse social problems from the renewed neighbourhood. The class effects of such changes are unclear: they could result in class fragmentation, as existing neighbourhoods become more class-divided (including along lines of tenure) and working-class community networks become more attenuated over larger geographical areas; on the other hand, they could offer new opportunities for class-based organisation as working-class residents in poorer neighbourhoods gain access to wider social networks, reducing their social isolation and ghettoisation. Following Savage's arguments, it would appear that perhaps the most likely outcome of policy-led regeneration is an ever-deepening (but ultimately ineffective) cultural colonisation of working-class areas by middle-class 'professionals' (Cowburn 2002), thus continuing a long tradition in 'professional' community work and community development (Popple 1995). Such regeneration issues are discussed in more detail in Pierson and Worley (this volume).

Recent research on community control (Somerville 2003), however, suggests that, in certain circumstances, it is possible for working-class communities to take advantage of the government's 'looseness' on organisational mechanisms to achieve a high degree of autonomy of action. To take just one example: Shoreditch Our Way, a New Deal for Communities project, is democratically controlled by local people at a number of different levels and is moving towards taking on responsibility for most activities in its area currently carried out by the local authority. In this and similar cases elsewhere, the task is now to take these local working-class gains forward into a wider social and political arena.

A crucial issue in neighbourhood regeneration is that of sustainable economic development. There is some research suggesting that community enterprise can pose a practical alternative to the corporate capitalist economy, which is responsible for class divisions in the first place. Arguably, therefore, the expansion of the community economy is essential for the transformation of class society in the long term (see, for example, Douthwaite 1996; Begg 2000; MacIntosh 2001). Other research, however, is less sanguine, concluding that alternative economies as currently constituted:

> may merely supplement and/or ape the mainstream while remaining in a structural sense separate from it. Alternatively, they may offer support for the mainstream by providing material and social supplements yet not mount a challenge to its material or social power.
>
> (Lee and Leyshon 2003: 197; see also Amin et al. 2002)

This difference of opinion could reflect a difference between what alternative forms of economic activity are actually like and what they could be like, or between descriptive and normative approaches to the subject. Either way, if sustainable economic development is the aim, the strengthening of the co-operative (housing) movement seems a sensible way forward. To use Mike Savage's terminology, the increasingly individualised character of class relations makes co-operative strategies of commitment (De Vos et al. 2001), based on rationalised 'projects of the self', more appropriate for the achievement of social transformation.

Conclusion

The argument in this chapter has appeared to travel far from its original discussion of social mobility. In reality, however, the theme remains that of how the working class can emancipate itself, specifically through the housing and neighbourhoods in which working-class communities live. Individual mobility up a Weberian class hierarchy is always going to leave most working-class people behind and makes little or no difference to the overall structure of domination characteristic of late capitalist society. Collective social mobility, of the working class as a whole, however, is a tall order and conveys an impression of utopianism. This impression can be dispelled perhaps only through the adoption of a rigorous action-theoretic approach, using a non-fundamentalist version of Marxist theory (for example, following Gramsci or Arendt) or radical theory of some other kind (see Stewart 2001, for a general evaluation of such theories). Focusing specifically on housing, it can be seen that, maybe because housing typically functions as a surrogate for class, it is possible to identify housing policies and housing-related policies as major sites of class struggle. A concentration on housing *per se*, however, seems to lead to pessimism about the prospects of working-class emancipation. In contrast, viewing housing within a wider social and political context appears to hold out a degree of hope, however small. This is an important lesson to be learnt from the attempt to explore the interface between housing and social policy. In particular, there is evidence to show that concerted action within local working-class communities, not restricted only to housing issues, can be successful in lifting those communities out of their depression, at least temporarily, and in establishing genuinely co-operative and empowering ways of working.

Notes

1 Another example of opportunity hoarding is 'nimbyism', whereby areas with more affluent residents are defended against the threat of an influx of poorer households. At a more institutional level, the owner-occupied housing market itself operates, in some areas, as a means for better-off households to accumulate ('hoard') wealth through the increasing value of their equity.

2 The options relate mainly to education, social capital, and taxation.

3 It should be noted, however, that these are simplistic and stereotypical representations of the 'origin' and 'destination' of council housing as a tenure. The more complex reality is that, although much (but by no means all) of council housing was commissioned and owned by Labour-controlled local authorities, it was largely built by private companies and managed by middle-class officials. On the other hand, even after fifty years of residualisation, a significant proportion of council tenants continue to live in good quality housing and are not in receipt of state benefits.

4 According to Byrne (1997: 23), 'It was not a social movement, because its target was one specific policy; once the policy was changed, the *raison d'être* of the campaign disappeared, as did the protest'. This comment, however, misses the point that a successful protest campaign can promote further mobilisation and political action – it is no accident, for example, that Tommy Sheridan, one of the leaders of the anti-poll tax campaign, is now leader of the Scottish Socialist Party.

References

Acheson, D. (1999) *Independent Inquiry into Inequalities in Health Report*, London: Department of Health.

Adonis, A. and Pollard, S. (1998) *A Class Act – The Myth of Britain's Classless Society*, Harmondsworth: Penguin Books.

Aldridge, S. (2001) *Social Mobility: A Discussion Paper*, London: Cabinet Office Performance and Innovation Unit.

Allen, J. and Cars, G. (2001) 'Multiculturalism and governing neighbourhoods', *Urban Studies*, 38, 112: 2195–209.

Amin, A., Cameron, A. and Hudson, R. (2002) *Placing the Social Economy*, London: Routledge.

Anning, N., Wates, N. and Wolmar, C. (eds) (1980) *Squatting: The Real Story*, London: Bayleaf Books.

Anthias, F. (2001) 'The concept of "social divisions" and theorising social stratification: looking at ethnicity and class', *Sociology*, 35, 4: 835–54.

Atkinson, R. (2002) *Does Gentrification Help or Harm Urban Neighbourhoods? An Assessment of the Evidence Base in the Context of the New Urban Agenda*, CNR Paper 5, London: Centre for Neighbourhood Research.

Bauman, Z. (1998) *Globalization: The Human Consequences*, Cambridge: Polity Press.

Beck, U. (1992) *Risk Society*, London: Sage.

Begg, A. (2000) *Empowering the Earth: Strategies for Social Change*, Dartington: Green Books.

Blossfeld, H.-P. and Shavit, Y. (eds) (1992) *Persistent Inequality: Changing Educational Stratification in 13 Countries*, Boulder, CO: Westview Press.

Bradley, H. and Hebson, G. (1999) 'Breaking the silence: the need to re-articulate "class"', *International Journal of Sociology and Social Policy*, 19, 9/10/11: 187–214.

Bramley, G., Pawson, H. and Third, H. (2000) *Low Demand Housing and Unpopular Neighbourhoods*, London: DETR.

Breen, R. and Goldthorpe, J. (1999) 'Class inequality and meritocracy: a critique of Saunders and an alternative analysis', *British Journal of Sociology*, 50, 1: 1–27.

Byrne, P. (1997) *Social Movements in Britain*, London: Routledge.

Castells, M. (1983) *The City and the Grassroots*, London: Edward Arnold.

Cole, I. and Furbey, R. (1994) *The Eclipse of Council Housing*. London: Routledge.

Cowburn, W. (2002) 'Why we must stop confusing class with ability', *New Start*, 13 December: 16.

Crook, S., Pakulski, J. and Waters, M. (1992) *Postmodernisation: Change in Advanced Society*, London: Sage.

Damer, S. (2000) '"The Clyde rent war!" The Clydebank rent strike of the 1920s', in M. Lavalette and G. Mooney (eds) *Class Struggle and Social Welfare*, London and New York: Routledge: 71–95.

Daunton, M.J. (1987) *A Property-Owning Democracy?* London: Faber and Faber.

Davies, J.S. (2001) *Partnerships and Regimes*, Aldershot: Ashgate.

De Vos, H., Smaniotto, R. and Elsas, D.A. (2001) 'Reciprocal altruism under conditions of partner selection', *Rationality and Society*, 13, 2: 139–83.

Douthwaite, R. (1996) *Short Circuit: Strengthening Local Economies for Security in an Unstable World*, Dartington: Green Books.

Eder, K. (1993) *The New Politics of Class: Social Movements and Cultural Dynamics in Advanced Societies*, London: Sage.

Erikson, R. and Goldthorpe, J. (1992) *The Constant Flux – A Study of Class Mobility in Industrial Societies*, Oxford: Clarendon Press.

Forrest, R. and Murie, A. (1989) 'Differential accumulation: wealth, inheritance and housing policy reconsidered', *Policy and Politics*, 17, 1: 25–39.

—— (1995) 'Points of departure', in R. Forrest and A. Murie (eds) *Housing and Family Wealth: Comparative International Perspectives*, London and New York: Routledge: 311–15.

Fotopoulos, T. (2000) 'Class divisions today – the inclusive democracy approach', *Democracy and Nature* 6, 2: 211–51.

Friedrichs, J. (1997) 'Context effects of poverty neighbourhoods on residents', in H. Westergaard (ed.) *Housing in Europe*, Horsholm: Danish Building Research Institute: 141–60.

Gershuny, J. (1994) 'Post-industrial career structures in Britain', in G. Esping-Andersen (ed.) *Changing Classes*, London: Sage.

Goldthorpe, J. (1996) 'Class analysis and the reorientation of class theory: the case of persisting differentials in educational attainment', *British Journal of Sociology*, 47: 481–505.

Goldthorpe, J. and Mills, C. (2000) *Trends in Intergenerational Class Mobility in Britain in the Late Twentieth Century*, Working Paper.

Gordon, D., Adelman, L., Ashworth, K., Bradshaw, J., Levitas, R., Middleton, S., Pantazis, C., Patsios, D., Payne, S., Townsend, P. and Williams, J. (2000) *Poverty and Social Exclusion in Britain*, York: Joseph Rowntree Foundation.

Grayson, J. (1997) 'Campaigning tenants: a pre-history of tenant involvement to 1979', in C. Cooper and M. Hawtin (eds) *Housing, Community and Conflict: Understanding Resident 'Involvement'*, Aldershot: Arena: 15–65.

Heath, A. and Clifford, P. (1996) 'Class inequalities and educational reform in 20th century Britain', in D.J. Lee and B.S. Turner (eds) *Conflicts About Class*, London: Longman: 209–24.

Heath, A. and Payne, C. (2000) 'Social mobility', in A.H. Halsey (ed.) with J. Webb *Twentieth Century British Social Trends*, Basingstoke: Macmillan.

Hoggett, P. (ed.) (1997) *Contested Communities: Experiences, Struggles, Policies*, Bristol: Policy Press.

Hoggett, P. and Burns, D. (1991) 'The revenge of the poor: the anti-poll tax campaign in Britain', *Critical Social Policy*, 33: 95–110.

Johnson, A. (2000) 'The making of a poor people's movement: a study of the political leadership of Poplarism, 1919–25', in M. Lavalette and G. Mooney (eds) *Class Struggle and Social Welfare*, London and New York: Routledge: 96–116.

Johnstone, C. (2000) 'Housing and class struggles in postwar Glasgow', in M. Lavalette and G. Mooney (eds) *Class Struggle and Social Welfare*, London and New York: Routledge: 139–54.

Lash, S. and Urry, J. (1987) *The End of Organised Capitalism*, Cambridge: Polity Press.

Lavalette, M. and Mooney, G. (eds) (2000a) *Class Struggle and Social Welfare*, London: Routledge.

—— (2000b) 'Introduction: class struggle and social policy', in M. Lavalette and G. Mooney (eds) *Class Struggle and Social Welfare*, London and New York: Routledge: 1–12.

—— (2000c) '"No poll tax here!" The Tories, social policy and the great poll tax rebellion 1987–1991', in M. Lavalette and G. Mooney (eds) *Class Struggle and Social Welfare*, London and New York: Routldge: 199–227.

Lee, R. and Leyshon, A. (2003) 'Conclusions: re-making geographies and the construction of "spaces of hope"', in A. Leyshon, R. Lee and C.C. Williams (eds) *Alternative Economic Spaces*, London: Sage: 193–8.

MacIntosh, A. (2001) *Soil and Soul: People versus Corporate Power*, London: Aurum Press.

Maclennan, D. (2000) *Changing Places, Engaging People*, York: Joseph Rowntree Foundation.

Mann, K. (1992) *The Making of an English 'Underclass'? The Social Divisions of Welfare and Labour*, Buckingham: Open University Press.

Marshall, G., Swift, A. and Roberts, S. (1997) *Against the Odds? Social Class and Social Justice in Industrial Societies*, Oxford: Clarendon.

Melling, J. (1983) *Rent Strikes: People's Struggle for Housing in West Scotland 1890–1916*, Edinburgh: Polygon.

Munro, M. and Smith, S.J. (1989) 'Gender and housing: broadening the debate', *Housing Studies*, 4, 1: 3–17.

Office of National Statistics (ONS) (2000) *Family Spending 1999–2000*, London: ONS.

Pakulski, J. and Waters, M. (1996) *The Death of Class*, London: Sage.

Piven, F.F. and Cloward, R.A. (1977) *Poor People's Movements: Why They Succeed, How They Fail*, New York: Pantheon Books.

Popple, G. (1995) *Analysing Community Work: Its Theory and Practice*, Buckingham: Open University Press.

Rose, N. (1996) 'The death of the social? Refiguring the territory of government', *Economy and Society*, 25: 327–56.

Saunders, P. (1981) *Social Theory and the Urban Question*, London: Hutchinson.

—— (1990) *Social Class and Stratification*, London: Routledge.

—— (1995) 'Might Britain be a meritocracy?' *Sociology*, 29: 23–41.

—— (1996) *Unequal But Fair? A Study of Class Barriers in Britain*, London: Institute of Economic Affairs Health and Welfare Unit.

—— (1997) 'Social mobility in Britain', *Sociology*, 31, 2: 261–88.

Savage, M. (2000) *Class Analysis and Social Transformation*, Buckingham: Open University Press.

Scott, J. (2002) 'Social class and stratification in late modernity', *Acta Sociologica*, 45, 1: 23–35.

Social Exclusion Unit (SEU) (2000) *Joining It Up Locally*, PAT 17 Report, London: Cabinet Office.

—— (2001) *A New Commitment to Neighbourhood Renewal: National Strategy Action Plan*, London: Cabinet Office.

Somerville, P. (2003) *Community Control: A Position Paper*, Lincoln: University of Lincoln.

Somerville, P. and Knowles, A. (1991) 'The difference that tenure makes', *Housing Studies*, 6, 2: 112–30.

Somerville, P., Steele, A. and Sodhi, D. (2000) *A Question of Diversity: Black and Minority Ethnic Staff in the RSL Sector*, London: The Housing Corporation.

Stewart, A. (2001) *Theories of Power and Domination: The Politics of Empowerment in Late Modernity*, London: Sage.

Ward, C. (1976) *Housing: An Anarchist Approach*, London: Freedom Press.

Weeks, M. (2002) 'Just say no', *Property People*, 28 November: 10–11.

Young, M. (1958) *The Rise of the Meritocracy*, London: Thames and Hudson.

6 Ethnicity, 'race' and policy issues

Malcolm Harrison

This chapter highlights key features in the social policy and housing agenda related to minority ethnic households in Britain. It should be noted at the outset that much has changed in the past three decades, both in the housing experiences of minorities and in public policy responses. Observers have become increasingly aware of a diversity of housing and locational trajectories for minority ethnic households and groups, and of many personal successes, while overt racisms have had a greatly reduced impact on official policies and service delivery. Yet there has also been a degree of continuity of shared disadvantages for communities, affecting resources and hedging in housing choice.

We begin below by setting the scene with background on conditions, trends and the information base. The chapter then comments on developments in policy and the policy environment, and on ways in which today's research and policy preoccupations differ from those of the past. Third, we identify a set of overlapping key policy topics that seem crucial. Parts of this chapter build on two previous publications arising from a national review commissioned by central government, and these may be consulted for more extensive data and analysis on specific points (Harrison with Phillips 2003; Harrison 2003).

Conditions and trends

A longstanding problem facing officials and politicians charged with policy development concerns the information base. In writing elsewhere we have indicated the richness of existing empirical research material, but also the many gaps in knowledge that make conclusive judgements about events, policy outcomes or conditions difficult (Harrison 2003). Matters should improve as more investigations using new census data come 'on stream', but deficiencies will remain. For example, there is too little contemporary in-depth information about private sector activities in lettings, financial services, or property management. Recently Phillips has surveyed estate agents in Leeds and indicated that discriminatory practices may be persisting (see Phillips, in Harrison with Phillips 2003: 46), but such work seems rare. Other important under-researched topics concern housing quality and the costs experienced by households (which perhaps should be connected up with data on incomes, capital values, housing debts, affordability and financial services). For minority groups we also know too little on housing in relation to gender, children, chronic illness, impairments, and 'newer' or 'less visible' minority and migrant categories (for a recent study of such a group, see Cole and Robinson 2003). There is still also little research on disadvantaged white minorities, although some households amongst these may experience problems to a degree similar to those of non-white groups (perhaps particularly some elders or recent arrivals). Writing has however touched on inequality and the sense of hurt for people of Irish origin at the way that they have been treated (Hickman and Walter 1997). More generally, few analysts have as yet investigated housing 'pathways' and trajectories for minority ethnic households or their communities (although see Bowes *et al.* 1997a, 1997b; and Phillips, in Harrison with Phillips 2003).

Despite data limitations, there is nonetheless ample evidence pointing to continuing relative disadvantage. If our need is for reasonable general indicators for policy purposes, along with insights from localised and case study work, then the information base often proves 'fit for purpose'. The term *difference within difference* is applicable, conveying the view that there is still an uneven patterning of material outcomes in which a general 'white/black minority ethnic' divide remains important, but that diversity at household or minority group levels can be substantial (Harrison with Davis 2001).

It has been recognised officially that in comparison to their representation in the population, people from minority ethnic communities are more likely than others to live in deprived areas, to be poor, to suffer ill-health, and to live in over-crowded housing (Cabinet Office 2000: 17). One feature is that low income home ownership has persisted as an important aspect of black and minority ethnic experience, with potentially problematic consequences for owners if repair and maintenance costs have been high, conventional mortgages difficult to obtain, neighbourhood environmental quality unsatisfactory, or property values insecure. Use of social rented housing is also significant, reflecting low incomes and specific situations pushing people towards this tenure (as with many single parents). Homelessness provides a specific indicator of ongoing housing pressures, and recent data here point clearly to disproportionately high overall levels for black and minority ethnic people (Harrison with Phillips 2003: 30–1; see also Cole and Robinson 2003: 44–5; and Harrison 1999). Local housing research has reinforced the impressions of difficulties facing particular minorities, revealing substantial problems of long-term illness or impairment, or drawing attention to practical issues such as inability to use central heating fully because of the expense (see Ratcliffe 1996; Gidley *et al.* 1999).

Significant differences have been noted for some years between various minority ethnic groups in terms of household composition, tenure, dwelling types, settlement geographies, or density of occupation (see Ratcliffe 1997). Household sizes and structures and population age structures are important, while different groups have differing population growth rates and potential for new household formation (Phillips 1996). There may be severe problems if population growth is rapid within low-income communities confined to housing markets where there is already extensive overcrowding and a shortage of affordable dwellings. Specific groups have been found to have extremely low incomes (see especially Platt and Noble 1999: 20–3, referring to Birmingham). In recent years, writers have highlighted Pakistanis and Bangladeshis as living in very deprived housing conditions, both groups having been affected by high levels of overcrowding and issues such as lack of central heating (see Ratcliffe 1997: 141–3). In Wales, people of Black African or Pakistani heritages are the most likely to live in acutely overcrowded conditions, while people of Bangladeshi or Pakistani heritages are the most likely to live in accommodation with no central heating (BME Housing Project 2003: 12). The UK picture is complicated by geographical variations in market conditions and supply, with housing opportunities open to people from specific minority ethnic groups differing greatly from place to place.

Experiences within particular minority ethnic groups may vary according to age, generation, gender, household type, chronic illness or impairment, community or settlement histories, specific religious or kinship affiliations, and socio-economic status. Development of a 'minority ethnic middle class' may have been associated with the emergence of a degree of suburbanisation (Phillips 1998), and, although this may be more marked for some minority ethnic or religious groups than for others, there is likely to be a degree of socio-economic differentiation within most communities. Thus, while people assigned to specific ethnic categories (such as the Indian group) may now appear to be extremely successful on several fronts, even here we might expect to find a gradient linked to class, occupation, etc. Household structures and composition within particular ethnic groups are also important for housing needs (as with high proportions of female-headed, lone-parent families, or of extended households).

The geographical concentration of the UK's black and minority ethnic populations particularly into housing areas within parts of urban England is widely known, but a concentration in itself does not necessarily indicate or cause 'social exclusion'. Although many black and minority ethnic people would prefer improved housing, some favour areas of existing settlement, wishing to avoid tensions and isolation that may arise in other places, and needing access to specific facilities. Racist harassment generates barriers to movement for people from many minorities, through the risks faced in living outside the main areas of settlement, even though residence patterns and boundaries are potentially fluid rather than static. As well as offering relative safety, inner urban areas may also have crucial processes of what might be depicted as local cultural, community or political inclusion, often facilitated through affiliations linked to ethnicity (see Harrison 2003: 110–12; and, for fuller analysis, Phillips, in Harrison with Phillips 2003). Although one cannot deny that aspects of life in inner city areas may carry penalties, or that housing choices are constrained, there are benefits from living in proximity to people of similar culture and language.

Changing preoccupations for policy, analysis and research

For housing, ethnicity and 'race' there has been a gradual shift over time towards greater sophistication as far as organisations' activities are concerned, together with something of a change in the focus and purposes of policy analysis and research. Reference has been made elsewhere by the present writer to two over-lapping periods (Harrison with Phillips 2003: 78–9), the first running from the 1960s through to the early 1990s, and the second from then to the present. Dividing things up in this way over-simplifies, and a more refined chronology could be drafted, taking account of legislation on 'race' relations, key events like the appearance of the Stephen Lawrence inquiry report (Macpherson 1999), migration and asylum debates, and changes in governments. Nonetheless, although we lack a detailed chronology, some trends can be readily perceived. If we looked at the agenda of the 1960s, 1970s, or even the early 1980s, it would probably seem very different from that of today.

The reform preoccupations of the earlier decades cast anti-racism strategies largely in terms of monitoring and resisting direct discrimination, exposing and seeking change in systematic bad practice around a 'black/white' divide, starting to tackle broad 'racial inequalities', bringing resources into specific inner urban localities to counter economic decline, and (as time passed) promotional and exploratory work on equal opportunities through codes of practice and investig- ations (for a fuller account of change, see Law 1996: Chapter 1). Several factors led to this agenda gradually becoming more complex in housing practice and allied fields. The rise of the black voluntary housing movement brought new voices into prominence, helping redirect policy towards community empowerment and cultural sensitivity. More generally, the governmental agenda gradually changed in the face of recognition of increasing diversity and 'difference' across households and localities, and the growth in numbers of minority ethnic people. With these changes came a heightened interest in autonomy and involvement for groups, or at least a discourse that has touched upon such matters positively. Meanwhile, processes of monitoring, regulation, advice and audit developed considerably in penetration, reach and complication. Some of the advice and training available today to organisations is highly sophisticated and extremely well informed (see, for example, Blackaby and Chahal 2000), while 'official' organisations like the Housing Corporation have engaged in proactive promotional or research work of considerable significance (see Harrison with Phillips 2003: 87–8, 90–1). Central government itself has contributed substantially to the emergence of better practice. Recent policy development, strategy and training ideas have shown in many respects a level of understanding much advanced on that of earlier periods (for instance, see DTLR 2001; BME Housing Project 2003; Tomlins 2003). Finally, law has tightened over time as far as responsibilities are concerned, with enhanced duties for organisations under the Race Relations (Amendment) Act 2000. None of this is to argue that further change is unnecessary, but simply that the policy scene differs from that of fifteen to twenty years ago. Despite their political and media impact, recent crude and reactive developments in policy on asylum and immigration have probably been running somewhat 'against the grain' as far as general trends in anti-racist and equal opportunities practices have been concerned.

If we turn to research and analysis, we find clear differences from the past, suggestive of changed practice environments. Direct or 'straightforward' racist activities or outcomes have become far less dominant in the research agenda. Many 'classic' housing and 'race' studies of earlier years dealt directly and critically with the performance of housing organisations on 'racial' equality, and especially with negative discriminatory practices in council housing allocation processes. Black and minority ethnic households faced barriers in obtaining social rented dwellings, and in gaining entry to the better estates. Today, however, overt racisms have been very much reduced in social rented housing practice, and this is reflected in research priorities. Researchers in the late 1980s continued to find problems, Jeffers and Hoggett (publishing in 1995) providing especially interesting findings about disadvantage for minority ethnic households in accessing good quality council housing, despite an apparently more responsive official outlook. Much of the most recent research in England has related to housing associations, raising questions about several dimensions of their performance (Somerville *et al.* 2000; Tomlins *et al.* 2001; Robinson *et al.* 2002). Their equality policies may lack depth and breadth (although they have become more comprehensive), and there are doubts about the adequacy of record-keeping and monitoring, consultation with communities, outcomes on contractors and consultants, employment of staff, lettings, and investment. Nonetheless, the thrust of research has altered, not only because housing associations are now more central in the policy forum, but also because equal opportunities expectations have become much more generally established, with pressures for adoption and implementation of particular strategies and forms of improved practice. At the same time there has been increasing acknowledgement of the significance of cultural sensitivity for service design and delivery.

Some key policy issues

Rather than offering now a detailed catalogue of specific political, legal, administrative or financial events, we highlight some selected overlapping issues and topics that can be particularly relevant for many minority ethnic households, but also important for 'mainstream' housing policy.

Conditions, affordability and security

A policy portfolio relating to urgent immediate needs would probably include a range of strategies to improve access to affordable and good quality dwellings, to improve secure and safe possession, and to counter homelessness. In addition, policy makers could give more direct attention to groups that are presently neglected as regards provision and choice, including young single people. A key policy concern in some localities is the shortage of reasonable quality accommodation on manageable financial terms for poorer households, including many people in minority communities. We have already noted some of the features of disadvantage, overcrowding being a strong indicator of possible problems. Data suggest that white households are less likely to be overcrowded than households of other ethnic groups, and are also less likely to have poor housing conditions (unfitness, substantial levels of disrepair, need for essential modernisation) or live in poor conditions (local concentrations of housing in substantial disrepair, vacant/derelict housing or sites, other forms of neglect or misuse) (Harrison with Phillips 2003: 21–2).

In recent years the local needs study has perhaps come to be seen as a potential standard tool for acquiring information on conditions, for feeding ideas into the policy process, for helping with target setting, or for facilitating the social audit of ongoing housing agency performance (see Harrison with Phillips 2003: 50). The methodologies, measures and indicators available for such studies are varied, and there is potential for disagreements about how far a specific type of information is actually a good guide to needs in a particular locality or community. For instance, established approaches to indicators of households' relative needs may not place weight on matters such as isolation or potential harassment. There may also sometimes be a poor fit between available local strategies and investment targeting on the one hand, and the needs and preferences of minority ethnic groups on the other. Insofar as policy and investment preoccupations continue to be focused on social rented housing rather than the private sectors, there may be too few means of responding to housing and associated disadvantages faced by some minority ethnic communities living in private housing neighbourhoods. Available strategies and funds (particularly in respect of owner-occupied housing) can be inadequate for responding to needs or preferences.

Homelessness is in a sense that part of the 'housing disadvantage iceberg' which is highly visible, and therefore offers warnings of possibly more extensive problems lying out of sight. While minority ethnic groups differ in the extent and nature of the homelessness experience, disproportionately high overall rates of homelessness indicate real difficulties in affordable housing supply. Beyond official data on processed applications, there can be 'hidden' (or perhaps more accurately 'unrecognised') homelessness, and 'concealed households' pushed into staying with friends or relatives. Chahal suggests that minority ethnic homelessness 'is less about street homelessness and much more about being hidden', with minority ethnic people tending to use friends and relatives more than white people (Chahal 1999:1). In any event, policy responses to homelessness over the years often sought solutions after the event, highlighting crisis management rather than developing long-term strategies and discovering appropriate points for prior intervention or support. This may have reflected homelessness manifested as a street event to which a rapid reaction seemed vital, rather than an element within complex housing pathway experiences that could be the focus of preventative strategies. A comprehensive approach might include efforts to scrutinise any significant patterns of institutional and actor behaviour (in private, voluntary and public sectors) playing a role in creating conditions for homelessness.

One aspect of shared disadvantage directly linked to the sense of security is continuing exposure to harassment and violence. Racist hostilities have immediate and longer-term effects on individuals and families, and can influence people's choices of housing and localities. Significant roles can be played by housing organisations in preventing unpleasant incidents, supporting those at risk, or taking action against perpetrators. A particularly insightful study by Chahal and Julienne examines the impact of racist victimisation on daily lives, touches on strategies that families and individuals adopt in response, summarises criticisms made in earlier writings about official responses, and notes negative effects on household choice (Chahal and Julienne 1999). We know that perception of racist harassment as a problem differs as between white and black minority ethnic groups (see Harrison with Phillips 2003: 23), and some minority ethnic households certainly will be prepared to forego higher dwelling quality to achieve more security.

Responding to differences and diversity

We have already commented on differences related to ethnicity, but these are cross-cut by other markers of differing experiences. Disability, age and gender are important here, with potential policy implications in specific contexts.

Several writers have commented usefully on provision and problems in relation to disability, chronic illness, and older age. Issues raised for providers have included minority ethnic under-representation amongst households with medical priority, and a low percentage of minority ethnic households receiving Disabled Facilities Grant (Law 1996: 101,106), older disabled people from black minority ethnic communities being more likely than white counterparts to face problems like extreme isolation and very low incomes (see JRF 1993), and a considerable and developing need for sheltered bed-spaces, very sheltered units, aids, adaptations and residential care among Asian elders (Sandhu 1998). Chahal and Temple (2000) observe that different minority ethnic communities have differing and changing expectations about both service provision and the changing structures of family life (cf. Karn *et al.* 1999), yet aspirations and expectations of older people from minority ethnic groups remain under-explored. Stereotypes about ethnicities may lead to over-optimistic assumptions about the preparedness or capacity of people's relatives and social networks to provide informal support, while lack of directly expressed demand for services may be interpreted mistakenly to suggest lack of need (disregarding possibilities that problems of information, communications, access or cultural insensitivity may have restricted take-up). Some households may indeed cater for elders within extended families, needing less separate elders' accommodation and more large family dwellings, but situations within communities are not static, while some people certainly may be 'left out' of kinship arrangements.

Adaptation of homes may be very important for elders. Given potential over-crowding and a shortage of larger dwellings, allocation of adjacent properties might be useful, perhaps with thought given to possibilities such as a connecting door, or simply members of an extended family living next door to each other (see Karn *et al.* 1999: 134). Nationally, the predicted increase in numbers of elders within certain communities, coupled with an altered ratio of younger to older people, is likely to enlarge the demand for community services, with diminished potential for households to arrange informal care. Factors making forms of accommodation acceptable to elders could include low risks of harassment and crime, culturally sensitive staffing, outreach or support services, intelligent design taking culture into account, and proximity to family, community, shops and places of worship.

Turning to disability research we find a useful study indicating difficulties faced by minority ethnic families with disabled children, including the unsuitability of much of the accommodation that they occupy (Chamba *et al.* 1999). An investigation on housing and mental health care needs for Asian people points to inappropriate housing, difficulties with neighbours, burglaries, harassment, fears for personal safety, insufficient support, and culturally insensitive services. Ways forward might include making available a range of good quality supported independent housing and residential care, specialist housing catering for the needs of Asian people with mental health care problems, and trained outreach support workers to service residential projects and people living more independently in the community (see Radia 1996: 1, 2, 22–5).

A number of problems have been identified that affect black and minority ethnic women, including unrecognised (or 'hidden') homelessness associated with dependence on temporary accommodation with family or friends, lack of neighbourhood choice or satisfactory provider responses in social renting, isolation or stigma linked with separation from families, partners or communities, access and dwelling quality disadvantage in private markets because of low incomes, and poor housing outcomes and choices following domestic violence and separation (for an overview on women and social exclusion, see Gill 2002). Gender is significant for housing tenure destinations, intersecting with other variables (income, age, ethnicity, etc.) to give complex housing outcomes. Disadvantage can be expected for numerous female-headed households, whether single person or larger (for relevant discussions see Phillips 1996, also 1997: 175; Peach and Byron 1993, 1994). Given low incomes, there may be a tendency for dependence on social renting, and it appears that more new lettings have been made recently to women than to men by housing associations (Lemos and Crane, undated: 1, 5–6). Female tenants' needs may deserve specific attention from social landlords.

Women separating from partners may encounter considerable difficulties. Rai and Thiara (1997) explored the needs of black women and children in refuge support services, and indicated a low level of awareness or knowledge about such services among large numbers of women. Most women preferred to go to a refuge outside their locality for reasons of safety, and also wanted to be housed in areas with substantial minority ethnic populations, to avoid racism and to be able to use specific facilities. In addition, black women often faced 'the dual problem of racism from the wider society and rejection from their own communities', while 'specific needs of children of mixed parentage often remain unrecognised' (Rai and Thiara 1997: 9). Ahmed and Sodhi (2000) found that few black and minority ethnic women knew about supported housing, and lack of knowledge was a barrier. Service providers pointed to a range of provision in terms of accommodation type and levels of support to meet the diverse needs of women, and highlighted specific gaps for women with high support needs. Very few Asian women identified a need for supported housing, but many identified a need for support, and some wanted to be close to cultural facilities. Ahmed and Sodhi indicate a need for greater provision of women-only, age- and culturally-specific schemes, and more discrete provision for those fleeing domestic violence. We should add that what happens to women when they approach more long-term housing providers is an important allied topic.

The housing situations of young minority ethnic men deserve more attention, given that in some communities they are faring badly in economic terms, and bearing in mind their sometimes negative interactions with the criminal justice system. It would be useful for policy makers to consider trajectories, barriers and opportunities more systematically, and to develop more proactive housing policies complementing homelessness and emergency services.

Participation and voice

Involving housing consumers in consultative and decision-making processes has been given higher priority by governments in recent years, at least at the level of general expectations. For urban regeneration, minority ethnic participation and leadership are sometimes seen as crucial to success, with community engagement perceived as essential (although this may not be easy to sustain outside *ad hoc* short-term projects). Attention has also been given to improving housing career opportunities (through positive action strategies focused on training, etc.), and to development of housing organisations run directly by black and minority ethnic people.

Enhancing tenant participation has become increasingly emphasised in official perspectives on social rented housing, but the general literature (albeit rather anecdotal) suggests that black and minority ethnic tenants of councils and housing associations may often have been excluded rather than fully involved. Similar criticism is sometimes voiced about urban renewal processes. Unfortunately there is little detailed information about recent participation practices or developments for women, specific minority ethnic or religious groups, elders, or disabled people. Fuller consultation and participation could be very important here in relation to improved provision and services. There is a need for more knowledge of aspirations and expectations, but also an understanding of households' circumstances and realistic options in contexts of local markets, available finance, and community characteristics. For elders and disabled people, emphasis should be on helping participants retain or develop choice and independence. When considering women in all age groups it is desirable to avoid stereotypes about supposed passivity or lack of involvement in housing decisions, and to consult properly.

Much has been written about black and minority ethnic-run housing associations. The Housing Corporation's five-year strategies for them (running from the mid-1980s onwards) represented a distinctive and important social policy innovation, effectively 'top-slicing' a mainstream spending programme to encourage development of organisations run primarily by minority ethnic people. Although their impact has been mostly within England, establishing such organisations has been on the agenda in other parts of the UK too (for Scotland, see Bowes *et al.* 1998: 21, 92–6; for recent ideas in Wales, see BME Housing Project 2003: 23–4). Lemos and Crane (undated) state that on a range of indicators – stock, staff, lettings and new housing – black and minority ethnic registered social landlords (RSLs) represent about 1.5 per cent of RSL activity, and own and manage over 21,000 units. Despite their small stock sizes, the black and minority ethnic housing associations have played crucial roles in giving minority ethnic participants voices in policy and implementation, have provided potential comparators for white-run bodies on equal opportunities and lettings, have sometimes tried to promote the employment of black-led contracting firms, and have developed 'housing plus' services going beyond bricks-and-mortar housing management (for insights into housing association lettings performance, see Robinson *et al.* 2002, Chapter 3). The vulnerability of some associations to pressures relating to their financial circumstances, small size, and limited assets has often raised possibilities of mergers with larger white-run organisations, or of group structures within which autonomy might vanish or diminish. Perhaps there might be some potential for constructing federal forms, within which organisations of differing sizes and resources might share more equally in the collective management of partnerships or consortia. Conceding equality of influence, however, might require significant incentives for larger players if financial and staff resources were to be pooled. In any event, given contemporary pressures to act commercially and competitively, minority ethnic associations may not always find it easy to remain close to their community roots, and sometimes there might in any case be limitations on their capacity to respond to the interests of very diverse potential local constituencies (cf. Cole and Robinson 2003: 34–5). Nonetheless, they have been a crucial channel of communication and participation.

Choice and outward movement

In the present period it is impossible to know how far particular groups of tenants or prospective tenants encounter deficient services or restricted housing choices through the effects of discriminatory attitudes and stereotypes, investment priorities, or practitioner assumptions about appropriate and comfortable neighbourhood destinations for minority ethnic households. Given the relatively sophisticated policy environments of today, more research might have been expected into specific areas of consumer/provider interaction; including access in cases of medical need, access by women (and particularly women escaping from domestic violence or unwelcome community pressures), supported housing and responses to specific impairments, access to agency services and improvement funds, access by specific religious or ethnic groups, and access to better quality dwellings. Some minority ethnic households already established in social renting may be facing obstacles in moving to higher status dwellings or areas, but it is difficult to appraise the situation. It would be of considerable value to have systematic and substantial research material on the recent locational options and destinations of specific groups (such as homeless people, female-headed households, long-established tenants, or small, newer minorities), as well as research into areas of strong demand with low tenancy turnover.

Considerable debate has developed, however, about movement from established areas of residence in older (often private) housing into areas of social rented housing outside existing areas of minority settlement. Tenancies may be available in specific neighbourhoods which no longer attract as many applications from white households as previously, while at the same time low income minority ethnic households (especially from Asian communities) may be established elsewhere in the same urban areas in overcrowded, poor quality, older, private sector dwellings. Whilst significant numbers of minority ethnic residents may wish to move out of inner-city areas, take-up of council tenancies may have been slowed by worries about the absence of other minority ethnic households and associated facilities and shops in estates, as well as fear of potential harassment (see Birmingham City Council 1998: i). Several reports have cited or illustrated negative perceptions amongst households about particular estates or localities (probably most recently in Wales; see Tomlins 2003: 41–2, 47). Concerns about harassment may be complemented by reservations about what are thought of as crime-prone and 'rough' (primarily white) neighbourhood cultures (cf. Bowes *et al*. 1998). More 'respectable' or higher status white-occupied estates may be further from established areas of residence, have higher demand, and feel unwelcoming (having few existing black tenants). Housing association accommodation managed by black-run RSLs attracts minority ethnic tenants, but may offer limited choices of dwellings, and few estates located away from central districts. Risks of racist abuse and violence from local white populations may deter some housing associations from developing schemes aimed at minority ethnic tenants away from 'core' areas of settlement (see Robinson 2002: 101).

Phillips and Unsworth indicate a need for sensitive policies to support minority ethnic households wishing to rent in non-traditional areas of social rented housing. They observe that some housing providers have begun implementing strategies of creating 'settlement nodes' or clusters in more outlying areas, perhaps underpinned by inter-agency initiatives and tenant support (Phillips and Unsworth 2002: 85). Perhaps components of a sensitive strategy might include conversions to create larger dwellings (or re-conversions of sub-divided properties), adaptable housing where units can be combined or subdivided later, opportunities for low-cost home ownership (where viable), and substantial targeted allocations of tenancies, possibly connected with ownership or management arrangements facilitating involvement of black-run housing organisations. Reports for specific cities have suggested various ways of overcoming barriers, including improving housing related services, supporting provision of cultural and religious amenities, improving the standard and cultural sensitivity of service delivery, more joined-up policy-making between organisations, developing appropriate property types/sizes (including houses for shared ownership and outright sale), developing community support networks, aiming for linked lettings where families are rehoused together to improve security, and providing better public transport connections to inner-city locations (Birmingham City Council 1998: i–ii; cf Karn *et al*. 1999: 8, etc.; Ratcliffe *et al*. 2001: 32–3). Even with supportive multi-organisational community development strategies, it may not prove easy to facilitate the movement of minority ethnic households into areas with high proportions of white residents. Nonetheless, enhancing access to social renting is important, especially since new or growing households in some places could face increasingly severe difficulties in obtaining adequate accommodation within 'traditional' areas of residence (cf. Ratcliffe *et al*. 2001: 8).

Sustainability, ownership and asset-based welfare

Surprisingly little is known about the durability, limitations and effectiveness of physical improvements in inner areas, the contributions that policy interventions make there to ongoing financial success, autonomy or difficulty for minority ethnic households, or the manageability for tenants and landlords of rented dwellings over time. These issues all relate to sustainability, which in its social and economic as well as physical senses is potentially an important part of the policy agenda.

From a sustainability perspective one key concern over the past decade has been the restricted character of governmental support for low-income owner occupation. Even after a change of governing party, there is still not much evidence of coherent policies for pre-1919 housing in sustainability terms, so that locally there are often few effective policy levers to assist minority ethnic home owners living in poor quality dwellings. One criticism has been that minority ethnic households in some localities have gained little through the focusing of mainstream capital programmes on regenerating areas of social renting, because they often live in mixed tenure neighbourhoods. It is difficult to weigh up the benefits that may have reached minority groups through large-scale programmes recently (see Harrison with Phillips 2003: 65–7), but uncertainties persist about success. Meanwhile, despite official interest, strategies for assistance with full purchase or shared ownership perhaps remain under-developed, with ongoing doubts about affordability and feasibility (see Harrison with Phillips 2003: 74–6).

A concept of *social* sustainability implies taking account of people's individual, household or collective preferences and strategies, and bearing in mind the dynamic nature of these (see also our conclusions section below). More active support for 'down-market' owners might include increases in direct improvement funding, more state-sponsored protection to reduce financial risks, easier arrangements for changing tenure (in whichever direction was appropriate) while staying in the same house, and enhanced funding and choices for moves out of run-down areas into replacement housing. Preferences for ownership, however, may not be fixed or universal, being affected by experiences of poor dwelling quality, repair problems, and changing housing and labour market conditions, as well as by any governmental moves affecting viability of tenure options. Crucial foci for further policy analysis and development might include the potential integration of central governmental strategies across the tenures, more sophisticated improvement policies, and more effective development of shared ownership and of collective forms of ownership such as co-ops and self-build schemes. A dynamic view would also need to take into account the possibility of social renting being perceived more deliberately as a transitional stage for some households heading for ownership.

The control of assets and management is potentially significant for households and groups, and another important issue for a sustainability agenda. Contributions might be made through low-cost ownership, the right-to-buy, 'staircasing', 'equity stakes' in rented housing, and collective forms of ownership and self-management. Questions about collective ownership, community ownership and control have taken on enhanced immediate significance because of the desire to utilise potentially 'surplus' municipal stock, and (more important) the ongoing processes of large-scale stock transfer from local authorities to other landlords. Possible fragmentation of former council stocks might have negative implications for offering an integrated service, or for segregation by ethnic group, but also open up new possibilities for participation. Despite the swift pace of council stock transfer, however, potential roles for minority ethnic housing organisations and federal organisational structures in housing management remain under-researched.

We have indicated elsewhere that one possible route for contemporary housing policies lies in the direction of 'assets based' concepts of need and welfare, in which support might focus more on helping people establish or sustain a share in housing property, individually or collectively (Harrison with Phillips 2003: Chapter 10). We have noted that this might be for individual households (as with the right to buy), or for larger groups (for instance via co-ops). To be effective, policies focused on ownership would take account both of preferences and of financial and income realities in specific localities, as well as acknowledging any distinctive neighbourhood problems such as weak demand or potential 'abandonment'. Despite problems of financial viability and affordability, however, being able to purchase in the long term remains important as an element in household strategies. Perhaps there is potential for developing existing 'gateway' roles that black and minority ethnic housing associations play (for tenants considering social renting), in the direction of a wider range of functions connected with ownership, shared equity, maintenance, social support for owners, and sustainability. Developments here could be facilitated by more frequent inter-organisational collaborative and federal arrangements, or pursued by individual associations if resources were adequate. In any event, information on steps taken so far along this path is limited. Little is known, furthermore, of any attempts to develop the right to buy as a possible component in local authority or housing association planning for minority ethnic choice. Some black and minority ethnic households in council housing have exercised the right to buy, but it is difficult to evaluate this in terms of neighbourhood features or dwelling quality, or to make predictions about ongoing purchases. For conventional social renting, sustainability could have several dimensions concerning autonomy, rights, security and safety, but also clearly a financial one. When regeneration or improvements occur, gains made on matters such as health might be offset by increased household costs (for insights, see Ambrose 2000; Ambrose and MacDonald 2001). It should not be forgotten that outside owner occupancy low rents and servicing charges are often crucial components of a sustainable and stable housing environment.

Turning to collective rights and ownership, options could be considered more systematically for transferring council dwellings to black and minority ethnic-run housing associations, neighbourhood-based associations, non-profit companies, and co-ops, or involving black-run organisations in joint enterprises and federal structures for taking over control or collective ownership as transfers took place. Perhaps possibilities might also include transferring estates in need of renovation to bodies that would give minority ethnic and other tenants opportunities to acquire equity through contributing their labour (as in some self-build schemes). Although policy debates have touched on questions of community or neighbourhood control, and on community ownership in the Scottish agenda, there seems to be only limited information for the UK on the prospects for (or experiences with) collective forms of ownership or equity acquisition for minority ethnic groups (through co-ops, self-builds, estate transfers to tenant ownership, community land ownership, etc.) (cf. Clapham *et al.* 2001). Ways towards community control in the context of stock transfer have come under investigation in England, with the Confederation of Co-operative Housing working with the Housing Corporation to develop best practice (see Harrison with Phillips 2003: 76–7), but transfer has been occurring rather hastily. Thus an adequate debate about options for community-controlled housing for minorities may not have been occurring often enough in those English districts where possibilities of 'bending' the transfer process might appear most viable. Nonetheless, alongside positive discussion in governmental circles of resident-controlled housing, there has been mention of the potential for community-based and black and minority ethnic RSLs (including co-ops) to take on ownership or management of stock (Housing Corporation 2000: 4).

Equality testing or proofing

Although expectations about better monitoring practices and audit processes have spread, systematic analysis of outcomes from specific policy or legal measures is still not by any means automatic. Ideally, implemented policies should be kept under review in the light of their impact for particular types of households (choice based lettings schemes, developments in homelessness practices, etc.). Going further, there is an urgent need to test policy proposals before they become entrenched in governmental programmes. One reason is that there may be indirect and unanticipated side-effects from policies which at first glance seem to have little direct connection to equality of opportunities. The *Race and Housing Inquiry Challenge Report 2001* indicates that 'equality testing' should be a standard element of public policy development (see National Housing Federation *et al.* 2001: 4), and clearly this could apply to policies dealing with issues ranging from rents to the mandatory house sellers' information pack. Several phrases are presently in use (equality testing, equality proofing, disability testing, ethnicity proofing, and so forth), but the main point is that government should evaluate its proposals in the light of their potentially differential impacts across differing groups. Perhaps it is over-optimistic to expect this in any comprehensive form in present national political environments, but it is nonetheless a practice to be pressed for by all those favouring better-informed policy-making and genuinely 'evidence-based' policy.

Conclusions

Rather than summarising what has been said above, we conclude by emphasising the dynamic nature of housing consumption, and the implications this has for future policy analysis and research. Policy-makers should be aware of area and tenure preferences, and of choices about proximity and co-residence. Ideally, analysts should explore how specific policy development options might fit with or inhibit aspirations and preferred future pathways over time, taking account of inter-generational differences, the cumulation of household experiences, patterns of relative disadvantage, and locality factors. In the long term, we should work towards a more holistic understanding of people's needs and strategies, taking account of finance, employment, religion, ethnicity, and social support, although such a perspective would be hard to achieve. What is required is detailed knowledge of the present, but also insight into routes and paths from the past and into the future. It would be useful to gather materials from which to derive more dynamic accounts of household activity, opportunities and constraints, and of probable future trends in settlement and housing for wider communities. This is however a potentially difficult task, even with in-depth fieldwork. There could be differences between people's broader aspirations and their real prospects (which might themselves change), while lack of information on an option such as shared ownership might mean that it played no part in a household's planned pathway. Some types of studies achieve considerable depth (see Bowes *et al.* 1997a, 1997b), but even with complex methodologies it is easier to look backwards than forwards. At the outset, however, something may be gained by being cautious about stereotypes, and by consulting regularly. It might also be possible to obtain information on emergent needs by more regular use of 'administrative' and monitoring data. For instance, there is no comprehensive up-to-date account of the nature and scale of demand from minority ethnic households for social renting. In some districts expressed demand may be high relative to the capacity of housing organisations to meet it with tenancy allocations in acceptable areas, and data on applications, preferences and take-up might provide helpful insights. More generally, improving policy analysis requires as comprehensive an understanding of expectations, aspirations and processes as possible, for which we may need to seek out a wide range of indicators and informants.

References

Ahmed, A. and Sodhi, D. (2000) *The Housing and Support Needs of Women Especially Those from Ethnic Minorities*, Rochdale: Rochdale WHAG.

Ambrose, P. (2000) *A Drop in the Ocean*, Brighton: Health and Social Policy Research Centre, University of Brighton.

Ambrose, P. and MacDonald, D. (2001) *For Richer, For Poorer?* Brighton: Health and Social Policy Research Centre, University of Brighton.

Birmingham City Council, Housing Department (1998) *Black and Minority Ethnic Communities' Access to Outer City Housing*, Birmingham: Birmingham City Council.

Blackaby, B. and Chahal, K. (2000) *Black and Minority Ethnic Housing Strategies: A Good Practice Guide*, Coventry: Chartered Institute of Housing, Federation of Black Housing Organisations and The Housing Corporation.

BME Housing Project (2003) *BME Housing Project Feasibility Study, Final Report*, Cardiff: National Assembly for Wales.

Bowes, A., Dar, N. and Sim, D. (1997a) 'Tenure preference and housing strategy: an exploration of Pakistani experiences', *Housing Studies*, 12, 1: 63–84.

—— (1997b) 'Life histories in housing research: the case of Pakistanis in Glasgow', *Quality and Quantity*, 31: 109–25.

—— (1998) *Too White, Too Rough, and Too Many Problems: A Study of Pakistani Housing in Britain*, Housing Policy and Practice Unit Research Report No. 3, Stirling: Department of Applied Social Science, University of Stirling.

Cabinet Office (2000) *Minority Ethnic Issues in Social Exclusion and Neighbourhood Renewal: A Guide to the Work of the Social Exclusion Unit and the Policy Action Teams so far*, London: Crown copyright.

Chahal, K. (1999) *Minority Ethnic Homelessness in London: Findings from a Rapid Review*, for NHS Executive (London), Preston: Federation of Black Housing Organisations and University of Central Lancashire.

Chahal, K. and Julienne, L. (1999) *We Can't All Be White!: Racist Victimisation in the UK*, York: Joseph Rowntree Foundation.

Chahal, K. and Temple, B. (2000) *Older People from Minority Ethnic Communities: A Housing Research Review*, Report by the Federation of Black Housing Organisations (FBHO) commissioned by Anchor Trust and Manningham Housing Association, London: FBHO.

Chamba, R., Ahmad, W., Hirst, M., Lawton, D. and Beresford, B. (1999) *On the Edge: Minority Ethnic Families Caring for a Severely Disabled Child*, Bristol: Policy Press.

Clapham, D., O'Neill, P. and Bliss, N. (2001) *Tenant Control and Social Exclusion*, Birmingham: Confederation of Co-operative Housing.

Cole, I. and Robinson, D. (2003) *Somali Housing Experiences in England*, Sheffield: CRESR, Sheffield Hallam University.

Department for Transport, Local Government and the Regions (DTLR) (2001) *Addressing the Housing Needs of Black and Minority Ethnic People*, A DTLR (Housing Directorate) Action Plan, London: DTLR.

Gidley, G., Harrison, M. and Robinson, D. (1999) *Housing Black and Minority Ethnic People in Sheffield*, Sheffield: CRESR, Sheffield Hallam University.

Gill, F. (2002) 'The diverse experiences of black and minority ethnic women in relation to housing and social exclusion', in P. Somerville and A. Steele (eds) *'Race', Housing and Social Exclusion*, London: Jessica Kingsley: 159–77.

Harrison, M. (1999) 'Theorising homelessness and "race"', in P. Kennett and A. Marsh (eds) *Homelessness: Exploring the New Terrain*, Bristol: Policy Press: 101–21.

—— (2003) 'Housing black and minority ethnic communities: diversity and constraint', in D. Mason (ed.) *Explaining Ethnic Differences: Changing Patterns of Disadvantage in Britain*, Bristol: Policy Press: 105–19.

Harrison, M. with Davis, C. (2001) *Housing, Social Policy and Difference: Disability, Ethnicity, Gender and Housing*, Bristol: Policy Press.

Harrison, M. with Phillips, D. (2003) *Housing and Black and Minority Ethnic Communities: Review of the Evidence Base*, London: Office of the Deputy Prime Minister.

Hickman, M. and Walter, B. (1997) *Discrimination and the Irish Community in Britain*, London: Commission for Racial Equality.

Housing Corporation (2000) *Communities in Control*, London: The Housing Corporation.

Jeffers, S. and Hoggett, P. (1995) 'Like counting deckchairs on the Titanic: a study of institutional racism and housing allocations in Haringey and Lambeth', *Housing Studies*, 10, 3: 325–44.

Joseph Rowntree Foundation (JRF) (1993) 'Ageing with a disability', *Social Care Research Findings*, 34.

Karn, V., Mian, S., Brown, M. and Dale, A. (1999) *Tradition, Change and Diversity: Understanding the Housing Needs of Minority Ethnic Groups in Manchester*, Source Research 37, London: The Housing Corporation.

Law, I. (1996) *Racism, Ethnicity and Social Policy*, London: Prentice Hall/Harvester Wheatsheaf.

Lemos and Crane (undated) *Black and Minority Ethnic Registered Social Landlords*, Sector Study 4, London: The Housing Corporation.

Macpherson, W. (1999) *The Stephen Lawrence Inquiry: Report of an Inquiry*, by Sir William Macpherson advised by T. Cook, J. Sentamu and R. Stone, Cm 4262–I, London: The Stationery Office.

National Housing Federation (NHF), Commission for Racial Equality, Federation of Black Housing Organisations and The Housing Corporation (2001) *Race and Housing Inquiry: Challenge Report 2001*, London: NHF.

Peach, C. and Byron, M. (1993) 'Caribbean tenants in council housing: "race", class and gender', *New Community* 19, 3: 407–23.

—— (1994) 'Council house sales, residualisation and Afro Caribbean tenants', *Journal of Social Policy*, 23, 3: 363–83.

Phillips, D. (1996) 'Appendix 2: an overview of the housing needs of black and minority ethnic households; census analysis', in M. Harrison, A. Karmani, I. Law, D. Phillips and A. Ravetz, *Black and Minority Ethnic Housing Associations: An Evaluation of the Housing Corporation's Black and Minority Ethnic Housing Association Strategies*, London: The Housing Corporation: 50–65.

—— (1997) 'The housing position of ethnic minority group home owners', in V. Karn (ed.) *Ethnicity in the 1991 Census: Volume 4, Employment, Education and Housing among the Ethnic Minority Populations of Britain*, London: The Stationery Office: 170–88.

—— (1998) 'Black minority ethnic concentration, segregation and dispersal in Britain', *Urban Studies*, 35, 10: 1681–702.

Phillips, D. and Unsworth, R. (2002) 'Widening locational choices for minority ethnic groups in the social rented sector', in P. Somerville and A. Steele (eds) *'Race', Housing and Social Exclusion*, London: Jessica Kingsley: 77–93.

Platt, L. and Noble, M. (1999) *Race, Place and Poverty: Ethnic Groups and Low Income Distributions*, York: Joseph Rowntree Foundation.

Radia, K. (1996) *Ignored, Silenced, Neglected: Housing and Mental Health Care Needs of Asian people in the London Boroughs of Brent, Ealing, Harrow and Tower Hamlets*, York: Joseph Rowntree Foundation.

Rai, D. and Thiara, R. (1997) *Re-defining Spaces: The Needs of Black Women and Children in Refuge Support Services and Black Workers in Women's Aid*, Bristol: Women's Aid Federation of England.

Ratcliffe, P. (1996) *'Race' and Housing in Bradford*, Bradford: Bradford Housing Forum.

—— (1997) '"Race", ethnicity and housing differentials in Britain', in V. Karn (ed.) *Ethnicity in the 1991 Census; Volume 4, Employment, Education and Housing among the Ethnic Minority Populations of Britain*, London: The Stationery Office: 130–46.

Ratcliffe, P. with Harrison, M., Hogg, R., Line, B., Phillips, D. and Tomlins, R., and with Action Plan by Power, A. (2001) *Breaking Down the Barriers: Improving Asian Access to Social Rented Housing*, Coventry: CIH, on behalf of Bradford Metropolitan District Council, Bradford Housing Forum, The Housing Corporation, and Federation of Black Housing Organisations.

Robinson, D. (2002) 'Missing the target? Discrimination and exclusion in the allocation of social housing', in P. Somerville and A. Steele (eds) *'Race', Housing and Social Exclusion*, London: Jessica Kingsley: 94–113.

Robinson, D., Iqbal, B. and Harrison, M. (2002) *A Question of Investment: From Funding Bids to Black and Minority Ethnic Housing Opportunities*, London: The Housing Corporation.

Sandhu, H. (1998) 'Home affront', *Housing Today*, 1 October: 19.

Somerville, P., Sodhi, D. and Steele, A. (2000) *A Question of Diversity: Black and Minority Ethnic Staff in the RSL sector*, Source Research 43, London: The Housing Corporation.

Tomlins, R. (2003) *BME Housing Project Research*, Cardiff: National Assembly for Wales.

Tomlins, R., with Brown, T., Duncan, J., Harrison, M., Johnson, M., Line, B., Owen, D., Phillips, D. and Ratcliffe, P. (2001) *A Question of Delivery: An Evaluation of How RSLs Meet the Needs of Black and Minority Ethnic Communities*, Source Research 50, London: The Housing Corporation.

7 Housing, gender and social policy

Joan Smith[1]

This chapter discusses both the particular and different problems of accessing adequate housing faced by many women and men, the special housing needs of women associated with their own need for shelter and safety in a society in which they are likely to earn low incomes, and the housing needs of women who are responsible for children. It also considers evidence of gendered routes into homelessness and the potentially gendered impact of current housing policies and new homelessness legislation.

Women, the need for shelter and economic disadvantage

As many writers have recognised women have a specific need for safe shelter, whatever their household circumstances or their age. It is possible to argue that women value their homes in a distinctive way (Gurney 1990, 1991; Darke 1994), associating them with important life-events, and relate to them both in relation to the burdens they represent (housework and bills) and to the security they offer. The issues surrounding a 'place of safety' are, however, complex. Women are much less likely than men to sleep on the streets, or in public places, partly because of their physical needs (keeping clean, dealing with menstruation) and also because of fear of sexual attack and harassment (Golden 1992; Jones 1999; Sahlin and Thorn 2000). On the other hand, many women face their greatest threat within their home and domestic violence has been recognised as a major cause of homelessness among women within UK homelessness legislation. Women facing domestic violence have to create a safe home for themselves or themselves and their children through the support of the state and organisations established to defend women, including Women's Aid. For these reasons and reasons associated with women's economic disadvantage, social housing provision plays a greater role in housing women compared with men.

The housing provision enjoyed by women has come increasingly to rely on resources she can access, rather than resources of a domestic partner. Family stability shifted decisively in the UK in the 1970s when both separation and never married cohabitation became increasingly common (Joshi 1989), precisely at the time that the predominant housing tenure became owner-occupation. After the house price rises of the early 1970s, late 1970s, mid-1980s and now late 1990s–2000s, the majority of households require two incomes in order to enter home-ownership, a major risk in a period of domestic partnership instability, or to rent. For women to run their own independent household requires either one very good income or a housing safety net that is especially protective towards women, compensating for their lower average earnings compared with men.

Although social housing is a particularly important tenure for women, the special needs of women are rarely acknowledged as such. Women have been able to access social housing in the past, either as part of a couple or as a single parent, through the fact that they were mothers rather than their own lack of income and vulner-ability in the housing market. Despite the increasing absolute numbers of single parent fathers, during the dissolution of a partnership it is still overwhelmingly the case that women take responsibility for the children of a partnership. Survey data records a rate of 94 per cent of women among all lone parents, and 6 per cent men, although official statistics place the distribution at between 8 per cent and 10 per cent men (Marsh et al. 2001: 35). The lack of good quality affordable child-care in the UK and the heavy load of working, parenting and running a household means that single parent mothers are most likely to either remain on benefit or work part-time. The Third Report on the National Minimum Wage reported that only a quarter of all women over the age of 22 years worked full-time and 19 per cent part-time, compared with 47 per cent of all men working full-time and only 3 per cent part-time (Low Pay Commission 2001, Volume 2: Table A1.4).

Recently, there has been greater encouragement for lone mothers to work, even at a minimum wage, because of the additional benefits of Working Families Tax Credit (WFTC), now Working Tax Credit (WTC). WTC has to be set at a high enough rate to offset the loss of housing benefit and other associated benefits. One example given by the Low Pay Commission is of a lone mother with one child aged under sixteen years, working thirty-five hours a week at the minimum wage earning net pay of £125.25 per week. Under new benefit rules she would receive 70 per cent of child care costs, raising the wage to £161.45 per week and a further £143.66 a week in (then) WFTC. Overall this lone mother would receive over £300 a week rather than £125.25 (Low Pay Commission 2001: 149).

The establishment of WTC, support for childcare costs and Job Seekers Allowance interviews, all designed to encourage claimant mothers back into work, marks a shift in practice towards lone mothers. One of the two pillars of welfare policy had been a regard for family responsibilities as well as work responsibilities, a family ethic alongside a work ethic. In the current political climate, however, social policy is increasingly dominated by the work ethic. In requiring single mothers to prove their commitment to the labour market, the UK is following US practice, albeit more moderately. As Orloff has argued, the emerging model of motherhood in the US is of women combining motherhood with paid work; in the US welfare 'reform' was built on antagonism to black welfare recipients and the punishment of women of colour for single motherhood (Orloff 2002). In the UK single motherhood and welfare claiming is not associated in the public mind with any particular ethnic group, but with a particular form of tenure – a fact that bemused the US new right guru Charles Murray as he attempted to apply his theories of welfare 'reform' to *white* working-class single mothers living in social housing (Murray 1990).

Housing as private investment and the rising cost of shelter

In the last quarter of the twentieth century, governments across Western Europe moved away from the perspective that included housing as part of the post-Second World War welfare settlement. Increasingly, governments adopted a view of housing as an economic investment on the part of private households rather than a social good (Ball and Harloe 1998), although previous material encouragement for this investment through tax concessions on mortgage interest has now ceased. In both the US and the UK a view of housing as the most secure long-term investment for a household produced a decisive shift in tenure and strongly influenced Labour thinking in relation to housing policy. Under New Labour there has been an acceptance of social housing as a minority tenure and a rejection of the idea that social housing should be run by local authorities; this is a decisive shift in Labour values from those of Old Labour. The provision of municipal housing to replace unsanitary and overcrowded private housing was an early demand in the platforms of both Trades Councils and local Independent Labour Party branches from the late nineteenth century. John Wheatley, the first Labour Minister of Housing in 1924, began his socialist career as leader of the Independent Labour Party in Glasgow, campaigning for municipal housing in one of the worst housed industrial cities in Britain.

As described by Spink (this volume), social housing provision became established in the 1920s, building on the Act of 1919 but, with the defeat of the Labour movement after the 1926 General Strike and the establishment of the 1931 National Government, housing policy changed and house-building was encouraged through government subsidies to private house builders. It was in this period that the suburbs around British towns were built; these houses cost from £350 to £750 around London – much more than even a worker in work, on £4 a week, could afford. In 1950 over half (53 per cent) of households still lived in private rented accommodation, nearly a fifth (18 per cent) in local authority housing and under a third (29 per cent) in owner-occupation. But part of the post-Second World War consensus was not just equality of opportunity in education, and free universal health but also the provision of adequate housing for all. Only ten years later, less than one-third lived in private rented accommodation (32 per cent), one-quarter in social housing (26 per cent) and the rest in owner-occupation (42 per cent).

The peak of social housing provision came in the 1960s and 1970s; by 1981 one third of all households lived in social housing (30 per cent in local authority accommodation and 2 per cent in housing association accommodation), whilst only one-tenth lived in private rented accommodation (11 per cent) (Balchin 1995: 6, Table 1.3). It is important to emphasise that in the 1950s and 1960s many workers aspired to become local authority tenants, and local authorities were proud of their housing provision. To become a local authority tenant meant moving from poor quality private rented accommodation, with coal-fired hot water, or even no proper bathrooms or inside toilet, to housing with bathrooms and running hot water, and heating by electricity. It reduced the work of both women and men, although principally women, in washing and cleaning.

But, also by 1981, a majority of households lived as owner-occupiers (57 per cent). Home-ownership aspirations had been boosted by house price inflation in the early 1970s when large price rises appeared to be a way of not only saving money (compared with renting) but also making money. Rising house prices produced a perception among employed social housing tenants that they were being denied entry into the world of home-ownership. Working-class tenants in good quality accommodation supported Conservative local councils who offered them the chance to buy their homes at a discount. Under the Conservative government of 1979 sales of local authority properties to sitting tenants became public policy imposed on all local authorities, whatever the extent of local housing need. This was a political decision to win votes from existing tenants and to break up areas of Labour support in local authorities, but it was also part of the 'privatisation' and monetarist agenda of that government.

'Right to buy' policies led to the immediate sale of over a million social housing units, reducing the proportion of households living in social housing from one-third of all households to one quarter in a decade (Balchin 1995: 6, Table 1.3); by 2000, 1.85 million social housing units had been sold (Ford *et al.* 2001). The sale of better quality social housing reduced both the quantity and the quality of public stock, as semi-detached and terraced houses were sold first, leaving flats and less desirable properties. Local authority housing stock in rural areas became reduced to estates in market towns, with many families 'helping' their parents to buy in local villages in order to inherit the property.

As well as selling stock, the Conservative government closed down local authority building programmes. Between 1979 and 1989, government expenditure on housing fell by 79 per cent. Overall UK capital investment in housing (private and public) as a proportion of the gross domestic product, and the number of dwellings built per head of population, were the lowest in Europe when averaged over the years from 1970 to 1992 (Oxley and Smith 1998: Figures 3.1, 3.4, 3.5). Partly this was a function of lower economic growth rates in the UK compared with other European countries, but it was also a result of housing investment being confined to private new build. In 1980 new build local authority stock was 67,000 units, but in 1998 only 251 were completed; over the same period, housing association new completions rose slightly but were not much higher than in 1980 (R. Smith *et al.* 2001).

Over ten years (1981–91) 'right to buy' policies and discounts helped raise the proportion of owner-occupiers from 57 per cent to 66 per cent. It exacerbated a tendency, which was already apparent, for social housing to become a *residualised* tenure for social welfare claimants and homeless people (Hills 1993), albeit a tenure that was most scarce in areas of highest housing prices and extreme housing need as stock was sold in precisely those areas that most needed social housing. By the 1991 census two-thirds of all households were owner-occupiers (66 per cent of all households), one-quarter were social housing tenants (21 per cent local authority, three per cent housing association), and one-tenth were private tenants (Balchin 1995). However, couple households were much more likely than others to be owner-occupiers; in 1991, three-quarters of couples were owner-occupiers (77 per cent), compared with a half or less than half of households headed by single, divorced or widowed women. The situation for single women and men was also quite distinct – only 44 per cent of single women and 46 per cent of divorced women were owner-occupiers, compared with 54 per cent of single or divorced men. Only widowed women were as likely to be owner-occupiers as widowed men – 51 per cent and 50 per cent (Gilroy 1994).

The shift to owner-occupation as the tenure of choice, insufficient new build (both private and social) and a housing policy that introduced 'market rents' in local authority housing, led to a rise in the cost of housing in the UK, for both buyers and renters. In the UK, as in the US, the wages of the lowest paid have not kept pace with house and rent inflation. As Ehrenreich wrote in her study of the low paid in the US:

> The problem of rents is easy for a non-economist, even a sparsely educated low-wage worker, to grasp: it's the market, stupid. When the rich and the poor compete for housing on the open market, the poor don't stand a chance. The rich can always outbid them, buy up their tenements or trailer parks, and replace them with condos, McMansions, golf courses, or whatever they like.
> (Ehrenreich 2001: 199)

Ehrenreich reports that in the 1960s the food bill in the US took 24 per cent of the average family budget, and housing costs 29 per cent; by 1999 housing costs had risen to 37 per cent and food fallen to 16 per cent. For the UK Wilcox has estimated that the poorest one-fifth of homeowners spend 42 per cent of their income on housing costs, including mortgages and repairs (Wilcox 1999, quoted in Ford *et al*. 2001: 48).

Owner-occupation, private renting and the demand for social housing

Because of the rising cost of any form of housing, many households on very low incomes sought to become owner-occupiers or remain owner-occupiers, after family breakdown. In the twenty years after 1979, home-ownership with a mortgage grew by 18 percentage points (Ford *et al*. 2001: 47). In this period households who could *least* afford high housing costs were pushed into owner-occupation for lack of a viable alternative. Of the poorest one-tenth of households before taking housing costs into account, 57 per cent were owner-occupiers (half with and half without a mortgage) and 43 per cent were renters (Ford *et al*. 2001: 47, Table 2.7).

Janet Ford, in previous research on mortgage debt over a five-year period, estimated that one-fifth of mortgagors had problems with paying their mortgages (Ford 1995 quoted in Ford *et al*. 2001), and Holmans has estimated that one-fifth of owner-occupiers may face repossession during the lifetime of a mortgage (Holmans 2000, quoted in Ford *et al*. 2001). In the years 1995–6 to 1998–9, householders, responding to the Survey of English Housing (SEH) question on mortgage repayment arrears, gave a variety of reasons for being in arrears: 61–71 per cent gave loss of income as a reason for arrears, 26–30 per cent gave household change including separation and divorce, and 24–30 per cent gave increase in mortgage or other payments (Ford *et al*. 2001: 45, Table 2.6).

As home-ownership spread to all sections of society, mortgage arrears became a social issue associated with unemployment, low wages, the 'reform' of the welfare safety net, and also the problem of low-income women subsequent to a dissolved partnership. Home ownership became unsustainable for some households, particularly women on their own, as employment became less stable and mortgage debt was no longer eroded by inflation. Mortgage arrears today are higher among lone parents and among those who have exercised the right to buy. Over one-third of lone parents report mortgage arrears and also report that they are finding payments 'difficult' or 'very difficult' (Ford *et al*. 2001: 34, Table 2.4). In 1998–9 20 per cent of households that contained someone who had had their home repossessed were lone parent households (compared with 10 per cent for all other households), and 30 per cent of such households included someone divorced or separated (compared with 13 per cent for all households) (Ford *et al*. 2001: 28, Table 2.2).

Therefore, women heads of household faced an increasingly difficult housing situation. Many lone women heads of household have sought to become or remain owner-occupiers on very low incomes. Ford *et al*.'s (2001) study of repossession of housing after mortgage arrears, and Christie's (2000) study of women facing repossession following family breakdown, point to particular problems facing women after domestic partnership breakdown. Many women faced not only mortgage and utility bills arrears but also liability for their partner's debts or the house being re-mortgaged to support a business. Under the impact of both changing patterns of marriage, divorce and cohabitation, which gave rise to an increasing number of lone mothers, and the 'feminisation of poverty', social housing has become an increasingly *gendered* tenure. Overall two-thirds of lone parents live in independent households and half of these rent from local authorities (49 per cent compared to 22 per cent of the general population) and 14 per cent rent privately (compared to 9 per cent), and the remainder, 37 per cent, seek to retain owner-occupation status (Webster 2000).

Private renting has been the alternative tenure proposed by Conservative and Labour administrations in the past twenty-five years, but the cost of private renting is not just high financially but high in relation to family security and stability. In a recent study by the author of 84 applicants accepted as homeless by Herefordshire Housing Options Team it was apparent that a new layer of applicants were being made homeless by the working of the private rental market. One lone mother had finally applied as homeless after losing her accommodation when the owners decided to sell. She had no formal renting agreement: 'It would have cost £80 to set it up... it was based on trust', and had decorated the house herself before it was sold off. She was working and reported:

> I have had seven tenancies in the past eight years, my oldest girl is 8. That's private renting for you ... It was too expensive too ... but that's how private is. When they sold it they made £40,000 in two years. That was why I was in housing difficulties. When I had notice from them I found that housing costs had gone sky-high.
>
> (Single mother, two children)

Her previous tenancies had included a local authority top floor flat that she could not manage with her disabled child, two private rented tenancies where the rent was increased beyond her means, and two private tenancies where the houses were sold. She has now moved into a small house owned by a local housing association (Smith 2003).

This level of insecurity was also found to apply to single parent fathers (still a small minority of single parents) and to older couples who had worked in pubs or in service with accommodation. One single parent father could not keep his children with him:

> Each tenancy expired and was followed by a new one. To move every six months or so is not a settled way of living in a modern society. It is extremely

stressful and distressing from start to end. I have never been able to peacefully enjoy my possessions … The law no longer protects tenants – instead it now protects the landlord.

(Single parent father, children with his mother)

In the cases of one pensioner and a pensioner couple it was a shock to find that they could no longer afford a month's deposit of £500–700 for rented accommodation and neither could they find the private rented accommodation they wanted. In many cases the first reaction of applicants who lost their tenancy was not to apply to the Housing Options Team or Home Point but to approach estate agents, look in newspapers, and seek private rented accommodation (Smith 2003).

As repossession of housing has spread and the private rented market has become increasingly volatile and expensive, the numbers and groups applying for social housing have grown. One of the reasons that social housing has become dominated by women headed households is the poverty of most women – single women or lone mothers on lower wages, lone mothers on benefits, or older women living as single person household pensioners. Only low-income couples with no earner or households with a disabled adult or child are as poor. A second reason is their greater responsibility for raising children. But another reason why women move into social housing is to escape violence against themselves and/or their children. Even though they try to avoid homelessness, and hide their homelessness when it occurs, many women still become homeless as a result of poverty and violence.

Homelessness legislation and the protection of dependent children and the elderly

One of the long-lasting outcomes of the 1960s' wave of concern about poverty and housing has been the provision of a 'homeless' route into social housing, for certain types of household, under the Housing (Homeless Persons) Act 1977. This Act gave local housing authorities a duty to secure accommodation for homeless households belonging to a designated 'priority need' group, principally homeless families with dependent children or older homeless people (over the age of sixty) or those especially vulnerable on the grounds of physical or mental health. The selection of these two particular groups of households for protection under the Act was a reflection of the principles that had sanctioned the use of state resources for welfare provision in the past, namely, the family ethic and the work ethic – offering housing support for those caring for dependent children, and those who are too old or ill to work. Two conditions were, and are, applied – that the applicant should not have made themselves homeless intentionally and that they should be a local resident or have local connections. As social housing in some areas has become scarce, the local connection rule has come to be applied more vigorously.

Children became amongst the chief beneficiaries of the homeless persons legislation, as by 1990 four out of every five households accepted as homeless contained children or a pregnant woman (Greve and Currie 1990: 10). As the primary care-givers of children, women had a statutory right to apply for social housing whatever the primary cause of their homelessness: domestic violence, welfare benefit poverty or low-wage poverty. In 1991 nearly a half (45 per cent) of divorced or separated women heads of household occupied social (local authority or housing association) housing compared with 28 per cent of divorced and separated men (Woods 1996: 69, Table 5.2). Burrows (1997: Table 5) calculated that the odds of a new lone parent with dependent children entering social housing increased by a factor of 3.6 over other newly formed households.

However, it is not just women with children who have been more likely to occupy social housing; Woods (1996: 69, Table 5.2) also calculated that in 1991 31 per cent of *single* women heads of household occupied social housing compared with 18 per cent of men. Therefore, by 1991, fourteen years after the 1977 Act was passed, it was seen as working in its central task of providing accommodation for homeless families, and the provision was of particular importance for women. Applications for housing under the Homeless Persons legislation trebled from 1978 (53,000 applications) to nearly 149,000 in 1991 (Balchin 1995; Bramley 1994). This peak of applications reflected a crisis in housing supply. At the time, however, public concern was most engaged with the overwhelming and visible problem of single homelessness, particularly among young people who were living on the streets.

The Conservative government reaction to the homelessness crisis of the early 1990s was two-fold. First, under pressure from the Audit Commission, the Rough Sleepers Initiatives (RSIs, discussed below) were established. Second, a Consultation White Paper was published in 1994, prior to the changes in the 1996 Housing Act, which suggested that rising housing need, as demonstrated by increased waiting lists and numbers of homeless applicants, arose from the homelessness legislation itself rather than the lack of investment in social housing. Homelessness legislation, the White Paper argued, had given the homeless and particularly homeless lone mothers, the right to 'jump the housing queue', preventing deserving couples securing social housing. To correct this, the 1996 Housing Act abolished the local authority's *permanent* duty to secure social housing and replaced it with a two-year temporary duty, and excluded homelessness from the list of grounds on which local authorities were required to give 'reasonable preference' in allocating their housing.

The 1996 Housing Act could have been disastrous for never partnered lone mothers and lone mothers who had to leave a violent relationship. Although lone parents may access support from their families, that support is frequently built upon the provision of social housing. Fathers and mothers, brothers and sisters, may decorate the social housing flat, provide curtains, some furniture, and some childcare. In most cases, however, this is the limit of what they can afford to do. It is possible to find a father (as we did on one Staffordshire estate) about to build an extension to house his daughter, a grandchild and a further grandchild on the way, but it is more usual to find support being given in ways other than by direct housing (Smith *et al.* 1998). Homelessness legislation has allowed women with children to access secure accommodation in a way that no other legislation has done.

One of the first acts of the new Labour Government in 1997 was to restore homelessness to the list of priority reasons for rehousing and to re-emphasise through the Code of Guidance to local authorities the need to protect women facing domestic violence. The Homelessness Act 2002 re-enacted the local housing authority's permanent duty to secure settled accommodation for those in priority need, added new priority need groups, and widened the authority's duties to advise those who are non-priority homeless. It placed a duty on local housing authorities to develop a homelessness strategy, including a prevention strategy and a multi-agency partnership to work to solve homelessness. It also required housing authorities to cease using bed-and-breakfast accommodation as temporary accommodation for priority homeless households. The legislation also acknow-ledged the needs of particular groups of single homeless people by including, among those designated as 'priority need', young sixteen and seventeen year olds (especially those previously in care), ex-prisoners and ex-armed forces; the latter two groups are much more likely to be male.

The expansion of 'priority need' categories in the homelessness legislation followed the development of the Conservatives' rough sleeper initiatives by the Labour government. The Labour government transformed the RSI into the Rough Sleepers' Unit (RSU), which greatly improved contact and assessment work with rough sleepers through the creation of area designated Contact and Assessment Teams (CATs), replacing a host of overlapping agencies. CAT teams include specialist workers for young people, or for rough sleepers with mental health problems. The work of the CAT teams is also followed up by workers from area-designated Tenancy Support Teams. This model has been adopted in other urban centres in the UK, with much improved results – avoiding overlapping agencies all working at outreach and contact, and providing a multi-agency resettlement path. However, even the work of the RSU has come up against the problem of the lack of new build social housing in London and other housing stress areas. Whereas in the early days of the RSI programmes some rough sleepers could be accommo-dated in local authority or housing association one-bedroom flats, today rough sleepers are being resettled into hostels and then into move-on accommodation. Nevertheless, in London and other cities where the Rough Sleepers' Strategy has been adopted, some social housing is now used to re-house those found sleeping rough on the streets. Given the profile of rough sleepers (85 per cent male) this also begins to impact on the availability of social housing for vulnerable single women whose homelessness situation does not appear as urgent as that of rough sleepers, and creates stress in relation to the availability of social housing for others, as a report into the experience of 'moving on' from a West London hostel demonstrates (Worley and Smith 2001; and see below).

The emphasis on rough sleeping in both Conservative and Labour government policy since 1991 also shifted the focus away from the crisis in family housing. It was noticeable that, as homelessness amongst young people became ever more visible, media attention turned from investigations into family homelessness and the appalling life of homeless families in bed-and-breakfast hostels to in-depth reports of the life of young street-dwellers or runaways. Homelessness became seen as a problem affecting young single people rather than families. Public attention was shifted from the issue of providing social housing for homeless families (and also for poor single people) to the problem of emergency accommodation and youth residential projects/foyers for young people. This shift in public awareness had a major impact, involving a transfer of attention from the housing problems of women and children to the housing and support problems of homeless men, who are more visible among the street population. It is only with the housing crisis that has occurred in the years 2000–2004 that attention has returned to the problem of housing families on low incomes.

The lack of available social and private housing for homeless families has also led to rising numbers of the families accepted as homeless by local authorities being placed in temporary and emergency accommodation because the local authority has nowhere else to house them. The crisis is particularly acute in London where in 2003 more than 61,000 households were living in temporary accommodation secured by London borough housing departments (according to the Mayor's office – www.london.gov.uk/mayor/housing). Many housing authorities in low-supply areas are therefore faced with a demand for social housing that they can only meet through very tight gate-keeping and the use of long-term temporary accommodation, or by transferring social housing applicants to other areas of the country – from Haringey and Camden to Leeds or Stoke-on-Trent.

Gender differences in single homelessness

Prior to the 1980s *single* person homelessness appeared to be an issue affecting some older men in their 40s and 50s, without families, who were largely accommodated in traditional hostels. Among the users of these hostels there were a few older women. From the beginning of the 1980s increasing numbers of young single people were found to be arriving at these traditional shelters. An early study of hostel and advice centre users found evidence of growing homelessness among young single people, that a third of service users were now women, and among service users aged under 29 years the proportion of women rose to 40 per cent (Drake 1981).[2]

By the mid-1980s the number of homeless young single people had grown sufficiently large for churches and voluntary agencies to begin providing additional night shelters and then residential accommodation specifically for young people; the YMCA, in particular, allocated an increasing proportion of their beds to homeless young people. As board and lodgings allowances and income support payments were withdrawn from 16–17 year olds in 1985 and 1988, rising numbers of young single homeless people meant that in London increasing numbers were also forced to live on the street (Evans 1996). The increase in single homelessness among young people led to the provision of additional specialist emergency and hostel accommodation, and the provision of specialised care and support, as well as the provision of employment, training and move-on accommodation, and the establishment of specialist foyers (Anderson and Quilgars 1995).

Early studies of single homelessness in the 1990s found a high preponderance of young men, around 70 per cent, among the single homeless population (Anderson *et al.* 1993; Stockley *et al.* 1993; Hutson and Liddiard 1994). Policy solutions to single homelessness were sought which dealt with the most extreme manifestation of the single young homeless – street dwellers – that had reached crisis proportions in London. Homeless situations became differentiated in relation to the vulnerability of the situation itself, relating to the level of security and support in each type of accommodation, rather than the vulnerability of the household (dependent children, older people, young women). The scale (1–7) described below reflects the severity of the homelessness situation among single people as viewed by many agencies and developed by the author in relation to a variety of agency studies:

1 Sleeping rough
2 Living in B&B and squatting
3 Living in institutions the week before coming to an agency (armed forces, hospitals or detox facilities, job accommodation, or in custody) who have no long-term accommodation or have lost it while in the institution
4 Living in direct access hostels and night shelters
5 Staying in youth and residential hostels
6 Living with friends or non-parental family members
7 Living in a parental household.

However, such assumptions about vulnerability in relation to homelessness situations lead to differential treatment between single men and women because of the far fewer numbers of women living in situations 1–4. Among the 'literal' homeless, to use the US term, who are sleeping rough or living in winter shelters or attending day centres, women comprise 16 per cent in the UK (a similar proportion to Sweden and other Northern European countries). Similarly, women are much less likely to have been released from custody, the predominant experience in situation 3, or living in single room occupancy bed and breakfast or squatting. Only in the last three categories do numbers of women begin to predominate. In youth and residential hostels young women comprise up to half of all residents, and this is also age-related; among the under twenty year olds women are a majority, but a minority over this age. They are also more likely at any age to present to a homelessness agency from living with friends, family members or parents.

An initial study of RSI provision found that only one quarter of those helped by the programme were young women, and this led the Housing Corporation to argue that women might by-pass the RSI entirely, though being offered accommodation because they were vulnerable (Douglas and Gilroy 1994: 134). A study undertaken by our research centre in 1996, however, found, on the contrary, that the different housing circumstances of young women (compared with young men) the night before they came to any agency led to both young single women and young single mothers being less likely to be classified as homeless, and therefore less likely to be accepted as homeless under the legislation, and less likely to be offered any kind of accommodation. This was particularly noticeable in the three London boroughs that provided housing department information (Smith *et al.* 1996).

The 1996 study of over 15,000 young clients of housing and homeless agencies has been described in greater depth elsewhere (Smith *et al.* 1996; Smith 1999). The important finding was that in any city approximately half of those aged 16–25 years who were recorded as homeless or in housing need were women. This finding occurred for two reasons: first, all young housing clients of any domestic or parenting status were included; and second, information was collected from *all* types of housing and homelessness agencies, and included, in particular, information on young mothers, and on single young women who approached a local housing authority or association but not a hostel. Previous research in Birmingham also found that homeless single young women were as likely to approach the housing department or a housing association as a hostel or shelter (Smith and Gilford 1993).

In the total 1996 data set, including all seven cities and three Inner London boroughs (a fourth, Lambeth, did not provide housing department statistics), housing departments rejected 35 per cent of single parent mother applications as priority need homeless though classifying them as being in housing need, whilst housing associations rejected 55 per cent. Overall, homelessness and housing agencies were more likely to classify young men as homeless compared with young women; 61 per cent of all women from the cities and London boroughs were classified as homeless compared with 71 per cent of men. The reason for this difference in classification is probably associated with the housing situation of young women the night before they came to any agency. Young men were more likely to present from rough sleeping, emergency accommodation and institutions, i.e. to present as 'literal' homeless rather than 'hidden' homeless.

In London the greatest difference between young men and young women related to whether they had slept rough the previous night; 22 per cent of young men had slept rough compared with only 11 per cent of young women. The difference in previous night's accommodation was not just due to the fact that some women had responsibilities for children and therefore avoided being on the streets. Considering the night before history of young single people only, even young *single* homeless women were much less likely to sleep rough than young single men. Whereas 23 per cent of young single men presented to agencies from no fixed abode/slept rough, only 11 per cent of young single women did so; and whereas a quarter of single young men presented from emergency hostels, only 12 per cent of young single women did so. Young single women were more likely to present from friends or families: 38 per cent, compared with 28 per cent for young single men. As would be expected, only 8 per cent of young single mothers/ pregnant women presented from no fixed abode or rough sleeping.

Outside of London, although the pattern of where they had slept the night before differed between young men and young women, differences were not as marked as in London because of the lower proportion of young people in the seven cities who had slept rough the night before (ranging from 3 to 8 per cent). In each city a higher proportion of young women presented as homeless from friends' and relatives' accommodation and from their own accommodation (Smith *et al.* 1996; Smith 1999).

Rough sleeping presents particular difficulties for all women, not only because of the increased danger of sexual harassment and abuse, but also because of the importance of cleanliness for women. Golden has argued that this is not only because of the problems of remaining clean during menstruation but also because remaining clean and respectably dressed at all times is a method of self-protection for women (Golden 1992). In their pattern of 'hidden' homelessness women display similar characteristics to men from ethnic groups other than white. In the 1996 study the percentage of young homeless people in London from ethnic origins other than white European was very high – nearly half of the study. In London, young women and men from ethnic origins other than white had the lowest proportion of reported rough sleeping (Smith *et al.* 1996). Therefore, equating homelessness with rough sleeping disadvantages homelessness applications from non-rough sleepers, particularly women from all ethnic backgrounds and men of ethnic backgrounds other than white. The establishment of the Rough Sleepers Initiative (RSI) in London in 1990, however, and the extension of this programme to other cities in 1996, followed by the work of the Rough Sleepers Unit, changed public perceptions of what is meant by 'homelessness'.

Clearly there are significant gender differences in the routes that single young people take into homelessness. A study of the family background of young homeless people in North Staffordshire suggests that there are also significant gender differences in the way young people leave the parental home. The most significant differences were found in non-disrupted households compared with disrupted households (Smith *et al.* 1998). In 'non-disrupted' households where a young person lived with the same 'parents' (including step parents) from an early age, gender differences in the reasons why young people left home were particularly noticeable. Although the numbers of households involved were not large, nearly all the young women reported that they had left because of friction over their relationships with young men who were involved in crime and drugs and in some cases were significantly older than themselves. Many parents said that they had hoped that their daughters would 'make something' of themselves or at least 'find a decent bloke' to leave home with. In fact, many young women were eventually asked to leave, or left, in an atmosphere of escalating conflict. Conflict between young men and their parents, however, took a different form in such households. It often began with trouble at school, through drug taking and/or stealing, as well as trouble with the police. More often than was the case with young women, 'back-chatting' their parents resulted in 'slapping', and this could escalate into violence between father and son. Eviction from the family home was often triggered by the young man stealing money or valuables from his parents or by his involvement with the police.

In 'disrupted' households, young people had experienced change in their parents' relationship, often involving a step-parent coming into the family or joining a new family. These young people were made homeless because their parental families broke up or their parent(s) started a new life without them. In some cases the household dissolved around young people when parents wished to make a new life for themselves and found teenage children getting in the way. A step-parent coming into what had been a lone parent family commonly triggered the conflict. In these situations, where households either dissolved or rejected children, there was little difference between young men and young women in their explanation of their homelessness and their description of their experiences. There was, however, some difference in the way in which they left. Young women were more likely to leave the parental home as soon as they were aged sixteen years, often following a major argument. Young men were more likely to move out when actually pushed out by their parents. Some parents tried to force young men to move out to any employment with accommodation. Among the young men interviewed, three had been pushed into joining the army.

The least difference in the circumstances of leaving home between young men and young women came from those who left abusive households. They reported facing similar home situations, and came mainly from disrupted households, though a minority had been in and out of care homes. Around a third of the young people interviewed reported physical abuse or neglect – from both step-parents and natural parents – and two girls reported sexual abuse (Smith *et al.* 1998).

Among all the homeless young women who were interviewed, whatever the situation behind them leaving home, there was a strong possibility that in the future they would become lone mothers. Young women from stable homes often left home in order to retain a relationship with a boyfriend who was not approved of. While young women from stable families often had children in order to be re-integrated into their existing family, young women from dissolving or rejecting families expressed a desire for children because they wanted a family of their own (Smith *et al.* 1998). Early pregnancy was more about the desire for a family, or rebuilding bridges with their own family, than anything else.

In two recent studies of homeless young people aged 16–25 years undertaken by the Centre for Housing and Community Research, it was noticeable that between one-quarter and one-third of homeless young women in Birmingham and the Cotswolds were either parents or pregnant. Many had left home before seventeen years of age and were pregnant by nineteen years. However, in both studies a similar proportion of single young men living in hostels reported that they too were parents. The difference was that they did not have responsibility for the child. Three-quarters of young men who reported being fathers in Birmingham also reported that they stayed in touch, compared with half of those in the Cotswolds (Smith 2000; Smith and Ing 2000; Smith *et al.* 2001).

Lone parents, domestic violence and the need for social housing

Most lone parents have previously been in relationships and are lone parents because of relationship breakdown; as reported above, they are more likely to be renters than home owners, unlike the general population. They are more likely to live in the worse parts of the rental sector and in poor neighbourhoods (Webster 2000; Lupton and Power 2001). Webster has argued that marital/partnership break-down is strongly related to economic conditions and charts the rate of lone parent-hood by male unemployment in local authorities providing a correlation of 0.846. He argues that: 'The combination of time series, cross-section and ethnographic evidence that the rise in lone parenthood has been mainly due to localised mass unemployment is extremely powerful' (Webster 2000: 119), and he dismisses the Policy Studies Institute's work on lone parenthood as being based on small national samples. However, as argued below, many lone parents are moved into remaining areas of social housing that also house couples on benefits i.e. unemployed males. Lone parenthood cannot be understood as a simple result of male unemployment; much of it relates to male violence, whether employed or unemployed.

Enders-Dragasser has described the situation of women who balance family and home as a 'modernity' trap:

> No matter how they decide about their way of living, whether in dependency on a partner as 'breadwinner' or in trying to reconcile employment and family work to be independent, whether leaving a violent partner or staying with him, they bear high personal risks and have problems with social security, with economic resources and with housing.
>
> (Enders-Dragasser 2001: 209)

Her work on women and homelessness in Germany has identified four risk factors in relation to women's housing: violence, poverty, health problems and gender stereotypes and prejudice. Enders-Dragasser argues that the attempt by women to conceal their housing problems and to find private solutions with friends or family members risks dependency and violence; it is for this reason that social housing is of particular importance for women.

In the 1970s domestic violence was 'rediscovered' through both the growth of the national Women's Aid movement (Wilson 1977) and Erin Pizzey's highly publicised writings on 'battered wives' at the Chiswick Shelter (Pizzey 1974). The Select Committee on Domestic Violence (1975) stressed the importance of housing provision as a safety net for women and children. Following divorce law reform in 1971, an increasing number of divorced and separated wives became dependent on social housing and this was acknowledged in the Finer Report (1974). It was in these circumstances that the Homelessness Act 1977 defined families with dependent children, including lone mothers, as having priority need for re-housing, and also specifically included women fleeing domestic violence, with or without children, as 'vulnerable' and therefore in priority need.

A recent survey by the Policy Studies Institute (PSI) (1999) of low-income families and *all* lone parent families, based on a national sample of households in receipt of child benefit, provides precise evidence on the proportion of previous cohabiting or married lone parents who had experienced domestic violence. The survey asked all ever-partnered lone parents they interviewed about violence in their previous partnership. Of all ever-partnered lone mothers, 8 per cent reported violence without injury, and 27 per cent violence with injury in the previous partnership (derived from Marsh *et al*. 2001: 90, Table 4.7; 91, Table 4.8). In all, therefore, 35 per cent reported violence within their previous relationship. The lack of good quality social housing and affordable housing also results in some women not declaring themselves homeless and instead staying in abusive relationships. Women's Aid Helplines and Outreach teams counsel women who believe their situation and responsibilities mean that they cannot walk away and subject their children to hostel life and temporary accommodation.

The PSI study identified four categories of lone mothers of almost equal proportions: never partnered, separated from cohabitation, separated from marriage, and divorced, with a fifth, widows, representing a smaller proportion of lone mothers but still an important group (Marsh *et al*. 2001: 83). Lone parents on benefits and low-income couples on benefits were almost equally likely to occupy a social tenancy (60 per cent of low-income couples on benefit, 66 per cent of non-working lone parents). The rates of social tenancy occupation among lone mothers were highest among single mothers never partnered (63 per cent) and single mothers separated after cohabitation (66 per cent). The highest rates of hardship identified in the survey were among non-working lone parents, who were one-third of all lone parents.

Whether or not violence is involved in the partnership, a common result of partnership dissolution is the loss of the home. Ford *et al.*'s study of repossession includes descriptions of the process from the perspective of both couples and lone mothers. Lone mothers were faced with dealing with the problem of their own distress and their children's distress, particularly when moving home involved moving schools as well:

> They were frightened. They were really quite frightened – what's going to happen, Mum? Where are we going to be? And they were asking quite grown-up questions, and they wanted to know why their Daddy wouldn't pay for the shortfall on the mortgage. Why couldn't the council just rent the house out to us? Why couldn't we pay the council rent? Why couldn't they buy the house?
> (Lone mothers, children aged 12 and 16, repossessed 1997)

> I've had to come to with it and I've had to come to terms with it quickly, with my son being upset. I mean he keeps asking for his friends that he used to have and he wants to go back to that school.
> (Lone mother, repossessed in 1998, quoted in Ford *et al.* 2001: 138–1)

Many women, therefore, find themselves living in unfamiliar areas, in housing of a lower quality than they have previously experienced. Young women who were never or only briefly partnered have also felt discriminated against in their desire to achieve a house in a respectable area that offered a future for themselves and their children. Such was the situation of most of the young single mothers interviewed in hostels in Birmingham, who felt particularly discriminated against in relation to the provision of social housing in a city with an adequate supply:

> I just want to meet nice people.
> …
> They always want to put you … Have you noticed? There are certain areas, just for people like us! Baby mothers! There's no other people around, just babies … single mums. You won't see mums and dads and two kids, you'll just see people like us…
> …
> But …. There are too many white people in Solihull and they're racist!
> …
> I was brought up in Sutton Coldfield and Erdington. So why should I… Why can't I go and live back there? Do you know what I mean?
> (Focus group, young single parent homeless, females, Birmingham, quoted in Smith *et al.* 2000)

For these young mothers a choice-based lettings system (where available housing is advertised on the internet, in shop windows, in local free papers, and other public outlets, and anyone can apply for it) would be helpful.

Lone parent households (94 per cent of whom are lone mother households) are included among those targeted by the Labour government in its efforts to move households off benefit. The comparatively high rates of benefit available through WTC are testimony to the determination of the Labour government to support households in paid work. This contrasts with the treatment of lone parents remaining on benefit whose entitlement to additional payments as lone parents was removed in 1998; the additional payments for children to all parents living on benefits has provided increased benefits for couples, but has only returned lone parents to their 1998 situation. The treatment of lone parents within the benefits system contrasts with the improved situation for both older people and couples.

Gender, age and the need for appropriate housing

Age is a difficult concept when discussing the problem of housing. In homelessness legislation an important qualifying age is sixty years. People above this age who apply for rehousing frequently cite medical grounds, and local authority housing departments typically accept applications from those seeking to move nearer to a carer and from carers seeking to move nearer to a relative. In studies of homelessness that concentrate on rough sleepers, however, rough sleepers can be categorised as older when they are over forty-five or fifty-five years of age.

In relation to the general population and the study of gerontology there is more interest in those aged seventy-five years plus, because it is at this age that major social and health problems are more likely to emerge. Women comprise two-thirds of the population aged seventy-five years plus in the UK, and nearly one in twenty of the population is a woman aged seventy-five years or over; by comparison, only one in forty of the population is a man aged seventy-five years or more. It is at this age that people are most likely to have to move into more suitable accommodation or to adapt the accommodation that they have. In his report on older people moving home, Sykes divides the older age group into the well-off 20 per cent, the not rich-not poor 40 per cent, and the poor 40 per cent, and points to the loss of income among older people, particularly older women. Income declines with the death of a spouse, although expenditure rarely declines proportionately, the 'old-old' are the poorest, and women have the lowest incomes in retirement (Sykes 1994).

Although nine out of ten older people continue to live in general housing and only one-tenth move into sheltered accommodation, residential care or nursing homes, the death of a spouse can be a strong push factor encouraging the remaining spouse (usually a woman) to move house. Some will 'trade down' to a cheaper owner-occupied house, but others will want to move out of owner-occupation into rented accommodation. Sykes quotes figures from Anchor that show that 30 per cent of their sheltered housing lettings are to applicants who were previously owner-occupiers. Alternatively, older homeowners may seek the support of a 'care and repair' service to maintain their home. Energy efficient housing policies are also targeted at older homeowners through the Warm Homes Scheme.

The Survey of English Housing sheds more light on the need of older person households for different types of accommodation. It reports that moving to a different property owned outright largely takes place at the end of the home-owning cycle when people have retired, and it estimates that 380,000 households moved to outright ownership in the previous three years. It was most common to move from a mortgaged home to outright ownership in south-east and south-west England, to move up to fifty miles away, perhaps to a seaside resort. It was also common to buy a different type of property: one-quarter bought a bungalow and one-fifth bought a flat (Green *et al.* 1999: 45). Of particular interest were the homeowners who expected to move in the next five years. One in nine of this group (11 per cent) expected to move from home ownership to the social rental sector. Forty per cent of these homeowners were living in one-person households, over half were retired, half were sixty-five years or over, and half were disabled (Green *et al.* 1999: 46). The provision of social housing is therefore essential in the context of an ageing population, and is of particular importance for women given their longevity.

It is important for older women that their households are offered a range of options for re-housing that include residential care, sheltered housing and purpose built housing. However, the needs of an ageing population have not been addressed. The model of 'lifetime' homes, which would ensure that all new housing is built so that it can be used by anyone who is older or disabled, is not one that has been adopted as standard (see Milner, this volume).

New Labour perspectives on social housing

As argued above, New Labour perspectives on social housing are critical for women because, although only one-quarter (25 per cent) of all households in England are headed by women, nearly half (44 per cent) of those with a female head are housed in the social rented sector (Green *et al.* 1999, reporting 1997 figures), reflecting the preponderance of women among lone parent households and single older person households. With regard to the low level of social housing supply, the Labour Government has a policy of 'planning gain', requiring private developers to include an element of social housing in their new developments, in partnership with a housing association. This is in sharp contrast to the policy of the 1960s. For example, although the housing crisis is now acute in London and south-east England and has led to shortages of accommodation for key workers in public services, the National Health Service disposed of 4,800 acres to a private developer housing consortium (the *Guardian*, 12 September 2002). That which was socially owned, paid for by national insurance and taxation, is now to be developed privately, as is the Millennium Dome site that could have provided a wonderful mixed development for London workers under the Greater London Authority.

Housing lettings policy has also become a priority in order to support two other New Labour agendas: the reversal of the 'social exclusion' processes that occurred under the previous Conservative administration leading to desperately run-down and impoverished neighbourhoods, and the development of policies of 'floating support' for new tenants:

> Changing messages about what lettings policy and practice should be aiming to achieve have emerged from the Government over the past year. The consistent themes are: building viable and sustainable communities, avoiding concentrations of people with certain attributes; and promoting choice for housing applicants.
>
> (R. Smith et al. 2001)

In relation to building viable and sustainable neighbourhoods there have been two relevant developments in lettings policy. In a study of housing exclusion in Stoke-on-Trent (an area of excess social housing) it was found that several strategies were used by different housing associations. Some housing associations have won the right to develop a local lettings policy, which effectively restricts lettings to people with an immediate local connection with an area (not just a local authority area) and with no reason for exclusion (such as rent arrears, anti-social behaviour/ violence, drug or other criminal record). Part of the agenda here is not just to remove drug dealers from the area but also women sex workers. The most common reasons for excluding women-headed households in particular are past rent arrears and a vandalised house. Some women will have had a relationship with a violent man who was also violent to neighbours and may have trashed the house. Even in areas of high housing supply the debt incurred as a previous tenant may prevent a new tenancy being offered (Smith 2002).

The second lettings development relates to the introduction of floating support schemes to help new tenants. Whereas previously local authorities commonly offered a property to a new tenant and undertook a review visit one month or so after the letting, it is now envisaged that there should be more interventionist support in order to prevent repeat homelessness and to help sustain tenancies. The 'Supporting People' pot of money, which includes all the payments outside of the rent payment that is part of housing benefit, has also been used in many areas to fund floating support for new tenants for the first three to six months of their social housing tenancy. This policy is an obvious response to government concerns about the problems of 'repeat homelessness' and repeat housing applications. However, in a study of Swedish social housing tenants (Sahlin 1995; see below), it has been suggested that the development of housing support workers, or housing social workers, has not been positive for all tenants.

In the 1980s and 1990s a decisive shift took place in Sweden in relation to housing policy: housing subsidies decreased, construction ceased, de-regulation was introduced, local housing companies shut down and municipal housing companies ceased to have their traditional advantages (Sahlin 1995; Sahlin and Thorn 2000). As part of this process, municipal housing companies (MMHCs) ceased to be required to house only those who could not be accommodated in the private market, and sought to rebalance their tenant profile by recruiting middle-class Swedish tenants to complement the low-income and immigrant households they were already housing. In Sweden, new tenants' legislation then came to include specific legislation on 'noisy neighbours' including procedures for their eviction, and renewal projects often led to welfare-recipient tenants being moved off estates to which many were never to return.

As MMHCs took less responsibility for people in housing need, so local authorities took a greater role, subleasing flats to homeless clients who had not been accepted by the MMHCs. Associated with these flats was specific training in 'independent living', and this was managed by newly appointed special social housing workers. Interviews with these special social housing workers on first appointment and four years later demonstrated that their perspective shifted through time so that they came to view the tenants as problem tenants and monitored them more frequently than the landlords demanded or had been planned (Sahlin 1995). As the process developed, more tenants were screened out of even this provision and tenants who misbehaved were permanently evicted. For the local social housing workers a 'failure' ceased to be that a homeless applicant remained homeless because they had previously failed in their tenancy and were therefore permanently excluded; it was more important that tenants who were accepted should behave themselves in their transition flats and moved on to a permanent tenancy – that was 'success'.

In retrospect, it was of special significance that in the UK the 1977 Homelessness Act transferred responsibility for housing priority need households from *social work* departments to local authority *housing* departments. This meant that local authority enquiries into the circumstances of the homeless household centred on their housing situation, priority need and local connection, not on the 'fitness' of the parent(s) to support their child or children. Although there might be medical evidence or even social work evidence on the needs of the children for housing support, the re-housing process was separated from a full social work inquiry. Therefore, the 1977 Act recognised that homelessness was to be solved through social housing intervention rather than social work intervention, and it was conceived as a housing crisis rather than a failure of the family. In some ways the provision of a universal floating support service by housing authorities could be argued to reverse this perspective, by identifying all social housing tenants, rather than some social housing tenants, as requiring a support worker.

One of the issues for the UK is what will happen when local authority statutory responsibility for housing homeless households is completely separated from the ownership and control of any stock, as is the Labour government's aim. Will housing associations act as the Municipal Housing Companies did in Sweden (and HLMs do in France) and seek to let to 'better tenants', as is the case in local lettings policies? Will a similar separation of functions occur as occurred in Sweden? Currently, housing authorities have accepted the fact that some families will re-apply and need re-housing, but will continuous monitoring of the families concerned, and greater involvement in their lives, lead to a development of the attitude described by Sahlin? In the study of homeless applicants in Herefordshire, where 'choice-based lettings' had been introduced, local housing associations were concerned that the 'best' properties were going to homeless applicants in the priority need band (as opposed to gold, silver or bronze band) and considered this unfair to their existing tenants who deserved the right to transfer to better properties (Smith 2003). There was also the beginning of monitoring of applicants who previously applied as homeless.

The situations in Sweden and the UK are not precisely the same. In the UK, 'floating support' services have been devolved to NGOs who specialise in working with the homeless, not to Social Work Departments. In a study comparing the support offered homeless young people by dispersed foyers (8), single site foyers (4) and floating support schemes (4), it was found that floating support schemes were financed through Supporting People but run by NGOs familiar with home-lessness issues. In Hertfordshire one agency that had run drop-in centres had the contract from the local authority to work with all new younger tenants including single parent mothers and single people. This was also the case in London where Patchwork, a housing association now specialising in young people, was providing support for a similar group of young mothers and young single people. In Birmingham a major contract had gone to a provider of support accommodation for young people from many different backgrounds whilst a similar scheme in Herefordshire worked with young single people, some of whom were living as 'hidden homeless' (Smith 2004).

Although housing departments have frequently been supportive of floating support services, attitudes differ between local authorities. Also, housing depart-ments in most areas are now the overall strategists for homelessness work but do not provide housing directly for homeless people. For women there are dangers in divorcing the management of social housing from the local authorities that have statutory responsibility to secure accommodation for homeless and needy house-holds. There is evidence that housing association practice towards women seeking support may be less helpful than that of local authorities. For example, Cathy Davis' research into how housing associations deal with housing applications from women escaping domestic violence found them seeking support letters, enquiring into previous housing history, and making judgements about the violence experienced; by contrast, no housing association in her study took action against the men who had been violent (Davis 2001).

Therefore, although under the Labour government the discourse that identified homeless lone parents as the cause of the housing crisis has been rolled back, present housing policy may still impact negatively upon women's access to social housing. This can happen as a result of, for example: increased monitoring of women households who become tenants (Are they re-applicants? Have there been previous complaints from neighbours?); imposition of anti-social behaviour orders on their children; large-scale voluntary transfers of local authority housing to other bodies; the lack of new build social housing leading to gate-keeping and 'rationing'; and gendered attitudes towards housing applications.

Conclusion

Social policy theory has never given housing a central role in social welfare. Books on welfare policy and on women and welfare policy have not paid attention to the role of housing in providing security and in stabilising people's lives. This chapter has argued that the provision of permanent secure low-cost shelter is particularly important for all female-headed households and especially important for women experiencing domestic violence (by enabling them to move out of that situation into a safe and cheap home). The housing policy of the New Labour government, however, has sought to address housing need through planning gain and the better use of existing stock rather than through a major investment in social housing. As the better stock has been sold, women who rely on social housing have increasingly been offered second or third best.

Therefore, although the Labour government has responded to the rough sleeping problem with well-targeted resources, it has not provided equally targeted resources for the delivery of social housing. Its response to the crisis of social housing has been to provide investment money for housing associations, demand that local housing authorities make better use of their existing stock, and provide floating support workers, a move that may turn social housing into 'assisted housing', as in Sweden. It has not reinstated the role of local authorities as housing providers, seeking instead that all local housing authority stock be transferred to other social housing providers, and falling foul of those tenants who refuse to vote for the transfer. It has not substantially restricted the right to buy, to stop the haemorrhaging of social housing into private hands. It has not re-allocated sufficient funds into social housing in order to close the gap that built up in the 1980s and 1990s between housing supply and housing demand across the UK as a whole. The situation now is that in London in particular more houses are being sold each year under the right to buy than are being built.

The government's response to the current housing situation was, first, to argue that it was not a housing crisis, but a crisis of supported accommodation. This position has now been officially dropped. Its new response to the current housing crisis of temporarily accommodated homeless families has been to create a new Homelessness Directorate, led by the previous Director of the Rough Sleepers Unit. It includes three different agencies: a Homelessness Unit given the task of preventing the using of inappropriate emergency accommodation for homeless families, particularly bed and breakfast accommodation; a Prevention of Rough Sleeping Unit; and a Homelessness Strategy Unit. It has also passed a new Homelessness Act (2002), discussed above, and proposed the use of private accommodation and assured shorthold tenancies for the discharge of the homelessness function by local authority housing departments. Alongside these developments there has already been, within criminal legislation, the development of anti-social behaviour orders for the eviction of undesirable tenants (see Cooper, this volume).

There are different contexts, therefore, within which the rights of women and children to housing are being eroded. First, as the number of young single homeless people rose in the UK, there was a shift of public attention away from the less visible problem of family homelessness towards the very visible problem of street homelessness. Initially, the Children Act 1989 gave local housing authorities and social services departments specific responsibilities for the housing of young people who had been in the care of the local authority. This followed a series of reports which had identified that up to one-third of the young people living in homeless hostels had had some experience of local authority care, either living in residential homes or in foster homes. This was followed by the Rough Sleepers Initiatives and then the Rough Sleepers Unit, which set an ambitious target of reducing rough sleeping by two-thirds in London, thus creating a new priority need group, with rough sleepers being given priority first for hostel places, and then for move-on accommodation. In London boroughs, with a very small supply of new social housing lets and a large demand, this meant that young single mothers, living with their parents or with other relatives or friends, could not be accommodated.

A further initiative was the Homelessness Act 2002, which requires local housing authorities to offer advice to single homeless people, and includes some young homeless people (16–17 years) in the category of 'priority need', along with ex-servicemen and ex-prisoners. In urban areas of scarce social housing, this could lead to young men being more likely to be classified as 'priority need' than young single mothers. This is for two reasons: first, young men are more likely to sleep on the streets, and be classified as at risk of rough sleeping; and second, the population of local authority 'looked after' children and young people includes more young men than young women, and ex-prisoners and ex-servicemen are overwhelmingly male.

Overall, therefore, although the homelessness legislation of 2002 finally recognises the priority need of some single homeless people (a measure suggested in 1977), there is a gap between its good intentions and the available provision. The separation of purchaser of services (housing authorities) from provider (housing associations, voluntary organisations), and the establishment of new lettings systems (bands rather than points, choice rather than guidance) also creates difficulties in matching local housing and homeless need with local available stock. Since nearly half of female-headed households are housed in social housing, it is particularly important that these policies are made to work.

Notes

1 Many of the homelessness reports cited in this chapter under my name and others derived from projects undertaken by a team of researchers at Staffordshire University where I was the Director of the original Housing and Community Research Unit (HCRU) from 1989. It was this team that first investigated the family background of young homeless people, interviewing both them and their parents, and also undertook record collection among agencies for the 1996 study of seven cities and four London boroughs, and interviews for the Birmingham studies. At the heart of the team was Pauline Ing. Originally from London, she moved to Stoke-on-Trent with her family and became a mature student of sociology at Staffordshire University. Her own life and work history meant that she had an empathy with young homeless people, carers, older people in residential homes, those with mental health issues, and the staff who worked with these client groups. But her understanding approach was also evident in interviews with ex-prisoners, young people from care, and women escaping domestic violence. It was not a rare event that an interviewee, or a parent, or a support worker, would phone and say what a difference talking to her had made. She strongly believed in being a voice for the excluded and that all our reports should reflect that voice. Unhappily she died on 24 June 2004 at the Douglas MacMillan Hospice, Stoke-on-Trent. Her death is a great loss.

2 The terms 'homelessness', 'hidden homelessness' and 'rough sleepers' are all used to describe homelessness in the UK; indeed the term 'rough sleeper' is solely used in the UK. Writers in the US make a different distinction between 'literal' homelessness of people living in the streets and/or in shelters and hostels, and homeless people who are 'doubled up', living with friends and families. In Northern Europe it is more common to find a three-fold distinction between the 'street homeless', those living in hostels, and the 'hidden homeless' or 'houseless homeless' (see the discussion on definitions of homelessness at www.cuhp.org, the website of the European Network discussing definitions of homelessness in Europe and different research methodologies).

References

Anderson, I. (1993) *Access to Housing for Low Income Single People*, York: Centre for Housing Policy, University of York.

Anderson, I. and Quilgars, D. (1995) *Foyers for Young People. Evaluation of a Pilot Initiative*, York: Centre for Housing Policy, University of York.

Anderson, I. and Sim, D. (eds) (2000) *Social Exclusion and Housing: Context and Challenges*, Coventry: Chartered Institute of Housing.

Anderson, I., Kemp, P. and Quilgars, D. (1993) *Single Homeless People*, London: HMSO.

Balchin, P. (1995) *Housing Policy. An Introduction*, 3rd edn, London: Routledge.

Ball, M. and Harloe, M. (1998) 'Uncertainty in European housing markets', in M. Kleinman, W. Matznetter and M. Stephens (eds) *European Integration and Housing Policy*, London: Routledge/Royal Institute of Chartered Surveyors.

Bramley, G. (1994) 'The affordability crisis in British housing: dimensions, causes and policy impact', *Housing Studies*, 9, 1: 103–24.

Bruegel, I. and Smith, J. (1999) *Taking Risks: An Analysis of the Risks of Homelessness for Young People in London*, London: Safe in the City/Peabody Trust.

Burghes, L. and Brown, M. (1995) *Single Lone Mothers: Problems, Prospects and Policies*, London: Family Policy Studies Centre.

Burrows, R. (1997) 'Powers of exclusion: residential mobility and the dynamics of residualisation', Table 5, paper to the British Sociological Association, April, York: Centre for Housing Policy, University of York.

Christie, H. (2000) 'Mortgage arrears and gender inequalities', *Housing Studies*, 15, 6: 877–907.

Darke, J. (1994) 'Women and the meaning of home', in R. Gilroy and R. Woods (eds) *Housing Women*, London: Routledge.

Davis, C. (2001) 'Gender and housing', in M. Harrison with C. Davis (eds) *Housing, Social Policy and Difference: Disability, Ethnicity, Gender and Housing*, Bristol: Policy Press.

Department of the Environment (1994) *Access to Local Authority and Housing Association Tenancies*, London: DoE.

Douglas, A. and Gilroy, R. (1994) 'Young women and homelessness', in R. Gilroy and R. Woods (eds) *Housing Women*, London: Routledge.

Drake, M. (1981) *Single and Homeless*, London: Department of the Environment.

Duncan, S. and Edwards, R. (1997) 'Single mothers in Britain: unsupported workers or mothers?', in S. Duncan and R. Edwards (eds) *Single Mothers in an International Context: Mothers or Workers*, London: UCL Press.

Edgar, B. and Doherty, J. (eds) (2001) *Women and Homelessness in Europe*, Bristol: Policy Press.

Ehrenreich, B. (2001) *Nickel and Dimed: On (Not) Getting By in America*. Henry Holt and Co. USA.

Enders-Dragasser, U. (2001) 'Women, exclusion and homelessness in Germany', in B. Edgar and J. Doherty (eds) *Women and Homelessness in Europe*, Bristol: Policy Press.

Evans, A. (1996) *We Don't Choose to Be Homeless*, report for the National Inquiry into Homelessness, London: CHAR.

Finer Report (1974) *Report of the Committee on One-Parent Families Vol. II, Evidence*, London: HMSO.

Ford, J., Burrows, R. and Nettleton, S. (2001) *Home Ownership in a Risk Society*, Bristol: Policy Press.

Gilroy, R. and Woods, R. (eds) (1994) *Housing Women*, London: Routledge.

Golden, S. (1992) *The Woman Outside: Meanings and Myths of Homelessness*, Berkeley, CA: University of California Press.

Green, H. (1994) *Shared Accommodation in Five Localities*, London: HMSO.

Green, H., Bumpstead, R., Thomas, M. and Grove, J. (1999) *Housing in England 1997/8*, London: Government Statistical Service, The Stationery Office.

Greve, J. and Currie, E. (1990) *Homelessness*, York: Joseph Rowntree Foundation.

Gurney C (1990) *The Meaning of Home in the Decade of Owner Occupation*, Working Paper 88, Bristol: School for Advanced Urban Studies, University of Bristol.

—— (1991) 'Ontological security, home ownership and the meansing of home: a theoretical and empirical critique', paper given at Conference on *Beyond a Nation of Home Owners*, Sheffield: Sheffield City Polytechnic, April.

Hallett, C. (ed.) (1996) *Women and Social Policy. An Introduction*, Hemel Hempstead: Harvester Wheatsheaf.

Hills, J. (1993) *The Future of Welfare. A Guide to the Debate*, York: Joseph Rowntree Foundation.

Holman A., Morrison, N. and Whitehead, C. (1998) *How Many Homes Will We Need? The Need for Affordable Housing in England*, London: Shelter.

Hutson, S. and Liddiard, M. (1994) *Youth Homelessness. The Social Construction of an Issue*, Basingstoke: Macmillan.

Jones, A. (1999) *Out of Sight, Out of Mind? The Experiences of Homeless Women*, London: CRISIS.

Joshi, H. (ed.) (1989) *The Changing Population of Britain*, Oxford: Blackwell.

—— (1991) 'Sex and motherhood as handicaps in the labour market', in M. Maclean and D. Groves (eds) *Women's Issues in Social Policy*, London: Routledge.

Kiernan, K. (1989) 'The family: formation and fission', in H. Joshi (ed.) *The Changing Population of Britain*, Oxford: Blackwell.

Kleinman, M., Matznetter, W. and Stephens, M. (1998) *European Integration and Housing Policy*, London: Routledge/Royal Institute of Chartered Surveyors.

Low Pay Commission (2001) *Third Report on the National Minimum Wage*, Vol. 2, London: Low Pay Commission.

Lupton, R. and Power, A. (2001) 'Social exclusion and neighbourhoods', in J. Hills, J. Le Grand and D. Piachaud (eds) *Understanding Social Exclusion*, Oxford: Oxford University Press.

Marsh, A., McKay, S., Smith, A. and Stephenson, A. (2001) *Low Income Families in Britain: Work, Welfare and Social Security in 1999*, Department of Social Security, Research Report No. 138, London: DSS.

Murray, C. (1990) *The Emerging British Underclass*, London: Institute of Economic Affairs.

—— (1994) series of articles in *Sunday Times*, May–June 1994.

Orloff, A.S. (2002) 'Explaining US welfare reform: power, gender, race and the US policy legacy', *Critical Social Policy*, 22, 1: 96–118.

Oxley, M. and Smith, J. (1998) 'Housing investment in Europe', in M. Kleinman, W. Matznetter and M. Stephens (eds) *European Integration and Housing Policy*, London: Routledge/Royal Institute of Chartered Surveyors.

Pizzey, E. (1974) *Scream Quietly or the Neighbours Will Hear*, Harmondsworth: Penguin.

Power, A. and Tunstall, R. (1995) *Swimming Against the Tide: Polarisation or Progress on 20 Unpopular Council Estates 1980–1995*, York: Joseph Rowntree Foundation.

Sahlin, I. (1995) 'Strategies for exclusion from social housing', *Housing Studies*, 10, 3: 381–401.

Sahlin, I. and Thorn, C. (2000) *Women, Exclusion and Homelessness in Sweden*, National Report 1999, Brussels: European Observatory on Homelessness/FEANTSA.

Smith, J. (1999) 'Gender and homelessness', in S. Hutson and D. Clapham (eds) *Homelessness: Public Policies and Private Troubles*, London: Cassell.

—— (2000) *Routes In and Out of Homelessness among Young People in Birmingham*, Stoke-on-Trent: Centre for Housing and Community Research, Staffordshire University.

—— (2002) *Exclusions from Social Housing and Hostel Accommodation. A Study for the 21st Century Homes Project*, Stoke-on-Trent: Centre for Housing and Community Research, Staffordshire University.

—— (2003) *A Report for Herefordshire Homeless Strategy Team*, unpublished, Stoke-on-Trent: Centre for Housing and Community Research, Staffordshire University.

—— (2004) *Dispersed Foyers*, London: Foyer Federation/London Metropolitan University. Available on-line: www.foyer.net.

Smith, J. and Gilford, S. (1993) *Young and Homeless in Birmingham*, London: Barnardos.

Smith, J., Gilford, S., Kirby, P., O'Reilly, A. and Ing, P. (1996) *Bright Lights and Homelessness: Family and Single Homelessness Among Young People in our Cities*, London: YMCA.

Smith, J., Gilford, S. and O'Sullivan, A. (1998) *The Family Background of Young Homeless People*, London: Family Policy Studies Centre; and York: Joseph Rowntree Foundation.

Smith, J. and Ing, P. (2000) *Towards A Youth Homeless Strategy for Birmingham: A Discussion Document*, Stoke-on-Trent: Centre for Housing and Community Research, Staffordshire University.

Smith, J., Ing, P. and O'Sullivan, A. (2000) *Routes In and Out of Homelessness among Young People in Birmingham*, Stoke-on-Trent: Centre for Housing and Community Research, Staffordshire University.

Smith, J., Ing, P. and Ing, M. (2001) *Making Youth Homelessness Visible: Youth Homelessness in the Cotswolds*, Stoke-on-Trent: Centre for Housing and Community Research, Staffordshire University.

Smith, R., Stirling, T., Papps, P., Evans, A. and Rowlands, R. (2001) *The Lettings Lottery. The Range and Impact of Homelessness and Lettings Policy*, London: Shelter.

Stockley, D., Bishopp, D. and Canter, D. (1993) *Young and Homeless*, Final Research Report, Guildford: Department of Psychology, University of Surrey.

Sykes, R. (1994) 'Older women and housing – prospects for the 1990s', in R. Gilroy and R. Woods (eds) (1994) *Housing Women*, London: Routledge.

Webster, D. (2000) 'Lone parenthood: two views and their consequences', in I. Anderson and D. Sim (eds) *Social Exclusion and Housing: Context and Challenges*, Coventry: Chartered Institute of Housing.

Wilson, E. (1977) *What Is To Be Done about Violence Against Women?*, London: Pluto Press.

Worley, C. and Smith, J. (2001) *Moving Out, Moving On ... From Foyer Accommodation to Independent Living*, London: YMCA.

Woods, R. (1996) 'Women and housing', in C. Hallett (ed.) *Women and Social Policy. An Introduction*, Hemel Hempstead: Prentice Hall/Harvester Wheatsheaf.

8 Disability and inclusive housing design

Towards a life-course perspective

Jo Milner

Introduction

Over the past three decades, the emergence and growth of political interest groups based on race, gender, sexuality, biological age, and disability, have posed a considerable challenge to the deeply embedded, stereotypical assumptions of 'normality' that have shaped the development of UK social policy. The hegemonic construct of the nuclear family, headed by an able-bodied, white, adult male has traditionally informed policy decisions as to which groups were identified as 'welfare' subjects (Hughes 1998). Older people and disabled people were socially constructed as 'dependent', and categorised on the basis of their lack of conformity with this universal representation. As recognition of the pluralist make-up of society increases, so the legitimacy of this stereotype is increasingly questioned as a means of defining needs, especially older and disabled people's needs, as 'special' or 'different'.

The disability movement, led by physically disabled people, gathered momentum at the end of the 1980s, and followed in the wake of the feminist, black, and gay struggles. The foundations of the movement were laid in 1976, when the Union of Physically Impaired Against Segregation (UPIAS) articulated the philosophy of the 'social' model of disability as a desirable objective, and contrasted this with the 'medical' (now termed the 'individual') model. Disability activists (Oliver 1990) argued that the state of dependency associated with disability originated not from an individual's impairment, the traditional view, but rather from discriminatory socio-economic and environmental policies and practice. Abberley explains:

> the 'medical' model locates the source of the disability in the individual's supposed deficiency and her personal incapacities when compared to 'normal' people. In contrast to this, social models see disability as resulting from society's failure to adapt to the needs of impaired people.
>
> (Abberley 1998: 79)

The 'social' model also challenged the deeply embedded 'medical' model on the grounds that it was based on the principle that disabled people had separate and/or 'special' needs arising from their impairment. It was argued that approaches informed by the 'medical' model perpetuated rather than reduced dependency, as they segregated and excluded disabled people from mainstream services such as employment, education, transport and the built environment, including housing.

Therefore, the problems related to disability were largely viewed as 'collective' issues to be resolved at a macro, 'social' policy level, as opposed to 'personal' issues to be resolved at an 'individual' or micro level. The 'social' model has remained at the heart of the movement's campaign to this day, and is reminiscent of the feminist slogan 'the personal is political', which stated that 'private troubles' can be translated into 'political issues'. By contesting the prevailing individualism of entrenched responses to disability, and focusing on legislative and policy reform, the 'social' model has served as a major catalyst in initiating debates as to the way forward for a new social settlement of welfare.

Housing policy, as a key component of the wider context of UK social policy, has been subject to the same debates as to how to reframe social constructions of 'normality', and move beyond stereotypical assumptions of disabled and older people's needs, to create more inclusive home and neighbourhood environments for a diverse population (Harrison 2001). Indeed, this issue has recently come to the fore within the area of housing quality and design, which is currently experiencing a re-negotiation of its boundaries, in the light of the disability movement's success in instigating stronger accessibility legislation. In 1999, Approved Document Part M of the English Building Regulations was amended, and now requires that all new private housing meet the minimal threshold of 'visitability' for all, including older and/or disabled people. No longer is it possible to conceive of physical 'accessibility' as a bolt on extra to housing quality criteria, as it has become an integral design feature. Although AD Part M has only been in place at the time of writing for four years, and is lauded by disability and older people's pressure groups as a major policy inroad, it is also widely perceived as an incremental first step towards 'lifetime' or 'universal' design standards (Milner and Madigan 2001). The former term refers to housing which is adaptable enough to enable older and/or disabled people to 'stay put' should their mobility requirements change, whilst the latter term refers to housing that allows for full wheelchair access.

This chapter focuses on the question of the most appropriate future direction for housing quality and inclusive design for all, including older and/or disabled people, and addresses this by examining a number of intersecting themes. It first explores the context of the shifting debates relating to the re-settlement of social welfare and discusses key issues relating to the positioning and re-positioning of social groups arising from this. It then moves on to examine the history of housing policy and the development of housing standards in relation to the hegemony of the nuclear family, and examines the policy influences that led to the stereotyping and exclusion of disabled people from mainstream housing. Finally, it discusses the policy thrust towards the inclusion of disabled people and the complex implications of the current gradual transition towards accommodating the difference and diversity of all individuals and groups.

End of post war consensus within social policy

Following the Second World War in the UK, the welfare state was underpinned by an economic, political and social settlement which endured for more than three decades, and revolved around assumptions of normality and difference based on the average, homogeneous nuclear family. However, as the Thatcherite era drew to a close in the early 1990s, and post-Fordist economic, technological, social and demographic changes took effect, a much more fragmented, less consensual picture appeared of a welfare state in organisational flux. The emergence of new constituencies based on identity politics, such as the women's, black, gay rights, and older people's movements and more recently the disability movement, played an important role in this shift and re-appraisal of the traditional patterns of distribution. They laid claim to marginalised status, welfare entitlements, and citizenship rights, and challenged and exposed underlying gendered, class, racist, ageist, and disablist discriminatory practices.

The rapid proliferation of protest groups (such as the UPIAS outlined above), and their subsequent fragmentation into further sub-groups (representing those with visual and/or hearing impairments, or other types of impairment or illness), raises questions as to where the 'new' (welfare) subjects might be positioned within the policy arena, as given their negotiated and (re)negotiated boundaries, their status as discrete and unambiguous categories is now continuously challenged (O'Brien and Penna 1998). Recently a number of theorists (Young 1990; Leonard 1997; O'Brien and Penna 1998; Carter 1998) have argued that social groups should not be considered in essentialist terms, that is, as in some way biologically fixed, unalterable, or homogeneous, but rather as sharing cross-cutting affinities and differences.

Re-appraising the 'social' model of disability

Recently the 'social' model of disability, derived from the definition outlined by UPIAS, has been criticised both from within and outside the movement on the grounds that it is reductionist, as it fails to reflect the many and complex factors which contribute to disability (Marks 1999: 87).

One key issue raised by critics such as Hughes and Paterson (1997) has been the exclusive focus of the 'social' model on 'disabling' structural issues, which if successfully addressed will remove the disability. However, as Watson (1998: 149) argues, this approach excludes the influence of impairment by suggesting that it 'is merely a biological description of the body and plays no part in determining a person's sense of self'. Watson draws on debates within medical sociology, which argue that this 'refusal to link disability to impairment', by playing down the role of personal experience of impairment and playing up the role of structural barriers, offers as partial and incomplete a picture as the 'medical' model. According to Watson (1998: 150), just as the 'medical' model risks portraying disabled people as victims of a personal tragedy, so the structural analysis 'risks portraying disabled people as victims, not of their impairment but of a society that fails to include them'. This latter analysis thus risks depicting disabled people as helpless and passive rather than as active agents able to engage in resistance.

Moreover, the 'social' model, having originated from a movement led largely by physically impaired male adults, developed to reflect the concerns of mobility impaired male adults, especially wheelchair users, who are least able to adapt their behaviour to environmental restrictions, such as steps and stairs. Not only did it fail to take into account the complexity of disability, which may be experienced on multiple, fluctuating, sensory, cognitive and emotional levels, but it led to policy responses largely directed at the needs of physically impaired people (Imrie and Hall 2001). So, just as the champions of the 'social' model challenged the normalising stereotype of the non-disabled, waged, adult, white male, which has traditionally informed policy definitions of dependency, they too have been criticised for promulgating a stereotyped image of disabled people as *white Western, male wheelchair users*' (Marks 1999: 87). Both Marks (1999) and Watson (1998) contend that this simplistic approach, although useful as a campaigning tool, failed to take into account the wide-ranging cultural factors, such as age, sexuality, race and gender, which also shaped the experiences of people with different impairments.

Clearly, there is a need to question the underlying premise of the 'social' model, and expose its weakness with a view to adopting a more balanced approach, which moves beyond the bias towards physical impairments, whilst taking into account the social meaning of impairment, the intersecting range of cultural factors, and the wider context relating to structural barriers.

However, in spite of such recent criticisms of the 'social' model, the disability movement has been instrumental in challenging the normative constructions of dependency that underpin redistributive welfare. Indeed, the subsequent shake-up and review of the policy framework in the light of the 'social' model has exposed the inherent individualism of many policies that have led to the marginalisation and segregation of disabled people (for further reading on the 'individual' and 'social' models of disability, see Barnes *et al.* 1999).

Towards a life-course perspective

As awareness of the need to move away from conceptions of group differences based on 'substantive characteristics and attributes' grows, along with awareness of the need for a re-positioning of (welfare) subjects that is 'relational' and multi-dimensional (Young 1990: 171), attention has now turned to sociological and policy constructions of the life-course as a unifying theme common to us all (Priestley 2001: 243).

Yet, analysis of traditional concepts of chronological progression shows that, like disability, they too are deeply embedded within an individualist framework of normative assumptions of dependency based on biological age. Until very recently, both sociology and social policy structured the life-course into a series of separate stages tied to social roles; for instance, whereas old age and childhood have been constructed as dependent phases, adulthood to the contrary is idealised as the high point or 'apex' of independence (Priestley 2001: 246). Further, the stereotyping of stages of the life-course has led to an oppressive normalisation, in which some stages, particularly childhood and old age, are valued less highly than others. This has resulted in confusion, especially in relation to the two groups constructed as dependent, older people and children, for they are viewed as separate from all other categories of need. This is evidenced, for example, by the development of discrete and parallel policy constructs and classifications for 'disabled people' and 'older people', which are at best misleading and at worst inaccurate. Priestley (2001: 597) argues that a contradictory trend has now emerged. For, although disabled people and older people share many overlapping concerns, especially as 'the majority of people with significant impairments are over retirement age, disabled politics has remained preoccupied with the interests of younger adults, and older people have remained under represented within the disability movement'.

Disabled and older people now have well-established political movements, which stress that their needs should be collectively defined in policy processes. This contrasts with children, whose directly expressed views were neither considered nor heard until very recently. To James and Prout (1997: 7), it was not so much that policy considerations of children's needs were viewed as of little importance, but rather that, as adults spoke on their behalf, their voices were 'muted' and 'silent'. Children occupied a marginal position within social policy, for they were constructed as passive and vulnerable dependents, and as of less than adult status. Conceptions of dependency associated with childhood have now begun to be challenged, and children are currently being reconstructed as having agency, that is, a measure of responsibility for their own actions. This development is having a significant impact on current debates concerning the re-negotiation of the life-course (Priestley 2000).

Traditional life-course constructions have been further challenged by significant social and demographic changes. The new category 'deep old age', for instance, emerged in response to an increase in life expectancy and decrease in the birth rate. Over just two decades, from 1980 to 2001, the proportion of men aged eighty-five and over increased from 3 per cent in 1980 to 7 per cent in 2001, whilst, over the same period, the proportion of older women aged eighty-five and over increased from 8 per cent to 11 per cent (General Household Survey 2002). Hockey and James (2003: 57) also point out that 'the relationship between age and key transitional moments in the life-course, such as leaving home, marriage and childbirth', is now reflected in a departure from traditional social norms 'and the significance these have for age based identities'. This can be taken to mean that there is increasing resistance to and rejection of the social roles traditionally attached to different life-cycle stages, for example, the assumption that only young people should be in full-time education.

Arguably, given that the life-course is a process shared by all human beings, it should comprise the starting point for any debate on the future of domestic design – particularly a debate on housing design standards, which have traditionally been informed by stereotypical assumptions about the dimensions of the human body and behavioural interactions.

Taking into account the risk of isolating the debate on technical design standards from the wider socio-economic context, the next section will first, chronologically chart the developments in housing policy that have shaped the regulatory frameworks for housing quality standards, especially 'accessibility'; and second, it will move on to identify the key factors that led to the repositioning of the formerly discrete concept of 'accessibility' into the centre of the debate surrounding the future of housing quality criteria.

History and development of housing standards

Following the First World War, the advent of interventionist housing policies, largely aimed at eliminating poor-quality housing and increasing the housing stock, gave rise to a complex weave of inter-related issues that remain to this day. Whilst these cover a very wide-ranging number of areas, such as policies aimed at rent control, this section will focus on those that have more directly influenced housing quality and design. These include determining: (a) the limits of public expenditure on housing, (b) levels of housing need in relation to categories of people deemed as 'deserving' and 'undeserving', (c) the extent of regulatory frameworks governing standards of housing quality and design, and (d) the extent of tenure change.

The 1918 Tudor Walters Report was the first manual offering guidance on housing design and amenity standards, ranging from overall layout and minimum room sizes to advice on heating and lighting. It also stressed the importance of building to a high as opposed to a minimum standard, arguing that this would prove more economical in the long term. This embraced what was to be an ongoing debate as to which regulatory measures and housing standards were appropriate to satisfy the largely conflicting demands of housing reformers pressing for higher standards, local authorities concerned about long-term durability, and governments operating within fiscal constraints.

The principle of design flexibility to cater for wide-ranging inter-generational demands on domestic space was emphasised by the Tudor Walters Report. This was to be achieved by the provision of a parlour and/or a third bedroom. Such was the recognition, at this point in time, of the need for adaptable housing to accommodate all of the family members, including children, older people and/or wheelchair-using First World War veterans, that in 1919 an architectural competition in Scotland entitled 'Homes Fit for Heroes' stipulated this in the design brief. It recommended that the first of three bedrooms, 'where provided at ground floor … could be used as a bedroom to suit an elderly or disabled person', and that the parlour may be 'required to accommodate a double bed and a cot, or a bed for a child' (Wren *et al.* 2000: Appendix C2).

In the light of an overall improvement in the standard of living, accompanied by rising expectations that housing should be spacious enough to incorporate the growing range of domestic appliances, the period immediately following the Second World War saw a further review of housing standards (Cullingworth 1966). The ensuing Dudley Report 1944 and an official Housing Manual 1944 adopted the same line as the Tudor Walters Report, by requiring that all local authority housing comply with the minimum room sizes and circulation space prescribed in the guidelines. This regulatory mechanism, when combined with adjustments to levels of subsidy, provided central government with a means of exerting control over local authority housing standards and, in this case, raising them, thus reversing the gradual 'retreat' from the Tudor Walters Report's pre-war recommendations (Malpass and Murie 1994; Cole and Furbey 1994). This period, overseen by a Labour Government until 1951, has now become known as the time when public sector housing reached the highest space and amenity standards ever. The continuing appeal of local authority housing built between 1946 and 1951 is a mark of its enduring quality, and perhaps justifies the initially higher level of financial outlay, which at the time 'provoked charges of extravagance' (Cole and Furbey 1994: 98). The long-term sustainability of housing built at this time also supports the then Labour Minister of Health, Aneurin Bevan's vision: 'While we will be judged for a year or two by the number of houses we build, we shall be judged in ten years' time by the type of houses we build' (Foot 1973: 82, quoted in Malpass and Murie 1994: 75).

This period of high investment in local authority housing was, however, short lived. The incoming Conservative government changed tack, by switching the emphasis from quality of output to quantity, which led to a decline in standards of floor space and equipment. To Cole and Furbey (1994: 98), this policy shift was also indicative of a longer-term aim to 'displace public housing as the dominant mode of provision' by concentrating on the expansion of owner-occupation. This aim marked an important juncture in housing policy, as it signalled the beginning of the gradual residualisation of public housing. Until that point, such housing had been directed at meeting the 'general' needs of the whole population but, after that time, the term became more narrowly interpreted to mean the needs of younger families only. This excluded not only disabled and/or older people but also larger families, who did not conform to the idealised norm of the stereotypical nuclear family.

The advent of the Parker Morris standards: 'family' and 'other' needs

By 1959, when the floor space standards had dropped to 897 square feet for the average three-bedroom house from 1,000 square feet just prior to 1951, mounting criticism of the clearly diminishing standards led to the establishment of a Committee chaired by Sir Parker Morris. Their brief was to 'consider the standards and equipment applicable to family dwellings and other forms of residential accommodation, whether provided by public authorities or by private enterprise, and to make recommendations' (MHLG 1961: IV).

Compliance with the Parker Morris standards was a condition of government subsidy for all new public sector housing from 1967 to 1982. Private sector housing, however, at least in England and Wales, was not required to meet these standards. Instead, regulations centred on criteria such as sanitation and safety, and were indicative of the reluctance of successive governments to intervene further within a market-driven industry without very strong justification (Goodchild and Karn 1997: 165). Private housebuilders adopted their own system of self-regulation, as a form of consumer protection, developed by the National House Builders' Registration Council (NHBC). To Goodchild and Karn (1997: 165), however, the NHBC criteria focused more on 'the quality of construction than the quality of design', and extended only to offering guidance on minimal room sizes and amenities, which fell short of the Parker Morris standards.

The Parker Morris Report (MHLG 1961) was published in response to perceived rapidly changing social and economic trends, which it described as a 'revolution'. A key aim was to accommodate these lifestyle changes within flexible living spaces, responsive not just to current but future patterns of use and to 'guard against [the] over-crowded or cramped conditions' (MHLG 1961: 3) of the past. Therefore, the improvement of floor-space standards and heating were singled out as priorities, as extra space would be redundant if some parts of the house could not be used during colder weather.

The requirement for minimum room sizes was dropped (as they were seen as too prescriptive), and replaced by the estimated space for a standardised range of household activities, furniture, equipment, storage and circulation, which when aggregated comprised the overall floor-space. Although the Parker Morris floor-space standards are widely regarded as a universal benchmark against which housing standards have since been measured, they did not exceed the recommendations of either the Tudor Walters or Dudley Reports (Cole and Furbey 1994). Indeed, Goodchild and Furbey (1986: 80) caution that 'the standard floor area was and remains a functional minimum'.

Level of occupancy was determined by the number of bed-spaces and remained the key indicator of the average total floor-space. As Goodchild and Furbey (1986: 81) point out, 'the same "tight-fit" assumptions are repeated in the report's approach to occupancy ... the report recommends different standards for different household sizes and these standards have generally precluded the possibility of children or adults each having a separate bedroom or a spare bedroom being available to visitors'.

As open plan designs were discouraged on account of noise and loss of privacy, conventional room layouts continued to be recommended. The report (MHLG 1961: 9), however, lauded the benefits of an 'adaptable house', which 'could be easily altered as circumstances changed'. Interestingly, the advantages envisaged related to the ease of accommodating the changing needs of families throughout their life-course though, as shown below, this definition of life-course did not extend to older people. The report stressed that at present the adaptable house was 'some way from a practical reality because of the high cost and other difficulties', but it predicted it would become a 'necessity' in the future.

Charged with the task of recommending improvements to housing standards 'applicable to *family dwellings* and *other* forms of residential accommodation', the Parker Morris report explicitly focused on the needs of nuclear families. 'General' needs became clearly defined as the needs of 'families with children'; any household that did not conform to this definition was to be catered for by 'other' accommodation. The report stated that 'the way of life of a family changes radically over twenty or thirty years of the average family's development', so effectively the report defined the needs of older families who fell outside this age span as needs not for family dwellings but for 'other' forms of accommodation. This reflected the hegemony of the idealised representation of family life within social welfare, a stereotype that was little questioned at the height of the postwar consensus within social policy (Milner and Madigan 2004).

For those who did not conform to this definition, that is, households defined in the report as comprising 'married couples', 'single people', and 'elderly people',[1] smaller more appropriate dwelling units were advised for their more modest requirements. The report justified the assumption that floor-space measurements should be apportioned on the basis of household size and characteristics by arguing that 'family homes have to cater for a way of life that is much more complex than in smaller households. They have to accommodate individual and group interests and activities involving any member, or all the family, with or without visitors'.

The report was supported, not by design manuals, but by a series of Design Bulletins, which marked a departure from its predecessors, and covered social and ergonomic data relating to the use of space, safety, and children's play areas both inside and outside the home. Bulletin 1 (MHLG 1963), for example, offers detailed information on patterns of use of space within domestic interiors by 'younger' and 'older' families. The typical younger family is seen as comprising parents and three children, of seven years and younger, whilst the older family also comprises parents (mother working part-time) and three children, aged twenty-three years and younger. For both families, the daily routine of household activities is mapped from 7 a.m. to 11.30 p.m.: at 9.30 a.m., for instance, the mother of the younger family is expected to 'put the baby out in the pram' whilst 'the toddler plays outside. The toddler wanders in and out of the house. Mother needs to be able to see the children easily while she works' (MHLG 1963: 4). This stereotypical account of family life was strongly criticised by Darke (1984: 425), who points out that the 'emphasis particularly in some of the early Design Bulletins, has been on the typical household rather than on a range of requirements ... the needs of the young family tend to be given greater weight than any other group'.

By listing a series of household activities, which were not tied to designated room functions, the Parker Morris report aimed to promote the importance of maximising the flexibility of the use of space. Nevertheless, this message is somewhat contradicted by the schedule of typical furniture within each room outlined by Bulletin 1: the 'living space', for instance, was seen as likely to incorporate two or three easy chairs, a settee, a television set and small tables, along with a reasonable quantity of other possessions, such as a sewing box, a toy box, radiogram and bookcase.

The Parker Morris housing standards: a review of research

Clearly, both the Parker Morris report and the Design Bulletins were based on wide-ranging assumptions about lifestyle and the use of domestic space. No substantive evidence to support these claims was referenced in either the report or the Design Bulletins but Wilson (1982: 401) explained that they were based on a series of domestic activity based studies. He pointed out that 'the number of data sources used for the Design Bulletins and the range of activities they covered were small' and that 'the criteria on which these original sources based their recommendations were often not specified clearly'. Moreover, Darke (1984: 425) dismissed the research within this area as biased, on the basis that it 'concentrated on family households with dependent children, which form a minority of all households'.

By the early 1970s, it had become clear that the design guidelines should be updated and expanded to take into account the needs of children, older and disabled people (Wilson 1982). However, as disabled people were considered to have needs that fell outside the 'general' needs category, two laboratory based experimental research projects were carried out on ergonomics and the use of domestic space (Milner and Madigan 2004). The first comprised children, older people and non-disabled males, and the second, undertaken in 1973 by the Institute of Ergonomic

Research, comprised physically disabled and non-disabled people, testing a range of standard issue wheelchairs within a model house (Goldsmith 1974).

Yet, as Goodchild (1997) noted, as the focus centred on the dimensions of the human body and the physical environment, the influence of social and psychological factors was little considered. Although the research was useful in generating basic technical measurements for domestic activity spaces, which fed into the revised standards, it only offered a partial insight into the complexities of people-environment interactions. For not only did disabled people's needs continue to be regarded as separate from 'general' needs, the multi-dimensional utility of domestic space failed to be fully considered. Goodchild (1997: 77) cites the Building Research Establishment's (BRE) example of the main functions of a kitchen, where it may be used as a site of food production and consumption, but also as a 'focal point for social activity in the household'. This latter activity, however, is unlikely to be picked up in a controlled laboratory setting. Darke (1984: 427) also focused on kitchens, to argue for a less positivist approach to research into housing design. She suggested that: 'rather than searching for, say, the differences in the proportions of particular types of household who wish to eat meals in the kitchen, it would probably help architects more if qualitative findings could be presented which could sensitise them to the variety of possible ways in which dwellings are used'.

Following the publication of the Parker Morris Report in 1961, the Ministry of Housing and Local Government (MHLG) extended the scope of the research into housing built to Parker Morris standards from the small-scale activity based studies, to large-scale social surveys investigating users' satisfaction with the internal and external environment. Research undertaken by the MHLG and its successor the Department of the Environment (DoE), between 1961 and 1975, on the user preferences of approximately 4,000 women living on nearly seventy housing estates, found widespread satisfaction with the quality of the housing interiors (IoH/RIBA 1983). A follow up survey by the DoE in 1979, however, showed that 'the external environment could, in certain circumstances, outweigh equipment and floor space standards as a determinant of housing satisfaction' (IoH/RIBA 1983).

This latter finding was further investigated in a 1982 study of 430 tenants on four estates in Sheffield, two of which were built to Parker Morris standards and two built to lower standards. The research, which was undertaken by Goodchild and Furbey, showed that:

> tenants notice even small reductions in floor space compared to Parker Morris. On the other hand, the results also suggest that, if standards are to be improved beyond Parker Morris, floor space is not the main priority … The statistical patterns of responses suggest that the appearance of the estate is the most important influence on overall satisfaction.
>
> (Goodchild and Furbey 1997: 106)

Overall, the review of research into housing designed to Parker Morris standards indicates a tendency to adopt a reductionist approach, which fails to reflect the diversity of the population, as it is heavily biased towards the needs of younger nuclear families. Moreover, as Darke (1984) points out, the positivist emphasis, which draws heavily on the empirical research approaches followed by natural science, offers an incomplete picture of the relationship between patterns of use within the home and the arrangement and size of domestic space. Since 1981, with the wholesale shift in government policy away from local authority housing and towards acceptance of owner-occupation as the dominant tenure, little research has been undertaken that examines a wide ranging profile of users' feedback on housing design, with a view to updating housing standards.

Disabled and/or older people: the journey from 'other' to 'special' needs

As the definition of 'general' needs contracted to focus on the nuclear family, so the concept of 'special' needs gained ground. By the late 1960s, this trend was established within housing policy in the Cullingworth Report (MHLG 1969). The report's guidelines for allocating council houses singled out 'the disabled', 'the elderly', 'the single', 'students', 'the large family' and 'the homeless', as groups with 'important' needs. The transition from an emphasis on 'blanket' to 'special' needs allocation procedures signalled a shift in policy, away from area-based approaches addressing housing disadvantage, to targeting groups identified as vulnerable and 'deserving'. Area-based approaches had been criticised on the basis that 'they were often of least benefit to those whose living conditions were the worst', as they did not adequately reflect the diverse characteristics and needs of the population (Clapham and Smith 1990: 194). The trend towards incrementally reducing the scale of public sector housing provision, to a point where it would have a minimal role as a safety net supporting groups identified as in most need, now underpinned all policy and practice. The revised categories of housing need were reflected in the marked change in the profile of public sector tenants over the period. Cole and Furbey summarised this change:

> In 1938, 47 per cent of heads of households, for example, were skilled manual workers; 46 per cent were semi or unskilled manual workers; and only 7 per cent were pensioners or widows. This tenure profile began to alter significantly from the early 1960s onwards, due to the influx of greater numbers of elderly people, large family households and Supplementary Benefit (SB) claimants … The proportion of council tenants who were economically inactive increased from a mere 4.8 per cent in 1961 to 28 per cent by 1981.
>
> (Cole and Furbey 1994: 83–4)

However, as definitions of need became more tightly specified within housing policy and ensured eligibility to strictly rationed resources, so a parallel trend emerged as stereotyped groups resisted the discriminatory labelling process as separatist. This inherent contradiction and tension between the policy drive towards 'segregation' and welfare reformers' drive towards 'integration' became manifest within the housing policies developed throughout this period. Clapham and Smith (1990) identified two strategies adopted by pressure groups for overcoming this dilemma: first, the 'incremental' approach to reform; and second, the 'radical' approach. Those who adopted the incremental approach accepted as a starting point their special needs status, as they did not want to jeopardise the legitimacy of their claim for resources, but they also sought to expand this to accommodate a much wider range of needs. Thereby, according to Clapham and Smith (1990: 201), through encouraging the development of policies that 'de-categorise rather than stigmatise assisted groups, they promote examples of good practice which are flexible, geared to the individual needs of residents and integrative, rather than separating the recipients from mainstream society'. Yet, as Clapham and Smith (1990) point out, although this may prove a very practical approach, its narrow starting point suggests that it may not be flexible enough to meet the wide range of needs it aspires to address. Housing associations, for example, centring on the 'special' needs of particular groups, such as people with learning disabilities, or younger physically disabled people, have now begun to embrace a more inclusive philosophy of providing for and/or supporting people within mainstream housing developments. Their funding provision, however, remains tied to specific groups.

The 'radical' approach broadly equates with the 'social' model of disability. Those preferring this approach rejected the incremental approach and sought structural reform, 'which challenged the very notion of "special" needs' (Clapham and Smith 1990: 201). This reform largely took the form of disability rights legislation and mainstream adaptable housing responsive to 'all' design needs.

The Chronically Sick and Disabled Persons Act (CSDP) 1970 comprised the first legislative measure developed to offer social service support via local authorities to people defined as disabled under the National Assistance Act 1948. Under the terms of Section 2 and 3 of the Act, local authorities are required to assess the numbers and needs of disabled people, including appropriate housing provision, and to provide 'assistance with home adaptations, or the provision of additional facilities designed to secure greater safety, comfort or convenience'. This marked a major advance in recognising the state's role in providing for the housing needs of disabled people, for as Bull and Watts (1998: 18) pointed out, 'local authorities ... became responsible for ensuring that their housing stock was designed to be accessible to disabled people'.

It was now clear that the narrow focus of the Parker Morris standards and Design Bulletins on the needs of the 'average' family was out of step with this shift in policy direction towards catering for 'special' needs, particularly the needs of disabled people. The growing recognition of the need to accommodate the diversity of the population, however, did not discredit the stereotype; indeed, separate guidelines were developed for a number of target groups. These built upon the earlier circulars, offering advice on housing provision for older people. The design prescriptions were published periodically throughout the 1970s to complement the existing Parker Morris guidelines. The Design Bulletin 'Housing for Single People' (DoE 1971) focused on young single people and middle-aged 'unmarried' women. This was closely followed by the Circulars 'Mobility Housing', aimed at ambulant older people and/or part-time wheelchair users (DoE 1974), and 'Wheelchair Housing', fully accessible for use by full-time wheelchair users (DoE 1975).

Yet, the development of the 'mobility' and 'wheelchair' housing guidelines offer an early example of the contradictory policy trends outlined above. The Cullingworth Report (MHLG 1969) had included an extract of a letter by P.J. Dixon, the then Director of Housing at Newcastle-upon-Tyne, which suggested that the cost of ensuring slight modifications to general needs housing, if included at the outset of the design process, would be minimal. Dixon stated, 'the homes provided would be quite acceptable to ordinary families but would, in the course of time, be available for re-letting, by which time there may well be families with a handicapped member wanting such accommodation'. Further, the publication of the UN Resolution on Adaptable Housing in 1974 reinforced Dixon's message, by calling for the development of accessible mainstream dwellings, which could be adapted for the needs of older and disabled people at low cost. Nevertheless, the policy guidelines developed at this time did not follow this recommendation. Instead, a DoE circular issued in 1974 stressed that whilst marginal adaptations to ordinary housing would suffice for many older and disabled people, 'mobility' and 'wheelchair' designs were the most appropriate alternatives.

It has been contended, however, that both design standards operate from a flawed premise. Whereas Clapham and Smith (1990) suggested that the 'mobility' guidelines reflect the 'incremental' approach outlined above, Stewart *et al.* (1999) argued that the wheelchair guidelines reflect the 'individual/medical' model as they take the line that wheelchair users require purpose-built housing tailored to their atypical, hence 'special' physical needs. This contrasts with the philosophy of fully inclusive mainstream housing, which is accessible to all, including wheelchair users.

'Mobility' housing comprises Parker Morris space standards 'designed to be usable by disabled people without the need to negotiate steps and stairs' (BSI 1978), and includes an accessible entrance, circulation space, and a toilet for use by wheelchair users at ground floor level. Yet, Goldsmith (1974: 43) clearly differentiates 'mobility' from 'family' housing, by arguing that 'as a general rule family housing is not modifiable – while it would be advantageous if it could be, the primary need in mobility housing is dwelling units for small households'.

This latter point is telling, for it largely derives from the policy drive to ration the distribution of council housing whilst minimising extra costs, especially costs arising from what was regarded as the under occupation of floor-space. The contention that disabled and/or older people lived in smaller households, as they did not conform to normative assumptions of the average family, and required smaller accommodation with less floor-space, became received wisdom and little questioned. The traditional housing stock, however, had been designed and built around 'family' needs, and comprised few smaller one- and two-bedroom dwellings. This posed local authorities with a challenge, for, on the one hand, they were exhorted to accommodate greater numbers of people with 'special' needs whilst, on the other hand, their housing stock was seen as unsuitable. The solution was to manage the allocation process more effectively, by first, increasing the supply of newly built 'specially' designed small dwellings and second, reducing the under-occupation of 'family' size dwellings by encouraging 'single' householders to move from larger to smaller homes. Such was the importance of 'ensuring that the accommodation people occupied accurately reflected their requirements' (Tinker 1996: 113) that two DoE Circulars, 'Housing Needs and Action' (1975) and 'Better Use of Vacant and Under-Occupied Housing' (1976), focused on this issue.

The introductory paragraphs in both the housing design guidelines for single people and ambulant older and disabled people (DoE 1971; Goldsmith 1974) developed this theme. 'Middle-aged single people, usually women, who had taken over rented houses from their parents' (DoE 1971: 2) were singled out as under-occupying space, along with older and disabled people. Goldsmith (1974: 43) argued that 'the greater need for smaller units is attributable to the very much higher prevalence of handicap among old people: some 58 per cent of adult handicapped people are aged 65 and over, and most of the time live alone or in two person households'.

Clearly, the evidence suggests that what started as a pragmatic policy to increase the efficiency of allocation procedures became an entrenched normative assumption that the majority of disabled and/or older people were single adults or couples who preferred to live alone and required specially designed small dwellings; or, if they occupied larger council dwellings, it was assumed that they would prefer to down-size to smaller units, and move on to make way for needy families.

Throughout the 1970s, local authorities were required by the CSDP Act 1970 to address older and/or disabled people's housing needs by building a small proportion (less than 5 per cent) of their new housing stock to mobility and wheelchair standards (Morris 1988). Ironically, however, the policy thrust towards special needs housing provision, which placed an emphasis on the need for pre-dominantly one-bedroom properties built to 'ambulant' or 'wheelchair' standards, also led to a problem anticipated by the Cullingworth Report a decade earlier (MHLG 1969), namely, the under-occupation and 'waste' of 'specially designed dwellings'. Morris's (1988: 5) study of the housing requirements of disabled people demonstrated that the stereotyping of older and disabled people's needs led to a clear mismatch between supply and demand, resulting in the under-provision of larger accessible dwellings. She found that 'whereas 59 per cent of the supply of special needs housing is of one bedroom properties, 65 per cent of the demand is for two, three and four bedroom properties'. A further problem, also highlighted by Stewart *et al.* (1999: 10), was the location of particularly wheelchair accessible dwellings, which were often sited alongside supported housing developments or 'another "special" facility such as a day centre for disabled people'. This practice further compounded the geographical segregation of disabled people into 'special needs' enclaves.

From 'special' needs to inclusive housing standards

The publication of British Standard (BS) 5619 in 1978 was the first Code of Practice for the design of housing suitable for disabled people, specifically aimed at raising the accessibility levels of new build 'ordinary' housing. This marked a departure from both the 'mobility' and 'wheelchair' housing design guidelines, as it now specifically embraced private as well as social sector housing, and indicated a turning point towards the recognition that the private sector house building industry should be encouraged to integrate access guidelines into their designs. Moreover, the wider remit of BS 5619 demonstrated the early influence of the disability movement, and its emphasis on integrative as opposed to segregative 'special needs' housing policies. However, just as disability campaigners criticised the 'general needs' housing standards for excluding their requirements, so the content of BS 5619, like the 'mobility' and 'wheelchair' guidelines before it, was largely informed by the 1973 research study by the Institute of Ergonomic Research based solely on the needs of adult wheelchair users (discussed earlier). This reflected the bias of the disability movement in favour of younger mobility impaired adults. Further, although BS 5619 was more generous than the 'mobility' standard, its adoption did little to increase the supply of accessible dwellings. This was due not only to the shortcomings of its content, which did not embrace the principle of 'adapt-ability' for all stages of the life-course, but also to the marked policy shift towards privatisation and de-regulation within housing policy and practice during the 1980s, which considerably weakened its influence.

Under the Thatcher government, both the repeal of the Parker Morris space standards in 1982 and the 1988 Housing Act had a significant downward impact on housing standards. By reducing the level of public subsidy (in the form of Housing Association Grant) available to Registered Social Landlords, and increasing the proportion of funding to be raised by private finance, the 1988 Act led to cutbacks in space standards and amenities. Research findings (Walentowicz 1992; Karn and Sheridan 1994) indicated that, whilst just over a half of housing association developments built in 1989/1990 fell more than 5 per cent below the Parker Morris minimum threshold, this proportion had increased to over two-thirds by 1991–1992.

It became clear from the above evidence, which examined both social and private sector housing design standards, that not only were private house-builders strongly averse to voluntarily incorporating access codes into their designs (Milner and Madigan 2001) but the average floor space of their properties was in fact falling (Karn and Sheridan 1994). This was largely due to the focus on the need to increase the supply of small starter homes at the bottom end of the housing market to encourage people who might have once rented local authority properties onto the first rung of owner-occupation.

Further, the implementation of the National Health Service and Community Care Act 1990 in 1993, led to two key outcomes: first, the acceleration of the rate of the resettlement of older and disabled people from long-stay institutions and hospitals into supported and mainstream accommodation in the community; second, the increased emphasis on enabling people to stay put within their own homes with appropriate packages of support. This led to further change in the profile of social rented tenants towards people with health and support needs. So, just as the number of affordable, accessible properties for rent was decreasing, so the number of people with health and support needs requiring suitable accommodation was increasing, resulting in a growing needs-supply gap.

Pressure from, on the one hand, disability campaigners, local authorities and housing associations, concerned about the housing stock's diminishing sustainability and ability to address people's needs, and, on the other hand, from the general public, who were increasingly disaffected with the size and quality of new build private sector housing (Angle and Malam 1998), led to a call for the regulation of accessibility standards in both social and private sector housing.

All this pressure and concern raised the question as to what type and level of accessibility was appropriate. By this point in the early 1990s, there were two main approaches to choose from: the 'visitability' standard, launched in 1985 by representatives from the private house-building industry, disability organisations and the government; and the 'Lifetime Homes' standard, launched in 1989 by the Helen Hamlyn Trust and later promoted by the Joseph Rowntree Foundation in 1992.

The 'visitability' standard largely derived from the 1974 'mobility' standard, but was now updated with the prescription that all new housing should be minimally accessible on the ground floor to wheelchair users and should have an accessible entrance level toilet. This marked a major advance as the previous 'mobility' standard had a limited application to predominantly one-bedroom, single-storey dwellings.

Alternatively, the 'Lifetime Homes' (LTH) standard had grown from the principles outlined by the UN Resolution on Adaptable Housing in 1974. Initiated with the aim of creating attractive, affordable, and flexible homes, LTH were designed to offset the fears of private house-builders and the house buying public alike that access features are costly and ugly additions, detracting from house value and marketability. The LTH concept rested on the principle that housing design should be more responsive to the changing needs of people throughout their life-course, and should therefore enable older and disabled people to 'stay put'. Based on sixteen key design criteria comprising a blueprint which can translate into most popular English house types, it embraced the idea that housing should accommodate a wider range of physical needs without any significant internal or external design features that mark the dwelling out as 'special' or 'different'. This blueprint is intended to enable wheelchair circulation and turning space on the ground floor level. Central to this life-course approach is the provision of sufficient space for conversion of a downstairs room to a bedroom and for a through floor lift should occupants' needs change (Carroll *et al.* 1999). It is important to point out, however, that LTH falls far short of a standard that would allow wheelchair users full independent living and unrestricted access to all living areas within a home.

The Housing Corporation introduced the Scheme Development Standards in 1993, which comprised a list of essential and desirable space and amenity criteria. All new housing association developments were henceforth required to comply with these standards to qualify for Housing Association Grant (HAG). The standards were revised in 1995 to include key accessibility criteria broadly approximating to the 'visitability' standards, which were less onerous than the LTH standards, although at that point the standards were so diluted that an entrance level toilet was only required in five-person units or above (Goldsmith 1997).

Although the strengthened controls relating to housing quality within the social rented sector marked a policy reversal from the repeal of the Parker Morris Standards in 1982, there was still considerable reluctance on the part of the then Conservative government to legislate for accessible new build private housing. This was due to strong opposition from the private house-building industry in a climate of de-regulation. The disability movement, however, proved an even stronger force to contend with. Indeed, the enactment of the Disability Discrimination Act (DDA) in late 1995 is a testament to the movement's achievements. After many failed private members' bills over the previous decade, disability rights were at last enshrined within legislation that challenged discrimination in a number of areas such as employment, education, and access to goods, services and facilities. The phased implementation of the Act has been ongoing until the time of writing, 2004. The measure 'imposes a duty on organisations as employers and service providers not to give a disabled person less favourable treatment where the reason for the treatment can be removed or made less than substantial by a reasonable adjustment' (NHF 1999: 4). This has wide ranging implications for all the services provided not only by housing associations but also by private sector housing developers, who must take measures not to discriminate against disabled people. The enforcement of the Act may prove problematic, because so much hinges on the debatable definition of 'reasonable'.

A key element of the new policy is the need to avoid stereotyping disabled people as a homogeneous group with similar housing needs, and to provide inclusive services that are responsive to their diversity and difference. It is now incumbent upon housing associations to monitor and review all their services with a view to moving away from the entrenched 'special needs' approach that has informed so much of past policy and practice. However, given that the differences between groups are complex and that their needs often conflict, as discussed earlier in this chapter, this aim is likely to prove very problematic when attempting to translate it into future approaches.

Although, as the Scottish Federation of Housing Associations (2002) points out, the DDA's remit does 'not apply directly to housing stock', the Act nevertheless provided a useful platform for campaigners to successfully lobby for the incorporation of mandatory access codes in all new private sector housing. This led in 1999 to the amendment of the Building Regulations requiring access for disabled people to public buildings (Approved Document Part M in England, Part Q of the Technical Standards, Scotland). These were extended to private dwellings, which are now required to meet the minimal criteria of 'visitability'.

Yet, in spite of the recent implementation of the regulations, they have been widely criticised by disability campaigners and social housing providers for neither being far-reaching enough nor incorporating lifetime homes criteria (Milner and Madigan 2001). A further problem identified by Imrie and Hall (2001: 43) is their bias in favour of people with mobility impairments. They argue that access standards have 'over the years tended to promote mobility impairment (related to wheelchair users) as the problem to be re-addressed rather than seeking to understand impairment as a myriad of possible, often changing, bodily conditions'.

In the light of the foregoing shortcomings of the 'visitability' standards, AD Part M is currently under review, and it looks likely that the standards will be incrementally developed along the lines of the Lifetime Homes design criteria. Yet, close analysis of lifetime homes shows that they too are based on a stereotypical assumption of the life-course, which centres on the needs of older physically impaired people and overlooks needs commonly occurring at earlier stages of the life cycle. A recent post-occupancy evaluation of 302 residents' perceptions of LTH homes found that the two key determinants of user satisfaction were 'the [older] age of residents and the presence or absence of children' (Sopp and Wood 2001: 6). Forty-four per cent of families with children had made changes to their homes, as compared with 25 per cent of those without children. The former group cited child safety as the key reason for carrying out such adjustments. The same group 'were also more likely to mention the size or shape of the rooms (22 per cent)' (Sopp and Wood 2001: 15), as well as stating a preference for 'an open plan design with few or no corridors ... the overwhelming reason was that it would feel more spacious or make better use of space' (Sopp and Wood 2001: 9).

Moreover, although it took just over twenty years to update the separate access codes to housing (BS 5619,1978) and public buildings (BS 5810,1979), and amalgamate both into one document (BS 8300 2001), the content of the revised standard continues to focus almost exclusively on the needs of physically impaired adults. It is noted in the foreword that: 'it has become clear that further research will be necessary into risks and inconvenience in buildings to people with sensory impairment'. It further adds that: 'this British Standard does not ... make specific recommendations relating to the use of buildings by children'.

Clearly, the problems identified within the 'visitability' and 'Lifetime Homes' standards derive from a narrowly conceived approach to disability and the life-course, yet this itself can be traced back to the dearth of empirical and interpretative research evidence informing the content of both these standards, much of which is over thirty years old. Both sets of guidelines comprise an amalgam of details drawn from previous design prescriptions, all of which are largely based on the small-scale activity based ergonomic studies undertaken between 1959 and 1973. True, Goldsmith's 1968 Norwich-based social survey (1974), investigating the perceptions of nearly 300 wheelchair users in relation to the physical accessibility of housing and public buildings, helped to shape his view that wheelchair users required accessible 'ordinary' housing. Essentially, however, Goldsmith saw mobility housing as a relatively inexpensive extension of ordinary housing, for ambulant and non-permanent wheelchair users, with little scope for adaptability. He envisaged that the achievement of full accessibility throughout the home would be available only to a small minority of permanent wheelchair users (in 'wheelchair housing'). He argued this for pragmatic reasons, on grounds of cost, but his approach may have served to reinforce the 'special needs' stereotype of disabled people as 'wheelchair-bound'.

This process of cobbling together and merging dated technical measurements and design notes, which in turn are based on dated lifestyle assumptions, when combined with the lack of recent research into the needs of disabled people, has rendered some of the standards so out of date as to be obsolete (Milner and Madigan 2004). This was a point stressed by Wren *et al.* who stated:

> any new standards would first require research into how people use their homes and what future trends may be. The implications of social and economic changes and increased use of technology in the home, all of which have accelerated in recent years, have not been studied in relation to the science of space standards as they have evolved since the Second World War.
>
> (Wren *et al.* 2000: 17)

This approach, albeit on a small scale, has recently been adopted in a research project undertaken by Allen *et al.* (2002), which examined the housing needs of a sample of forty-four visually impaired children. Adopting an ethnographic research method it highlighted how visually impaired children increasingly familiarise themselves with and memorise their environments to a point where they can successfully develop memory maps and navigate potential hazards. It was shown the problems lay less in the inherent design of the internal environment and more in the design of the external environment, where moving obstacles such as cars posed the greatest problems. This usefully offered not only an alternative to the predominantly positivist research approach adopted in this field to date, but also insight into a group who have been little studied due to the bias towards physically impaired adults.

The way forward: towards accommodating diversity and difference

The increase in social groups claiming marginalised status, combined with the reconstruction of their boundaries as intersecting and relational, has led to a policy shift in favour of the social integration of 'all', whilst at the same time retaining an awareness of group-defined identity. The phrase 'accommodating difference and diversity', coined to describe this agenda, is strongly reminiscent of the vision of democratic cultural pluralism outlined by Young (1990: 163), who argued: 'the good society does not eliminate or transcend group differences. Rather, there is equality among socially and culturally differentiated groups, who mutually respect one another and affirm one another in their differences'.

So what is the way forward for the development of housing standards? The foregoing evidence suggests the policy thrust should be less centred on the substantive characteristics and needs of social groups, such as older and/or disabled people, and more on fluid and dynamic individual and group differences. This objective is reflected in the White Paper recently published by the DTI (2004) which proposes replacing the Equal Opportunities Commission, the Commission for Racial Equality and the Disability Rights Commission with a single equality and human rights commission, which would be comprehensive enough to address the needs of 'all people', including those falling outside the parameters of the existing commissions.

This, however, prompts the question as to how such an aim might be achieved in practice. The proposed amalgamation reflects an attempt to embrace, integrate and value *all* human diversity, but there is a clear risk, in the process, of losing sight of group identities and needs in a melting pot of fractured individual differences. And what are the policy implications? Would this lead to reductionist interventions, comprising either 'a one size fits all' structural reform (favouring the dominant and/or majority culture, as evidenced by the bias towards mobility impairments within the disability movement) or approaches tailored to individual requirements that do not take into account the need for structural change?

The theme of 'accommodating diversity' has now been assimilated into the national Housing Corporation's key policy guidelines aimed at social housing providers such as the Scheme Development Standards (2000) and Good Practice Note 4: Race, Equality and Diversity (2002). Yet, the guidelines are often contradictory for, on the one hand, they assert the need to accommodate diversity, often in general and imprecise terms, whilst, on the other, they continue to promote separate policies relating to the housing needs of older people, disabled people and ethnic minorities. There is a clear need to review these stereotypical categories, because they overlook the intersecting and relational elements of group differences and indicate they have substantive differences and needs. They suggest, for instance, that older people comprise a separate social group from disabled people, and that ethnic minorities have little in common with either. This confusion reflects some of the complex philosophical and practical issues arising from the debate relating to mooted amalgamation of the three equality commissions outlined above. Clearly, it is of critical importance that housing policy makers engage with this debate and clarify issues of relevance to policy and practice, rendering them explicit prior to developing future research and policy strategies.

Conclusions

A review charting the chronological development of housing standards, as they relate to housing quality and design, from 1918 to the present day, has highlighted the changing definition of 'general' needs, which from the outset referred to 'family' needs. Yet, this early concept of 'family', which embraced older and/or disabled people's needs, along with larger families, became progressively eroded and re-defined to a point where it applied only to younger families in housing built after the Second World War. This change in household profile ran in parallel with a gradual policy thrust away from state housing towards owner-occupation. This led in turn to the progressive residualisation of local authority housing, which was intended to act only as a safety net for those deemed most 'deserving'. By the time the Parker Morris Report was published in 1961, the hegemony of the stereotypical 'younger' nuclear family had become entrenched within the post war social settlement of welfare and was reflected by the report's central focus on 'nuclear' as opposed to 'non-nuclear' households – or, to use the report's terminology, 'family dwellings', in preference to 'other forms of residential accommodation'. The latter phrase was later substituted by the now familiar term 'special needs' housing.

Just as this process of clearly differentiating between 'general' and 'special' needs became more established and tightly specified, so a parallel trend emerged as the older and/or disabled people's movements challenged the ideology of such separatist approaches. Although the increasing gap between 'general' and 'special' needs proved difficult to bridge, the philosophy of inclusive housing design, nevertheless, slowly and incrementally gained ground, to a point where current accessibility standards and recent legislative measures now espouse this approach. Indeed, the 'social' model of disability, derived from physically disabled activists, has been shown to be biased and slightly out of step with the current drive towards accommodating the full spectrum of diversity and difference in terms of individuals and groups.

This chapter has shown that the evidence underpinning housing design standards to date was produced by narrow and positivist research strategies and policy interventions. This in turn led to stereotyped design prescriptions that focused on the technical and quantifiable aspects of design, which failed to capture the full range of (a) users and (b) patterns of use within domestic space. This trend is exemplified by the current access guidelines relating to housing, which are based on research that is over thirty years old and biased in favour of wheelchair users.

In the light of the impact of rapid technological, demographic and socio-economic changes, there is an urgent need for a complete revision of existing housing design standards. It is clear that Darke's (1984) plea for more up-to-date empirical and interpretative research evidence to inform future standards continues to be relevant and should no longer remain unheeded.

It is suggested that, when considering dimensions of the human body and behavioural interactions within domestic space, one way forward would be to start with approaches based on the life-course as a unifying experience, which also intersects with all other types of social identity. However, it is important to be aware of the risk of lapsing into partial, stereotyped approaches that overlook or misrepresent the needs of, for instance, children, as occurred with the lifetime homes standard.

Note

1 Disabled people were considered to deviate from normative assumptions of the average family, to such an extent, that they were not even included under the category of 'other' accommodation in the Parker Morris report.

References

Abberley, P. (1998) 'The spectre at the feast: disabled people and social theory', in T. Shakespeare (ed.) *The Disability Reader: Social Science Perspectives*, London: Cassell.

Allen, C., Milner, J. and Price, D. (2002) *Home is Where the Start is: The Housing and Urban Experiences of Visually Impaired Children*, Bristol: Policy Press.

Angle, H. and Malam, S. (1998) *Kerb Appeal: The External Appearance and Site Layout of New Houses*, Report Number One, London: The Popular Housing Group.

Barnes, C., Mercer, G. and Shakespeare, T. (1999) *Exploring Disability: A Sociological Introduction*, Cambridge: Polity Press.

British Standards Institution (1978) *BS 5619: Code of Practice for Design of Housing for the Convenience of Disabled People*, London: BSI.

Bull, R. and Watts, V. (1998) 'The legislative and policy context', in R. Bull (ed.) *Housing Options for Disabled People*, London: Jessica Kingsley Publishers.

Carroll, C., Cowans, J. and Darton, D. (1999) *Meeting Part M and Designing Lifetime Homes*, York: Joseph Rowntree Foundation.

Carter, J. (ed.) (1998) *Postmodernity and the Fragmentation of Welfare*, London: Routledge.

Clapham, D. and Smith, S. (1990) 'Housing policy and "special needs"', *Policy and Politics*, 18, 3: 193–205.

Cole, I. and Furbey, R. (1994) *The Eclipse of Council Housing*, London: Routledge.

Cullingworth, J. B. (1966) *Housing and Local Government in England and Wales*, London: George Allen & Unwin.

Darke, J. (1984) 'Architects and user requirements in public sector housing: towards an adequate understanding of user requirements in housing', *Environment & Planning B: Planning & Design*, 11: 417–33.

Department for Trade and Industry (DTI) (2004) *Fairness for All: A New Commission for Equality and Human Rights*, White Paper, London: The Stationery Office.

General Household Survey (2002) *Living in Britain: Results from the 2001 General Household Survey*, London: The Stationery Office.

Goldsmith, S. (1974) 'Mobility housing', *The Architect's Journal*, 3 July: 43–50.

—— (1997) *Designing for the Disabled: A New Paradigm*, Oxford: Architectural Press.

Goodchild, B. (1997) *Housing and the Urban Environment: A Guide to Housing Design, Renewal and Urban Planning*, London: Blackwell Science.

Goodchild, B. and Furbey, R. (1986) 'Standards in housing design: a review of the main changes since the Parker Morris Report (1961)', *Land Development Studies*, 3: 79–99.

Goodchild, B. and Karn, V. (1997) 'Standards, quality control and housing building in the UK', in P. Williams (ed.) *Directions in Housing Policy*, London: Paul Chapman.

Harrison, M. with Davis, C. (2001) *Housing, Social Policy and Difference: Disability, Ethnicity, Gender and Housing*, Bristol: Policy Press.

Hockey, J. and James, A. (2003) *Social Identities across the Life Course*, Basingstoke: Palgrave Macmillan.

Hughes, G. (1998) 'Picking up the remains: the welfare state settlements of the post-second world war in the UK', in G. Hughes and G. Lewis (eds) *Unsettling Welfare: The Reconstruction of Social Policy*, London: Routledge/Open University.

Hughes, B. and Paterson, K. (1997) 'The social model of disability and the disappearing body: towards a sociology of impairment', *Disability & Society*, 12, 3: 325–40.

Imrie, R. and Hall, P. (2001) *Inclusive Design: Designing and Developing Accessible Environments,* London: Spon Press.

Institute of Housing and Royal Institute of British Architects (1983) *Homes for the Future: Standards for New Housing Development*, London: IoH/RIBA.

James, A. and Prout, A. (1997) 'A new paradigm for the sociology of childhood? Provenance, promise and problems', in A. James and A. Prout (eds) *Constructing and Re-constructing Childhood: Contemporary Issues in the Sociological Study of Childhood*, London: Falmer Press.

Karn, V. and Sheridan, L. (1994) *New Homes in the 1990's: A Study of Design, Space and Amenity in Housing Association and Private Sector Production*, Manchester: University of Manchester/Joseph Rowntree Foundation.

Leonard, P. (1997) *Postmodern Welfare: Reconstructing an Emancipatory Project*, London: Sage.

Malpass, P. and Murie, A. (1994) *Housing Policy and Practice*, 4th edn, London: Macmillan Press.

Marks, D. (1999) *Disability: Controversial Debates and Psychosocial Perspectives*, London: Routledge.

Milner, J. and Madigan, R. (2001) 'The politics of accessible housing in the UK', in S. Peace and C. Holland (eds) *Inclusive Housing in an Ageing Society*, Bristol: Policy Press.

—— (2004) 'Regulation and innovation: rethinking "inclusive" housing design', *Housing Studies*, 19, 5: 727–44.

Ministry of Housing and Local Government (the Parker Morris Report) (1961) *Homes for Today and Tomorrow*, London: HMSO.

—— (1963) *Space in the Home*, London: HMSO.

—— (1969) *Council Housing: Purposes, Procedures and Priorities*, Ninth Report of the Housing Management Sub-Committee of the Central Housing Advisory Committee, London: HMSO.

Morris, J. (1988) *Freedom to Lose: Housing Policy and People with Disabilities*, London: Shelter.

National Housing Federation (1999) *Equality in Housing: Guidance for Tackling Discrimination on the Grounds of Disability and Promoting Equality*, London: National Housing Federation.

O'Brien, M. and Penna, S. (1998) *Theorising Welfare: Enlightenment and Modern Society*, London: Sage.

Oliver, M. (1990) *The Politics of Disability*, Basingstoke: Macmillan.

Priestley, M. (2000) 'Adults only: social policy and the life course', *Journal of Social Policy*, 29, 3: 421–439.

—— (ed.) (2001) *Disability and the Life Course: Global Perspectives*, Cambridge: Cambridge University Press.

Scottish Federation of Housing Associations (2002) *The Disability Discrimination Act: Guidance Booklet No 13*, Edinburgh: SFHA.

Sopp, L. and Wood, L. (2001) *Living in a Lifetime Home: A Survey of Residents and Developers' Views*, Bristol: Policy Press/Joseph Rowntree Foundation.

Stewart, J., Harris, J. and Sapey, B. (1999) 'Disability and dependency: origins of "special needs" housing for disabled people', *Disability & Society*, 14, 1: 5–20.

Tinker, A. (1996) *Older People in Modern Society*, 4th edn, London: Longman.

Walentowicz, P. (1992) *Housing Standards after the Act: A Survey of Space and Design Standards on Housing Association Projects in 1989/90*, Research Report 15, London: National Federation of Housing Assocations/Joseph Rowntree Foundation.

Watson, N. (1998) 'Enabling identity: disability, self and citizenship', in T. Shakespeare (ed.) *The Disability Reader: Social Science Perspectives*, London: Cassell.

Wilson, J.R. (1982) 'The measurement of domestic activity space', *Ergonomics*, 25, 5: 401–18.

Wren, G., Rutherford, R. and Pickles, J. (2000) *Space Standards in Dwellings: Pre and Post 1987*, Edinburgh: Scottish Executive, Building Control Division.

Young, I. (1990) *Justice and the Politics of Difference*, Princeton, NJ: Princeton University Press.

9 Squatting since 1945

The enduring relevance of material need

Kesia Reeve

Introduction

Squatting is largely absent from policy and academic debate and is rarely conceptualised, as a problem, as a symptom, or as a social or housing movement. Drawing
on available literature about squatting in England immediately after the end of the
Second World War,[1] primary research examining squatting in London from 1968
through the 1970s,[2] and primary research into squatting in three English case
study locations in 2002,[3] this chapter explicates the link between squatting and
the housing policy context in which it exists.[4] It shows that in each of these periods
squatting provided a means through which individuals – in particular those excluded
from housing consumption through traditional channels – responded to their
positions of material need and inequality, rooted in those housing policies and
practices of which unmet housing needs, disadvantage and exclusion are a
consequence.

The chapter will also show that, in the 1960s and 1970s the focus on material
(in this case housing) need was overlaid by an emphasis on creating cultural
alternatives, of 'identity politics' and a positive acknowledgement that squatting,
as a tenure, lay out with the dictates of traditional channels of housing allocation
and consumption and traditional power relations between consumer and provider.
This 'cultural shift' in squatting is reflected in sociological debate, embodied in
New Social Movement (NSM) theory and the wider discourse of sociologists such
as Giddens and Beck. Broadly, these theorists suggest that fundamental changes
in the nature of modern society have rendered social and material needs and
inequalities less salient in contemporary capitalist societies. It is argued that there
has been a shift away from traditional economic or class issues towards concerns
focused on issues such as quality of life and identity. However, based on evidence
about squatting in these three eras, the chapter will argue that this debate, whilst
accurately reflecting some aspects of squatting in the 1960s/1970s, over-emphasises
the cultural and underplays the endurance and continued relevance of the unequal

distribution of material resources such as housing. Citizen concerns and conflict are reduced to a cultural 'post-class politics' realm which is removed from the reality of excluded social classes, who act to resolve their housing needs in the face of scarcity and differential access to resources, directly related to the policy actions of state institutions.

The changing nature of politics in modern society

According to the sociologists Anthony Giddens (1991, 1994), Ulrich Beck (2003, 1999) and those grouped under the banner of 'New Social Movement theory' (e.g. Touraine 1981; Melucci 1989, 1995; Offe 1985; Habermas 1985, 1987) the nature of politics has undergone profound changes over the last fifty years. Thus Giddens and Beck, for example, suggest that the modern period can be divided into two distinct phases: a primary (or early modern) and a secondary (or late modern) phase. NSM theorists similarly argue that there has been a qualitative shift in the nature of modern capitalism, towards a society which can broadly be termed 'post-industrial' but which is variously termed as 'complex' (Melucci 1989), 'programmed' (Touraine 1985) or 'advanced' (Habermas 1971). For Giddens (1991), the primary phase of modernity can be characterised by a concern with what he terms 'emancipatory politics', which is a:

> generic outlook concerned above all with liberating individuals and groups from constraints which adversely affect their life chances ... The objective of emancipatory politics is either to release under-privileged groups from their unhappy condition, or to eliminate the relative differences between them ... Emancipatory politics is concerned to reduce or eliminate *exploitation, inequality* and *oppression*
>
> (Giddens 1991: 210, 211; emphasis in original)

This means, of course, that politics in primary modernity is concerned with issues such as differential access to material resources, such as housing. Secondary modernity, on the other hand, is said to be characterised by culturally orientated 'life politics' which emphasises the normative and moral rather than the distribution of material 'goods' (Pakulski 1991), hence Beck's claim that '"the struggle for one's daily bread" has lost its urgency as a cardinal problem overshadowing everything else, compared to the material subsistence of the first half of this century' (Beck 2003: 20). Life politics, then, centres on issues of quality of life and identity (Inglehart 1977, 1990; Habermas 1987; Melucci 1995), and lifestyle choices:

> Life politics does not primarily concern the conditions which liberate us in order to make choices: it is a politics *of* choice. While emancipatory politics is a politics of life chances, life politics is a politics of lifestyle ... It is a

> politics of self-actualisation in a reflexively ordered environment ... Life politics concerns political issues which flow from processes of self-actualisation in post-traditional contexts.
>
> (Giddens 1991: 214)

In the first part of this chapter I argue that, in line with Giddens' and Beck's conceptualisation of primary modernity, squatting can be understood as an expression of inequality, life chances, and material subsistence. Squatting exists and emerges as an attempt by individual households, excluded from social housing, unable to access private accommodation or otherwise condemned to living in a high-cost, poor quality private rented sector, to meet their material need for low-cost housing – needs which are rooted in the particulars of the housing policy context in each era. In this part of the chapter, I also argue that in the postwar period and the 1960s and 1970s squatting can also be seen as a political *movement,* emphasising the legitimacy of squatting as a form of housing consumption given the failure of policy makers to provide any realistic alternatives. A key focus of squatting, then, has been on the politics of legitimate access to material resources, such as housing.

In the second part of the chapter, I concur with Giddens, Beck and NSM theorists that squatting can also latterly (in the 1960s and 1970s) be regarded as a form of lifestyle politics, fitting closely their conceptualisation of social action, social movements and concerns in secondary modernity (or post-industrial, complex, or advanced society, if adopting the terminology of NSM theorists). However, emphatically, this is not because squatters have been released from their 'unhappy condition'. Many have not. Indeed we will see that squatters in the 1960s and 1970s were as much concerned with 'material subsistence' as they were with developing alternative lifestyles, and the experiences of many present day squatters reveal the endurance of 'the struggle for one's daily bread'.

Squatting as an expression of material need

As the dominant tenure of the immediate postwar period, it was the private rented sector that provided opportunities to low-income households to satisfy their housing needs. However, although private house building increased in the inter-war years, the majority were built for owner occupation, a large proportion of private rented housing was transferred into the owner occupied sector and, combined with slum clearance, the private rented sector lost about half a million dwellings (Malpass and Murie 1994). This was followed during the war by a halt in house building, 200,000 homes were lost to bombing and a further quarter of a million were made uninhabitable. This left approximately 700,000 fewer dwellings in 1945 than there had been in 1939 (Branson 1989). In addition to increasing scarcity of private rented accommodation, conditions were often poor: rent control had been in effect in one form or another since 1915 (the Increase of Rent and Mortgage Interest [War Restrictions] Act) and, although this ensured *affordable* rent levels, it provided little incentive for landlords to repair and maintain their properties. The redirection of housing policy in the 1930s to address these poor conditions through slum clearance programmes made some headway but local authority estimates of the numbers of unfit properties had been grossly underestimated so that, despite the demolition of a quarter of a million slums between 1933 and 1938, a further quarter of a million homes remained unfit when Britain entered the war in 1939 and the programme was abolished.

These policies had a direct impact on the quality and availability of housing by 1945 and, correspondingly, we find postwar squatters emphasising their experiences of being homeless, living in severely overcrowded accommodation, or in acute conditions in decaying properties with infestations and lacking amenities. For example, one squatting family of four is recorded as having previously been living in one room with just a gas ring, no running water and without the space for their second child to live with them. Another family of four, previously living in two rooms, is recorded as saying 'we have had furniture dockets for nine months but we couldn't buy anything because there was no room to put it' (quoted in Hill 1946: 14). And another:

> He recalled that after returning home from the Far East where he'd been a prisoner of war, he joined his wife and two children at a house in Watford where he had been obliged to sleep on the floor. Bugs were running up and down and the door came off in his hand. They moved to Hammersmith where it was not bugs but mice which were the main problem; you could not tell where the decay stopped and the bomb damage started.
>
> (Branson 1989: 15)

When squatting emerged again in the 1960s, housing shortage in the low-cost private rented sector remained a pertinent issue, with the ideology of 1950s Conservative housing policy having had a direct impact on the supply of affordable private rented accommodation. For example, although designed to rejuvenate a diminishing private rented sector through rent decontrol, the 1957 Rent Act failed to halt this decline. By 1966 private rented accommodation accounted for just 24 per cent of the housing stock, compared to 61 per cent in 1947 (CHAC 1969), and rents had risen sharply. By 1960 '... the full impact of demand for housing in London was felt; rents were rising by 50,100 and occasionally 200 per cent' (Banting 1979: 19). The consequence of the massive shrinkage of this tenure, and the rising cost associated with it, was housing stress to low-income households. Banting, for example, comments that 'the poor, the elderly and immigrants were thus left to compete for a dwindling amount of decaying property. High rents, homelessness, evictions and exploitation were the consequences' (Banting 1979: 18).

These kinds of consequences and competition were commonplace experiences reported by squatters in the 1960s and 1970s. The scarcity of affordable private rented accommodation featured prominently as a factor shaping people's decisions (or necessity) to squat, as they described 'queuing round the block' for high priced bedsit accommodation:

> I got a job in Islington ... I desperately needed somewhere to live in Islington and there wasn't anywhere. There certainly wasn't anywhere affordable.
> (Squatter in London in the mid-1970s)

> I remember looking at private rented places at that time and the price still sticks in my mind. It seems ridiculously cheap now but it was 12 quid for a one bedroom flat which was just impossible then.
> (Squatter in London in the 1970s)

Thus, in both the 1940s and the 1960s/1970s the private rented sector was failing to satisfy the housing needs of many low-income households. The question, then, is whether the expansion of council housing adequately filled this void. This is also a pertinent question for present day squatters because, unlike in the previous two periods under discussion, in the early twenty-first century it is primarily social housing, rather than the private rented sector, which fulfils the function of affordable housing provision, and a 'safety net', for those in the most need. It is therefore policies impacting on the provision and distribution of social, rather than private, housing which provide the context in which present day squatting is rooted.

In terms of the social housing context of both the postwar and the 1960s periods, despite considerable advancement in social housing provision and an important ideological shift towards state intervention in housing, squatters in both periods were confronting the effects of a legacy of sporadic public housing subsidies, and an historical reliance on the market to meet general housing needs. For example, the subsidies created by the Housing and Town Planning etc. Act 1919, while marking an important ideological development in housing policy by placing a commitment to a council housing programme firmly on the agenda, were discontinued in the public spending cuts of 1921. These spending cuts were then followed by Chamberlain's 1923 Housing Act emphasising a bias towards building by private enterprise. Subsidies were raised substantially by the first Labour government in 1924 but were reduced once again in 1927. With the subsequent redirection of housing policy towards slum clearance, subsidies for general needs social housing ceased altogether in 1933 and were not reinstated until Labour came into power again in 1945. Housing expenditure was cut again in 1948. The Conservative government regained power in 1951 and their thirteen-year reign was characterised by policies looking to the market to provide general needs housing and restricting social housing output (for example by bringing rates of interest for local authority borrowing in line with market rates and imposing tighter conditions on local authority loan applications). During the 1950s there was also a second slum clearance drive which impacted on social housing output and availability by effectively ceasing the building of general needs housing and prioritising new allocations to slum clearance tenants. It is estimated, for example, that in Greater London in the early 1960s some local authorities were housing virtually no-one from the waiting list (MHLG 1965a) and by mid 1962 '…there were no less than 180,000 applicants on lists in Greater London, a figure almost equal to more than a third of the total local authority housing stock, which took 60 years to build' (MHLG 1965a: 127). When Labour regained control in 1964 they briefly returned to their pre-1950s 'high output' ideology on housing but the 1965 Housing White paper signalled a shift in direction: 'the programme of subsidised council housing should decrease … the expansion of building for owner occupation … reflects a long term social advance which should gradually pervade every region' (MHLG 1965b).

Consequently, despite the development of mass council housing since the end of the First World War, in the 1940s or the 1960s/1970s there was by no means a ready supply of new social housing, nor easy access to this tenure. In particular, single people's access to social housing in these periods was virtually non-existent, providing no 'safety net' for those without the economic means to secure adequate private housing. Council housing was for families who waited patiently on the waiting list. Until the Housing (Homeless Persons) Act 1977, local authorities had no statutory duty to provide accommodation, the conditions of acceptance to temporary accommodation were often strict and a 'welfare' and moralistic attitude encompassing notions of the 'deserving' and 'undeserving' prevailed so that 'council tenancies were to be given only to those who "deserved" them … Thus unmarried mothers, cohabitees, "dirty" families, and "transients" tended to be grouped together as "undesirable"' (CHAC 1969: 32).

Indeed many squatting families in the 1940s and 1960s/1970s had approached local authorities for re-housing to find they were ineligible or were discouraged, and many reported having been on the waiting list for years. Hill, who visited and spoke with some of those squatting in 1946, explained:

> with few exceptions *all* had applied to local authorities for new homes. The exceptions were those who had been discouraged from doing so. Many had been refused by Councils and some by their circumstances did not qualify for any list.
>
> (Hill 1946: 27; emphasis in original)

The social housing context for present day squatters, however, is markedly different. Local authorities now have a statutory duty to provide accommodation for those recognised as homeless and in 'priority need', and council housing is largely allocated on the basis of need. Rents are often low compared with the private sector and covered by housing benefit for those on low incomes. Single people, those in the most need, the 'less respectable', and the poorest sections of the population do, in theory at least, have access to decent affordable housing. However, despite high levels of 'need' evident in the population of homeless people squatting in the 2002 study (for example, 37 per cent reported mental ill health, 35 per cent had been in the care of the local authority, nearly 52 per cent had been in prison, and 46 per cent were drug dependent), only one-third of those who had sought accommodation from the local authority were recognised as homeless, and only 10 per cent as being in priority need. Time and again respondents reported being turned away from local authority homeless persons' units or not being deemed 'needy enough' to qualify for (immediate, or any) assistance. One nineteen-year-old woman, for example, had experienced bereavement, developed a crack cocaine habit, had her daughter taken into foster care and become homeless fleeing from her violent partner, who was trying to coerce her into prostitution. She explained that:

> they gave me emergency accommodation for three nights but after that I had to leave … they told me they couldn't help me, that's what they said, they said they can't help me because I'm not in a needy situation.
>
> (Squatter in London in 2002)

Two main reasons for this can be identified. First, where 'need' becomes the underpinning of social housing distribution, it becomes relative to the extent to which there is scarcity, and the assessment of need becomes the means through which to ration a scarce resource. In other words, in locations with an over-supply of social housing, local authorities can be more lenient in their assessment of need, resulting in a higher number of people to whom they owe a statutory housing duty. And in the two case study areas in the 2002 study where a rationing situation was evident, respondents were less likely to be recognised as homeless and in priority need than in the third case study area where the pressures on social housing were far from acute. Second, in some cases squatters' positions with regards to accessing social housing had been determined not by *ineligibility* or as 'losers' in the competition for a scarce resource but by *active exclusion* from social housing. For while 'need' has become paramount in social housing allocation, so has the policy agenda seeking to combat anti-social behaviour, create safe and sustainable communities, and balance rights against 'responsibilities'. So, for example, although the Homelessness Act 2002 extended the 'criteria' of priority need to additional groups such as those vulnerable as a result of leaving prison, this duty need not apply where applicants are 'guilty of unacceptable behaviour'. Many of those with additional vulnerabilities (for example, people with drug dependencies and offending histories) are often those very same people deemed 'anti-social', who have displayed problematic behaviour or been evicted from previous social housing tenancies. And indeed many present-day squatters reported having been barred from temporary housing provision or excluded from social housing tenancies, for example, because of a drug use problem, previous behaviour in tenancies or hostel accommodation, or rent arrears.

Although squatting results from individuals' material needs for housing in a context of lack of housing opportunity, a disjuncture between expectation and experience is also relevant in explaining the emergence of squatting in two of the periods under discussion. For example, in the immediate post war period squatting was partly a consequence of the disjunction between the reality of housing conditions and the expectation that, with increasing Labour influence in welfare policy during the coalition and with their election in 1945, the expansion of public housing would create the 'decent housing for all' which had been promised (Friend 1980). As one commentator argues, the emergence of squatting in the postwar period showed 'how far out of touch they [Labour government] were with the desperateness of the housing situation and with the mood of the people' (Anon 1963: 9).

Present day squatters in some ways also face a disparity between expectation and experience. The expectation associated with living in a welfare state society is that one's basic material needs will be met, while the experience of homelessness (or literal rooflessness in many of the cases) makes clear that those needs are not being met. Many of the individuals squatting in 2002 reported doing so because local authorities were unwilling to assist them, finding reasons to refuse access to this tenure, with officers acting as gatekeepers rather than providers:

> I only went to the council [here] once on the off chance they might be different. They give you a list of accommodation and services, it's just a way to get rid of you.
>
> (Squatter in Sheffield in 2002)

> I've given up on the council, they don't want to help me. The only contact I have with them is when they step over me to get into work.
>
> (Squatter in Craven in 2002)

> I went to the council after my mum's but I haven't been since … I thought the homeless section didn't really exist for my case, they didn't help, it was like I didn't exist. I would have liked them to, say, understand the situation and explain what they could have done to help me.
>
> (Squatter in Sheffield in 2002)

So, in the context of adverse housing circumstances, limited housing opportunity and frustrated expectations, squatters effectively remove themselves from and defy the norms of traditional channels of housing consumption and tenure power relations, bypassing the 'rules' of welfare provision.

The ways in which local authorities responded to squatting can be conceived as a form of 'punishment' of squatters for removing themselves from the rules of (in particular, social) housing distribution, and as a means through which to re-assert the corresponding norms of conduct. This was achieved in a number of ways. First, local authorities withdrew services from squatters. There is evidence, for example, that in the postwar period and the 1970s' squatters were removed from housing waiting lists and that 'banning squatters from waiting lists became quite a common tactic ...' (Platt 1980: 57). Similarly, the *Islington Gazette* reported in November 1975 that the council had voted to not automatically re-house families with children who had been evicted from squats. Other forms of 'punishment' included the refusal of milk rations (in the 1940s) and exclusion from services such as libraries, schools, and refuse collection (in the postwar period and the 1960s/1970s).

A second tactic employed by local authorities in the 1970s involved rendering their own (empty) properties uninhabitable, through a practice termed 'gutting', in order to prevent people housing themselves outside the dictated channels of housing distribution. 'Gutting' typically involved smashing ceilings and staircases, ripping out wiring, and pouring concrete down the drains. Many squatters commented on this:

> ... there was a lot of wrecking of houses going on in the 1970s by councils to prevent squatting ..., which it didn't. Westminster was terrible at that ... they smashed toilets, poured concrete down the drains, all sorts of stuff.
>
> (Squatter in London between 1974–8)

> by that stage the council, as a matter of course was smashing them up to stop squatters moving in. Things like pouring concrete down the toilet.
>
> (Squatter in London in the mid-1970s)

The Chair of the Housing Committee of one London borough explained the rationale behind this practice:

> If it wasn't for squatters in the first place we wouldn't have to take such drastic action securing to keep them out. We only make property uninhabitable to keep squatters out. We must keep them out because they delay our housing programme ...
>
> (Quoted in the *Islington Gazette*, 27 March 1975)

Third, a political rhetoric emerged to 'demonise' squatters. While squatters presented themselves as 'victims' of public housing scarcity and the logic of allocation systems, with squatting being a symptom of this, the Minister for Health accused postwar squatters who had occupied empty army camps of trying to 'jump their place' on the housing waiting list. In the same period a Cabinet memorandum discussing the occupation of a block of luxury flats in London states that the 'squatters [are] overriding the claims of many people who have been waiting a long time for houses ... [and] delay the completion of rehousing' (quoted in Friend 1980: 116). Squatters in the 1970s were similarly accused of 'holding up the housing programme' and taking houses from 'deserving' homeless families.

Thus far we have seen that in each period squatting was an attempt by *individual households* (i.e. in a non-politicised way) to meet their own material housing needs which, in turn, were firmly rooted in the housing policy context of each era. People squatting in the postwar period and the 1960s and 1970s, however, explicitly linked their adverse housing circumstances with the actions of the state, and clearly articulated the relationship between housing market conditions, as a consequence of historical housing policy, and squatting. In other words, squatting (and the material needs and inequalities which necessitate the act of squatting) was *perceived* by those involved as a direct consequence of these policies. For example:

> [people who squat] ... are people who have tried to rent property from the private rented sector which is totally impossible for a number of reasons; the level of rent, very high rent; landlords won't take couples with children; they invent all these various devices to get around the spirit of the Rent Act thus enabling them almost at will to evict tenants who have been maybe in the property for a very very long time so they can get high rents.
>
> (Squatter's audiotape recording of radio phone-in programmes about squatting broadcast during the 1970s; date unknown)

The connecting of subjective experiences of adverse housing circumstances and the policy actions of state institutions in these two periods resulted in a 'collectivising' of inequality, as illustrated in a statement by squatters occupying a block of luxury flats in 1946:

> We deplore the inhumanity of a law which can act so on behalf of property, and against the welfare of human beings. We came here, not for ourselves alone, but for the hundreds and thousands of others in similar plight ... those who were ignorant of our plight now know, and those who knew and ignored, are now shamed into a sense of urgency that London's homeless shall be housed ... we will continue to fight ... for all local authorities to bring a fresh urgency to the problem, never resting until property interests and the black market have been completely prevented from standing in the way of decent homes for London's people.
>
> (Reproduced in Branson 1989: 11)

Squatting in these two periods, then, developed into a struggle (or movement) to define squatting as a legitimate way of meeting housing need given the lack of alternatives provided. For example, the first households to squat in 1945 were ex-servicemen calling themselves 'The Vigilantes' who squatted luxury properties in coastal towns left empty by landlords to ensure high rent occupation during the summer. Their demand was for the immediate requisitioning of empty property to provide housing for the homeless. Similar demands were made in the campaigns initiated by squatters in the 1960s and 1970s, such as the London Campaign against the Housing Cuts. The documentation from this campaign highlights the problems of large numbers of: people on the council waiting list, substandard properties, homeless people, empty properties and rent increases, and sets these problems in the context of a government freeze on new building, and spending cuts. The campaign literature from an 'anti-gutting campaign' similarly highlights that habitable properties lay empty whilst people were homeless. There was a 'Squatters Convention on Housing' and a 'London Squatters Conference' holding workshops on council housing plans and policies and how to fight them, and the plight of the single homeless. Below are illustrative samples from two documents:

> Islington Council's housing record is a long line of lies, coercion, wastage, corruption, neglect, ignorance, shortsightedness and incompetence. With 3,000 empty houses in the borough, 59 guts in the Charteris Road area and a huge homelessness problem, this council is now attempting to evict 37 people from 7 houses in Charteris Road ... Our solution to the problem of homelessness is simple – <u>put people in homes</u>.
>
> (Information sheet entitled 'The housing crisis – who's to blame?' 1976; underline in original)

> Elgin Avenue squatters are fighting against homelessness. Squatting is not a 'Problem', the problem is the housing crisis. Council and Government should be forced to provide decent housing for ALL. No-one should have to wait for housing while 700,000 houses lie empty.
>
> (Information sheet entitled 'No evictions, housing for all', 1975; capitals in original)

Thus participants in post war squatting and in the 1960s/1970s did not just respond to their own material needs but contextualised their actions and housing experiences in the wider circumstances of housing policy and provision. They were not merely responding to their adverse housing circumstances *within* a certain housing context, but were actively confronting policy-makers in an effort to shape public policy.

Conversely, faced with limited assistance from local authority housing departments, or no right to housing under the terms of the Homelessness Act

2002, without the financial means to obtain private housing, and (for many) the daily experience of sleeping rough, squatting in the early twenty-first century is more of an 'instinctive' act. For example:

> Why did I decide to squat? Simple, it was cold, the middle of winter and I was sleeping outside in a graveyard, that's why.
>
> (Squatter in London in 2002)

> It's simple innit? It's either that [squat] or sleep on the streets.
>
> (Squatter in London in 2002)

> Was walking around town, it was cold and I just noticed it [the empty building] … there was nowhere else to go for shelter.
>
> (Squatter in Sheffield in 2002)

Many respondents in the 2002 study presented their decision to squat as an 'emergency last resort' with little recognition of the wider context in which they were acting, or of those policies and market conditions to which their position of exclusion was connected. Nor did they locate their experiences within a context of a collective experience of housing disadvantage. Unlike the postwar period and the 1960s/1970s, squatting in the early twenty-first century has not manifested as a collective mobilisation against restricted access to mainstream housing and inadequacies of welfare provision. It is the epitome of material housing need.

Squatting as 'lifestyle politics'

The discussion above has focused on squatting as existing (or emerging) as a symptom of, and response to, enduring material (and economic) inequalities rooted within a particular housing policy context. However, in the 1960s and 1970s this was overlaid by concerns, goals and practices shifting from the material to cultural ground. For example, squatters:

- explicitly conceived of squatting as a means through which to challenge the norms embedded within housing allocation systems and relationships between housing consumer and provider (whether landlord, mortgage lender, or local authority);
- challenged traditional notions of what constituted a 'legitimate' household or family unit;
- redefined housing as a cultural, not simply a functional, space; and:
- developed lifestyle and cultural practices, often centred on collective, communal and non-nuclear living.

Meanwhile, this shift in the nature of squatting is reflected in sociological discourse. Corresponding to a shift in the nature of modern society (for example, from primary to secondary modernity, or industrial to post-industrial society), the central concerns and conflicts within contemporary society are said to have shifted in focus to the development, definition and defence of cultural codes, and to developing alternative norms, cultures and lifestyles within everyday life:

> Social movements ... Seem to shift their focus from class, race, and other more traditional political issues towards cultural ground. In the past 20 years emerging social conflicts in advanced societies have not expressed themselves through political action, but rather have raised cultural challenges to the dominant language, to the codes that organise information and shape sexual practices.
>
> (Melucci 1995: 41)

For this body of social theory, the 'reflexive' nature of later-modern society is central to explaining the culturally orientated concerns of social actors (and new social movements) because societal values and social and structural relationships are consequently no longer imposed, but socially constructed, with all social actors having the capacity to produce the models by which they function: 'Through the unplanned sociocultural consequences of technological progress, the human species has challenged itself to learn not merely to affect its social destiny but to control it' (Habermas 1971: 61).

For Beck this is theorised in terms of 'de-traditionalization' as a product of reflexivity, so that 'people demand the right to develop their own perspective on life and to be able to act upon it' (Beck 2003: 92). Thus, people are released from ascribed roles and patterns of behaviour (as required and imposed by industrial societies) into: 'a reflexive form of life where social practices are constantly examined and reformed in light of incoming information about those very practices, thus constitutively altering their character' (Giddens 1991: 37–8).

The goals, concerns, and practices of squatters in the 1960s and 1970s lend support to these assertions about the character of late-modern, or post-industrial society, seen through the ever-present anti-dominant social values and a desire to be released from traditional power relations. As extracts from some contemporary documents demonstrate:

> Importance of squatting: ... People are taking their housing not waiting for it to be allocated or persuading landlords that they are suitable tenants. This is important because this method of obtaining housing is not in accordance with the methods laid down for us, i.e. the choice between buying, renting or council housing. In itself this fucks over the authorities because, to put it sociologically (joke) people aren't accepting the existing social norms ... It's important that

squatting continues to constitute a threat, because it's part of a wider movement of people not accepting what they are told to do … not to accept orders about housing is a really key thing. I.e. control over how/where/with whom one lives is central to control over one's life in toto.

(Document entitled 'London organization: some thoughts', 1977)

To squat is to challenge authority! To squat is to challenge property! … it is your right to house yourself. We must create our culture. It is our city, our world, our lives. These are our houses.

(Newsletter entitled *The Squatter*, Issue 1, 1975)

In the 1960s and 1970s, then, squatting represented a lifestyle choice, which explicitly redefined dominant meanings and social norms with regard to, for example, wage labour, the work ethic, sexual relationships, family, and education. This is seen clearly in the values expressed in many of the contemporary documents produced by squatters:

To me living in Villa Road means more than just squatting … it means living amongst people who are trying to set up alternatives for themselves, and anyone else who can no longer accept what society offers or is doing to itself; alternatives, for instance in housing and ways of living with people, education, community care, sex attitudes, work and technology.

(Newsletter entitled 'Villain', No. 21, 1977)

… there is a significant and large minority [of squatters] who refuse to accept the discipline of tedious work, the psychological and sexual torture of the nuclear family … Significant too, have been the women's and gay communes trying to provide more space for women's autonomy and gay love.

(Written review of, and response to, a published pamphlet entitled 'Squatting: what's it all about?' 1976)

Thus, in one squatting community, a 'work token' system was devised (whereby people received tokens for labour expended for the benefit of the community – such as housing repairs, building barricades to defend themselves against eviction, or street cleaning – which could then be exchanged for meals in the local squatters-run café) in an effort to move towards an exchange system and away from wage labour. Others commented that squatting represented a way of living 'outside' traditional patterns of employment:

Work in our society to me is a word which doesn't mean anything consistent apart from the fact that those who do work generally hate and resent every minute of it, and equally hate and resent those who have found an alternative to work ... Villa Road gives me the time and space to do what I want and live fairly contentedly in the present.

(Newsletter entitled *Villain* No. 22, 1977)

I think the squatters' movement, if there is a base to it, it was at the level of people sort of looking for slightly more depth to their realities than just the formal convention of going to work, getting married. They were looking for a little bit more.

(Squatter in London between 1974 and 1976)

In both these quotes we find the presence of the 'post-material' values said to be a key feature of contemporary social movements (Kriesi 1988), with an emphasis on 'quality of life' rather than material gain (Inglehart 1977, 1990; Habermas 1987). In the first we find that 'time and space to do what I want' is more important than 'work' and in the second we find that having 'more depth to their realities' is more important than other 'formal conventions'.

In a specific housing context, squatting represented, first, a rejection of the 'allocation' systems through which property is obtained, where people become 'units to be accommodated rather than people who have chosen to live in a particular house that suits them'[5] and a challenge to the power relationships seen to be inherent in traditional housing provision. For example:

We should hold out for the right to live as a community. This is a very important political aim. Society hates a community, especially if it works, however chaotically. People should be boxed up, preferably in concrete ... cut off, isolated, incapable of self help – which means they have to turn to state agencies, which equals feudalism: 'I look after you, you are therefore beholden to me' type of relationship.

(Document entitled 'A Written Proposal for a Common Negotiating Front' 1976)

Second, squatting represented a way of asserting one's right to determine, and define, patterns of occupation. Thus, the transforming of familial relationships and structures discussed by Beck in the context of women being released from their 'ascribed roles' and searching for 'a life of their own' (2003), and the ways in which traditional structures of interpersonal existence are said to be challenged and 'reformed lifestyles' practised in their place (Melucci 1989; Habermas 1985) can be seen in the communal (and non-nuclear family) living arrangements commonly practised by squatters in the 1960s and 1970s. For many, then, a communal way of life provided the means through which to subvert dominant meanings of 'family' and traditional (legitimised) patterns of occupation. For example:

... part of [squatting] was the whole thing about people living as nuclear families so for me squatting was also a part of breaking away from that as well, and living collectively and communally.

(Squatter in London in the 1970s)

Communal living, as well as serving the function of breaking away from traditional familial structures, also asserted the importance of one's relationship with the physical environment – for example in terms of the way in which housing environments impact on one's way of life and provide opportunities for lifestyle practices. Thus, 'the kind of housing available is very important. The council builds flats etc. but this insular privatised way of living is what we want to break away from'.[6] Other squatters made similar comments:

I saw housing as part of a process of ... the way that your housing situation, or how housing as a physical structure, influences the way that people live.

(Squatter in London in the 1970s)

For me personally it was the community side of it first and foremost so if the council had offered me a room on the nineteenth floor of a tower block I wouldn't have been interested at all ... coz it was the idea of living there in a different situation and having an organic community ... It was quite a stable community, coz once it caught on to the lifestyle you wouldn't really want it any other way.

(Squatter in London in the late 1970s)

The concept of housing was thus redefined as serving a cultural as well as an instrumental function. Many squatted properties were altered in order that cultural needs as well as housing needs were catered for through housing environments. For example, squatters knocked down dividing walls between properties to create a larger and more communal environment. Spaces were created within houses for darkrooms, band practice, silk screening, and rooms were left specifically for use as social spaces. As Ingham puts it, 'Houses have been tailored to fit occupants, rather than occupants simply fitting themselves into houses' (Ingham 1980: 166).

As a *visible* fight for recognition of these cultural orientations, and for recognition of the *legitimacy* of these redefined concepts of 'family' and 'household', squatters in one London borough, for example, questioned the Chair of Housing on whether the council was willing to 'do something about housing communities of people who want to live together'.[7] And correspondence and minuted meetings between a household of squatters and the local authority reveals overt attempts to persuade the council to recognise the validity of their living arrangements and household structure by accounting for them in allocation policies. For example:

We have been living as a group for the last 2½ years. There are three single people, three separated parents with three children … there is also one absent dependent child. We live as one household and wish to continue as such … people living in group situations like ours can give massive support to what would otherwise be isolated single parent families … the council must realise that we intend to remain as a household and that IF NECESSARY we will re-house ourselves within the borough.

(Correspondence from a squatting household to a London borough council, 22 May 1975; capitals in original)

The kinds of 'visible' fight for recognition of the legitimacy of 'alternative' cultural orientations and struggle over the control of the cultural models of a society (Touraine 1981) parallels, for example, Eder's analysis of women's and peace movements which found a struggle for recognition of their culture as a legitimate one, standing opposed to the prevalent morality (Eder 1985), and with the challenge of the women's movement to male dominated lifestyles (Habermas 1985). For theorists such as Habermas, some of the practices of squatters highlighted above would constitute an example of people changing the meaning and function of the physical environment in a defence (or development) of personal and collective space (Habermas 1985). For Beck, in a similar vein, it is a consequence of the de-traditionalisation of late modernity that provides room for 'new residential patterns' in the form of communal living arrangements to develop. He argues that because networks are chosen and reflexive, and people have the ability to determine their social relations, these will not necessarily be formed (or stratified) according to class or family but 'on the basis of interests, ambitions and commitments of individuals who regard themselves as organizers of their own circles of contacts and relationships' (2003: 98). There is also perhaps a parallel here with Touraine's analysis of the protest of school children in 1990, where he argues that this focused on a conflict between the 'goals of the educational apparatus' and the personal projects of the school children (1995). In the case of squatting in the 1960s/1970s, the goals of the 'housing apparatus' were in conflict with the goals of the squatters' movement and their personal projects.

Conclusion

There is no doubt that the nature of squatting has changed over time, and that squatting in the late 1960s and 1970s conforms closely to the suggested 'cultural shift' of late modern (or post-industrial) society. As such, theories of 'new social movements', as well as those of sociologists such as Giddens and Beck, are certainly useful for discussing the cultural goals and practices of squatting in this era.

However, the extent to which this theoretical debate has connected to the realities of social life for those with limited resources, and to the world of social policy that influences and affects our daily experience, is questionable. We saw in the second section of this chapter, for example, that squatters in the secondary modern period (present-day squatters and those in the late 1960s and 1970s) were certainly not removed or emancipated from inequality, exclusion, and enduring material need. And that, while Giddens' conceptualisation of the politics of the primary modern phase provides a useful framework for understanding squatting, it is in fact relevant to all periods of squatting, whichever phase of modernity it is located in.

In many respects, then, there are few fundamental differences between squatting in each period – an overall time in which the nature of contemporary society is said to have changed: yes, each is rooted in a particular social context to which it is related, and yes, 1960s squatting took on an *additional* set of values and practices. But, basic material need and an inability to meet this need, following the logic of the distribution of wealth and material goods or resources, were paramount in each period. In some historical contexts, squatting has occurred at the level of an individual household, while in other contexts it has resulted in the emergence of a social movement. Sometimes it has been an instinctive response to personal circumstances; at other times it has been publicly or politically organised. But it has always been a result of, and a conflict centred on, the distribution and allocation of material resources, namely, housing.

Notes

1 Much of the literature and documentation pertaining to squatting in the postwar period was written by, or incorporates the views of participants and eyewitnesses.
2 Undertaken as part of a PhD (Reeve 1999) and drawing on 430 contemporary documents, analysis of press reports, and interviews with people who had squatted during this era.
3 This study was undertaken for Crisis in 2002 (Reeve and Coward 2004) and explored squatting in three English case study locations through a survey of homeless people and in-depth interviews with squatters.
4 There are no accurate figures available about the extent of squatting in these three periods. Information which provides some indication of the extent of squatting includes: six months after squatting began in empty army camps in 1946 it is estimated that 1,038 camps were occupied housing 40,000 families (Ward 1982), although this may have included some who had been given licences to occupy by local authorities; it is estimated that in 1975 there were 50,000 people squatting in Britain (Wates and Wolmar 1980); and the 2002 study found that one in four of the homeless people interviewed had squatted during their current episode of homelessness.
5 Quoted from the minutes of an 'Islington Squatters' meeting, 10 June 1975.
6 Quoted from the minutes of an 'Islington Squatters Statement Meeting', 3 June 1975.
7 Quoted from the minutes of a meeting between 'Islington Squatters', the Chairperson of Islington Housing Committee and the Chairman of the Finance Committee, 7 November 1975.

References

Allen, C. and Sprigings, N. (2001) 'Housing policy, housing management and tenant power in the risk society: some critical observations on the welfare politics of radical doubt', *Critical Social Policy*, 21: 384–412.

Anon (1963) 'Direct action for houses: the story of the squatters', *Anarchy*, 21: 9–15.

Banting, K.G. (1979) *Poverty, Politics and Policy: Britain in the 1960s*, London and Basingstoke: Macmillan.

Beck, U. (2003) *Risk Society: Towards a New Modernity*, London: Sage Publications.

—— (1999) *World Risk Society*, Cambridge: Polity Press.

Branson, N. (ed.) (1989) *Our History: London Squatters 1946, Proceedings of a Conference held by the Communist Party History Group May 1984*, London: Community Party History Group.

CHAC (Cullingworth Committee) (1969) *Council Housing: Purposes, Procedures and Priorities*, London: Department of the Environment and Welsh Office.

Eder, K. (1985) 'The "new" social movements: moral crusades, political pressure groups, or social movements?', *Social Research*, 52: 869–90.

Friend, A. (1980) 'The post war squatters', in N. Wates and C. Wolmar (eds) *Squatting: The Real Story*, London: Bay Leaf Books.

Giddens, A. (1991) *Modernity and Self-Identity: Self and Society in the Late Modern Age*, Cambridge: Polity Press.

—— (1994) *Beyond Left and Right: The Future of Radical Politics*, Cambridge: Polity Press.

Habermas, J. (1971) *Towards a Rational Society*, London: Heinemann.

—— (1985) 'New social movements', *Telos*, 49: 33–37.

—— (1987) *The Theory of Communicative Action Vol. 2*, Cambridge: Polity Press.

Hill, D.M. (1946) 'Who are the squatters?', *Pilot Papers*, 1: 11–27.

Ingham, A. (1980) 'Using the space', in N. Wates and C. Wolmar (eds) *Squatting: The Real Story*, London: Bay Leaf Books.

Inglehart, R. (1977) *The Silent Revolution*, Princeton and Guilford: Princeton University Press.

—— (1990) 'Values, ideology, and cognitive mobilization in new social movements', in R. Dalton and M. Kuechler (eds) *Challenging the Political Order: New Social and Political Movements in Western Democracies*, Cambridge: Polity Press.

Kriesi, H. (1988) 'The interdependence of structure and action: some reflections on the state of the art', in B. Klandermans, H. Kriesi and S. Tarrow (eds) *From Structure to Action: Comparing Social Movement Research across Cultures*, International Social Movement Research, Vol. 1: 349–68, Greenwich, CT and London: Jai Press.

Malpass, P. and Murie, A. (1994) *Housing Policy and Practice*, London: Macmillan.

Melucci, A. (1989) *Nomads of the Present*, London: Hutchinson Radius.

—— (1995) 'The process of collective identity', in H. Johnston and B. Klandermans (eds) *Social Movements and Culture*, London: UCL Press.

Ministry of Housing and Local Government (MHLG) (1965a) *Report of the Committee on Housing in Greater London*, Cmnd 2605, London: HMSO.

—— (1965b) *The Housing Programme 1965–1970*, Cmnd 2838, London: HMSO.

Offe, C. (1985) 'New social movements: challenging the boundaries of institutional politics', *Social Research*, 52: 817–68.

Pakulski, J. (1991) *Social Movements: The Politics of Moral Protest*, Melbourne: Longman Cheshire.

Platt, S. (1980) 'A decade of squatting', in N. Wates and C. Wolmar (eds) *Squatting: The Real Story*, London: Bay Leaf Books.

Reeve, K. (1999) 'The squatters' movement in London: 1968–1980', unpublished thesis, Leeds: University of Leeds.

Reeve, K. and Coward, C. (2004) *Life at the Margins: The Experiences of Homeless People Living in Squats*, London: Crisis.

Touraine, A. (1981) *The Voice and the Eye: An Analysis of Social Movements*, Cambridge: Cambridge University Press.

—— (1985) 'An introduction to the study of social movements', *Social Research*, 52: 749–87.

Ward, C. (1982) *Anarchy in Action*, London: Freedom Press.

Wates, N. and Wolmar, C. (eds) (1980) *Squatting: The Real Story*, London: Bay Leaf Books.

10 Housing and urban regeneration policy

Citizen and community under new labour

John Pierson and Claire Worley

The extent of deprivation on many of Britain's social housing estates and inner-city areas has attracted unprecedented levels of government attention since the early 1990s. Driving the concern is the fear of deep social fissures and something like American ghettos taking root in the UK. At the same time, accumulating research has shown that the spatial concentration of poverty in specific urban areas affects every aspect of those residents' lives and is itself the product of many inter-related factors. New concepts such as social networks, 'neighbourhood effects', social capital, and social exclusion have been advanced to explain its impact on the social fabric of poor communities. In the wake of this newer understanding, regeneration initiatives have expanded dramatically in scope within a relatively short period. Yet, despite a decade and more of various initiatives, widespread poverty and social disadvantage still pervades many urban districts of the UK, including those that have been the beneficiary of regeneration programmes (Berthoud 2001).

As the field has expanded, so the focus on housing has changed. Broadly speaking, housing provision – its condition, tenure, market demand, and associated neighbourhood behavioural attributes – has become but one of several services targeted for intervention, and moreover acting in concert with other services. In addition, much of the recent research on implementation of regeneration policies has examined 'process' and in particular, whether that process has lived up to its participatory rhetoric (Hastings 1996; Oc *et al.* 1999; Hall 2000). There has been less interest in the role of mainstream services, particularly housing, and how effectively those services are absorbing regeneration objectives.

In this chapter, we seek to rebalance this relative neglect by focusing on the role of housing in regeneration policy. We regard housing, viewed ecologically as 'a set of social relations, including characteristic networks and patterns of activity' (Somerville 1998: 772), as a central instrument in the implementation of that policy. We also argue that a focus on housing casts a critical light on the limits of that policy and in doing so aids understanding of the structural reasons as to why poverty becomes spatially concentrated in certain areas and why social exclusion has a neighbourhood face.

Broadly, we argue that disadvantaged social housing estates and areas of low demand and housing abandonment are viewed by government as spaces where anti-social behaviour, parenting deficits, education deficits among children, and workless households have become the chief elements of urban disadvantage. The causes of these problems in social relations, in Ambrose's phrase, 'derive from the local shortcomings in management and service delivery, not with structural forces' (Ambrose 2003: 8). Disadvantaged estates are, in central government's view, the consequence of the failure of local services to work in a holistic or joined up way both with each other and with local residents. Seen in this light the problems of extreme urban disadvantage are spatially contained, affecting a limited number of people who are not coping very well and not the consequence of fundamental economic restructuring (Ambrose 2003). In an effort to re-assert social norms on 'failing' estates, communitarian concepts, such as 'participation', 'community' and the obligations of citizenship, have become fundamental to regeneration policy. On the basis of such concepts citizens are being invited to come out from their households into a well constructed, highly stylised public space, to invest their time, energy and personal resources in local partnerships. In return the local partnership – perhaps – acquires access to funding through special programmes that at best provide only 2 to 3 per cent of mainstream spend in those areas (Ambrose 2003).

Our intent, then, is to situate housing more clearly within Labour's regeneration initiatives and to examine the communitarian concepts behind those initiatives. In the first part of the chapter, we outline some of the major regeneration programmes and explain what they intend to achieve. These include the New Deal for Communities, Neighbourhood Renewal Pathfinders, Housing Market Renewal Pathfinders, and efforts to bridge the consequences of residential segregation through community cohesion initiatives. In the second part, we address the residents' own experiences within the regeneration process and in particular look at how the universalist notions proffered by government around participation, citizenship and community cohesion interact with residents' experiences of 'place' and 'neighbourhood'. We focus particularly on the gendered and racialised dynamics of regeneration, to suggest that the residents' perspective of the regeneration process is altogether more divided and fragmented.

Neighbourhood renewal and New Labour's regeneration policy

Before Labour

The riots and urban disturbances across Britain in 1991 served to highlight the continued marginalisation of disadvantaged estates. A major review of urban policy through the early 1990s concluded at the time that it was difficult to determine 'unambiguously what government has aimed to achieve … at any one time' (Robson *et al.* 1994: 2). As far as the creation of employment opportunities and improving the appeal for investors of such areas, the authors of the review asserted that 'policy has not been able to make significant inroads into the socio-economic problems' with 'continuing decline in the worst areas' (Robson *et al.* 1994: 49). Further, they argued for a re-focusing on people, mobilising the support of local residents, utilising their skills, and stressed the potential contribution of other stakeholders, such as non-profit organisations and local communities.

Accumulating evidence threw better light on the true extent of the problem: concentrated urban poverty had so many causal factors intertwined that any regeneration policy would have to be flexible and holistic to have a hope of success. Power and Mumford (1999) usefully described the process behind so-called 'failing' estates. Macro economic pressures, such as the demand of the labour market for a highly skilled, knowledge-based workforce, combined with adverse local conditions made certain estates 'hard to let' such as those with high rates of burglary, dilapidated housing or no on-site manager. As people failed in the labour market, there was increased pressure to house those with high levels of need. The result was a high concentration of tenants outside the labour market with a variety of needs, living in essentially unwanted areas with low levels of public services including transport, health, child care and schools (Power and Mumford 1999).

This was only beginning to be perceived in the early 1990s. Urban renewal policies in the late 1980s and early 1990s such as Estate Action and Housing Action Trusts had focused almost exclusively on the physical regeneration and tenure choice for run-down highly disadvantaged housing estates. The launch of the City Challenge Fund in 1991 and the subsequent consolidation of urban funding under the Single Regeneration Budget (SRB) in 1993, under the Conservative government, expanded the remit and aimed to improve levels of education, employment, health promotion, and community safety on such estates. They also attempted to gain legitimacy by widening the notion of partnership.

Regeneration policy after 1997

Under the two Labour governments from 1997, regeneration objectives widened even further to include changing the behavioural and cultural attributes of residents in highly disadvantaged urban areas. Tackling anti-social behaviour, tightening parental control over children's behaviour, raising educational attainment, reducing the fear of crime, and getting people 'job ready' all became recurrent features of regeneration packages. At the same time, Labour in government mandated higher levels of participation by local residents in the process, giving them wider roles in the governance of projects. Embedded in the policy was the assumption that local people and local organisations could and would call on their own resources and 'capacity' to help achieve these ambitious goals.

Numerous initiatives have emerged to embrace this wider brief: New Deal for Communities, Neighbourhood Management Pathfinders, coalfield regeneration, Health Action Zones, community cohesion initiatives, and Housing Market Renewal Pathfinders. The list is longer if one adds other programmes with an area based focus: Crime and Disorder Partnerships, Neighbourhood Warden Schemes, Sure Start programmes for children under five years old, and a host of smaller sports and arts schemes, many of whose objectives are also regenerative.

The publication of *A New Commitment to Neighbourhood Renewal* and the establishment of the Neighbourhood Renewal Unit in 2001 brought some coherence to this array of programmes. *A New Commitment* announced a strategy to address the needs of the 'hundreds' of poor neighbourhoods in the eighty-eight most deprived local authority areas that had seen their basic quality of life become increasingly detached from the rest of society. People, it announced, 'living just streets apart [have become] separated by a gulf in prosperity and opportunity' (SEU 2001: 7). The report drew on notions of the cycle of decay in poor urban neighbourhoods. It acknowledged the powerful consequences of industrial restructuring and out-migration, the declining popularity of social housing relative to owner-occupation. But in the main it focused on the impact of concentrated poverty on residents' behaviour: the consequences of criminal and anti-social behaviour, poor health, low educational attainment and poor housing environments.

The strategy establishes a connection between notions of 'community failure' and housing. As Maclennan (2000) notes, the housing system is the critical link between the Social Exclusion Unit's aims of reviving local economies and improving local services. It converts incomes into residential choices – or lack thereof – and thereby determines the quality of services that flow from those choices. Social housing estates are perceived as the instrument for concentrating poor people with high levels of need in given areas; in effect they underwrite poor communities in high cost cities by providing low cost subsidised homes for those in greatest need (Power and Mumford 1999).

In New Labour regeneration policy the concept of 'neighbourhood' is pragmatic in definition but at the same time also a proxy for 'community'. On the one hand, definitions of neighbourhood are based on local perceptions of what constitutes 'the neighbourhood' such as boundaries established by roads, changes in housing tenure or design, catchment areas for primary schools and shops or areas defined by transport links (SEU 2001: 13). They are invariably much larger than the layperson's understanding of 'neighbourhood', often comprising several thousand people. Interestingly, there is also now a tendency for 'neighbourhoods' to correspond to electoral wards where both statistical information and local political machinations can be more readily supplied. On the other hand there are expectations of engagement and participation laid on the residents of neighbourhoods with the implication that they have a fund of social capital to draw on. There are expectations too of positive responses to the range of behavioural programmes on offer – greater numbers of adults and school leavers in job training, pupils meeting improved educational targets, diminished levels of anti-social behaviour.

A new Neighbourhood Renewal Fund was made available to the local authorities with the eighty-eight most deprived wards in the country and their partners as a kind of top-up to ensure that core public services were improved in their delivery in the most deprived areas. Among the 105 commitments made were those tackling poor housing and the poor physical environment. Local authorities were admonished to integrate their investment in housing with wider regeneration policies. It also established the target of bringing all social housing up to a decent standard by 2010, with a third of that taking place by 2004 (SEU 2001). There were further pledges to take action on housing stock in areas of low demand and to reduce housing abandonment. There were also commitments to improving and making more visible local housing management, to establishing structures for tenant participation and to making social housing more responsive to tenants' needs including the introduction of choice-based lettings policies.

New Deal for Communities

Two of the most prominent regeneration programmes under the wing of the Neighbourhood Renewal Unit are the New Deal for Communities (NDC) and the Neighbourhood Management Pathfinders (NMP). Both programmes aim to reduce the gaps in services and quality of life between poorest neighbourhoods and the rest of the country and both cover relatively small areas, with social housing estates often, but not always, the focus.

Each of the thirty-nine New Deal for Communities projects covers an average of 4,000 households, with their funding of approximately £50 million guaranteed for ten years on the basis of rigorously constructed delivery plans, with the relevant government office in the region playing a strong hand in their construction. Common to all NDCs are five outcomes: reduction in crime, raising the level of educational achievement, improvement of health, improvement in housing and the physical environment, and action to increase employment opportunities.

The long-term funding for each NDC is meant to provide relative financial stability to local management boards as they tackle the multi-dimensional nature of urban disadvantage, in contrast to earlier single regeneration budget funding which was shorter lived and placed a premium on 'exit consciousness' (Oc *et al.* 1999). In fact, however, a high degree of factionalism and infighting over such large amounts of money has intruded into some NDC boards' affairs, which has resulted in delay and failure to meet targets. In the extreme, there have been allegations of corruption, votes of no confidence and other manifestations of local conflict.

While in concept NDC was not expected to be a housing-dominated programme, housing nevertheless has found a central role in delivery plans, partly as a result of resident pressure and partly because the logic of any 'place-based' initiative requires attention to housing and neighbourhood infrastructure. The most common housing outcomes adopted by NDC partnerships include improving the quality of housing, reducing the stock of unfit dwellings, reducing voids, eliminating derelict sites and improving open spaces and play areas. Such outcomes are to be achieved through Neighbourhood Management schemes, infrastructure improvement, demolitions, litter and graffiti clean up, and housing redevelopment (NRU 2003). The publication by the government of *Sustainable Communities: Building for the Future* (ODPM 2003) only further complicated the position of NDCs, which must coordinate housing interventions with those planned by other funders. Delivering housing investment in the future became more complex with local authorities required to develop appraisal of investment options by mid-2005, which could well override already existing NDC delivery plans (NRU 2003).

Although it is still early to establish definite patterns of success or failure, a range of findings from both national evaluation and reports on individual NDCs indicate a picture of mixed accomplishment. For example, in examining the impact of crime reduction by NDC partnerships, Bowers *et al.* (2003) found little evidence to support claims of progress. As for trust and 'feeling part of the community' the national evaluation found reasonable, even surprising, levels among residents across all NDC areas, with Asian residents the highest, with some 50 per cent considering themselves part of a community. Yet between 40 and 50 per cent of residents were also planning to move within two years across all NDC areas (NRU 2003: 240).

Community participation is now widely accepted as essential for effective regeneration programmes. Investment in the notion of communities as having an authentic voice was clearly highlighted in a report from the Social Exclusion Unit, in which Tony Blair argued that: '[t]oo much has been imposed from above, when experience shows that success depends on communities themselves having the power and taking the responsibility to make things better' (SEU 1998: 7, cited in Hoban and Beresford 2001: 313). This highlights not only the government's emphasis on the role of local residents within regeneration programmes, but also an acknowledgement of the failures of past regeneration efforts precisely for being 'top down' in their approach.

The key component for institutionalising resident participation is through partnership, the formal association of local authority services, voluntary organisations, business interests, and local residents that must be pulled together in order both to develop a delivery plan for the area and to oversee its implementation should its bid be successful. Partnership working, a mainstay of the Labour government, is seen as a crucial factor in both mediating community involvement in regeneration programmes and in expanding the potential for involving residents in decision-making processes (Smith and Beazley 2000). Indeed, regeneration partnerships are widely regarded as the primary vehicle through which local needs can be defined and addressed. They are also seen as a means of giving local people a voice, thus increasing the empowerment of local communities and their members. Consequently, partnerships are widely regarded as *the* new mode of local governance (Bentley *et al.* 2003), with the ability to engage key stakeholders across the community in the regeneration process.

Yet it is clear that NDC partnerships have struggled in many areas. The report on Aston Pride NDC for the national evaluation found that the partnership board had become stalled in its ability to operate effectively, had weak levels of community engagement and virtually no links with minority ethnic residents (Tyler 2003). NDCs have expended huge resources and effort in addressing a range of 'process' tasks – assembling partnerships, creating delivery plans, establishing management boards (provisional, then elected) for effective governance, promoting links with the community, and establishing inter-agency links (NRU 2003). The scale and demands on partnership of 'setting up tasks' are high. Partnerships have to hire – and then nurture – their own teams, establish long-term relationships with local agencies (who themselves need to develop a different culture and attitude), develop active lines of engagement with local citizens and learn to think strategically across a long time scale.[1] This can be a costly, time consuming, constant and often exhausting process (NRU 2003: 244).

In its partnerships the New Deals draw explicitly on the new compact between the enabling state and 'the active citizen'. They also highlight the tensions within that compact between communitarian definitions of responsibility and obligation and the fragmentation arising from smaller collectivities. Thus, individuals, organisations, parents, schools, hospitals, and housing estates take on a portion of the responsibility for solving extensive, intractable social problems (Rose 2000). As Rose puts it: 'Populations that were once under the tutelage of the social state are to be set free ... [y]et at the same time to be made responsible for their destiny and for that of society as a whole' (Rose 2000: 1400). 'Community' (and increasingly 'neighbourhood') becomes a critical element in central government policy, both an instrument for tackling the most difficult social problems and at the same time 'a space of emotional relationships through which individual identities are constructed through their bonds to micro-cultures of values and meanings' (Rose 2000: 1401). The instability of this compact has been amply demonstrated in certain key NDC areas with factionalism, infighting, and abrupt departures of staff in evidence (Tyler 2003). Baeten, commenting on the impact of regeneration partnerships in general, notes that they are dominated by urban elites who fail to acknowledge their paralysing effect on low income residents who become permanently entangled in the process (Baeten 2001). There is some evidence that particular NDC partnerships have had the effect of undermining local community organisations such as long established tenants' organisations and even been the source of outright corruption (Neil Jameson personal communication; Palmer 2003).

Neighbourhood management pathfinders

Neighbourhood management as a concept emerged from studies of particular estates that had re-established stability following periods of disruption, rising crime rates and abandonment (Power and Bergin 1999). The example of the Broadwater Farm estate in Tottenham was the most visible but others studied by Power and Bergin in the late 1990s included Poplar HARCA and Waltham Forest Action Trust. Essentially, neighbourhood management is a response to the incremental withdrawal of the front-line, street level, manual and low skill jobs which once were visible evidence on estates both of basic services being delivered and of informal control (Power and Bergin 1999; DETR 1999). It re-inserts a recognisable source of authority at street level through which the organisation, supervision and delivery of services occurs. In doing so, it provides intensive management of vulnerable housing areas with a greater role for staff such as concierges, caretakers, and 'super caretakers' (Taylor 2000). The objective is to establish a responsibility for standards within clear agreed lines of control and accountability.

To be successful neighbourhood management requires a small locally based, locally accountable staff team to implement decisions. It also requires a defined budget to fund the team and service delivery, a defined area of operation, a local base through which services can be organised, high priority to basic services for a visible impact, and clear lines of communication (Power and Bergin 1999). Housing is central to effective local management since only through housing can an authority be re-established as capable of focusing on rent accounts, allocation, advice, repair and maintenance, links with tenants and the enforcement of anti-social behaviour codes (Taylor 2000; Bright 2002). A range of other objectives also fall within the housing management remit such as controlling nuisance and anti-social behaviour, dealing immediately with arson and fire hazards, reducing drug taking, and responding to racial harassment, neighbour or family conflicts (Bright 2002).

The neighbourhood management pathfinders, following the recommendations of DETR (1999), have been established in areas where there is evidence of local 'capacity', that is where housing organisations such as estate management boards, tenant management organisations, housing action trusts or local authority housing departments have established lines of communication and authority. Pathfinders cover areas with a mixed range of housing conditions and tenures. The condition of housing in the Blacon NMP in Chester, for example, is relatively good, with only pockets of poorer, unlettable properties, while virtually half of all dwellings are owner-occupied. Yet poor recreational facilities, widespread fly tipping, abandoned cars, and arson all affect the lives of residents (Blacon NMP 2002).

In tackling such issues, neighbourhood management aims only to influence existing services rather than commission services directly. Teams are small and spend much time in negotiating and persuading partners, which means that progress can be slow. For example, abandoned and burnt out cars are concerns common to several pathfinders and high on residents' priority lists. Yet, NMPs can be stymied by multiple jurisdictions between police and highways and by the stand off between agencies over who is responsible (Paul Boylan, personal communication).

Like the New Deal for Communities, neighbourhood management pathfinders are intended to bring main services together in new integrated patterns of delivery. Like New Deals also, they emerge from a 'managed bidding' process in which delivery plans are steered in particular directions by regional government offices from designated localities intended to spare local partners the futility of preparing lengthy bids only to be disappointed in the end. Finally, their delivery plans intend to tackle the same problems: poor housing, poor local health outcomes, crime, low educational attainment and worklessness (Cole 2003). Compared with NDCs, however, the level of funding for NMPs is low, and this means reliance on the negotiating, bargaining, and modelling skills of the small NMP teams. They 'can't buy their way to success [so they] have no choice but to persuade' (Bright 2002).

Neighbourhood management objectives, as with the New Deals, directly lock the pathfinders into the expectation that they will tackle intractable local problems of behaviour by drawing on the presumed social nature of community, although the causes of these problems may actually lie well outside local control. The presumption is that a combination of better-managed services, more-joined up working and greater levels of community participation can resolve the acute problems of deprived neighbourhoods. The 'structure' that shapes such neigh-bourhoods – loss of jobs, out-migration of human capital, low levels of benefits and pursuit of internationally compliant economic orthodoxy – remains out of reach.

Housing Market Renewal Pathfinders

With the Housing Market Renewal Pathfinders, government is for the first time intervening systematically in the housing market in order to tackle low demand, and to ensure a balance between housing availability and demand. The extent of housing market failure has only recently been quantified. That the problem has now become a focus for policy is an admission that in certain areas the introduction of visible neighbourhood services, initiatives for tackling crime and anti-social behaviour, and the host of other behavioural targets, cannot in themselves rescue areas of low demand (Keenan *et al.* 1999). Abandonment and chronic low demand are not found only in areas of social housing; it is increasingly an interaction between tenures, for example private landlords renting to unemployed or student tenants (Bramley and Pawson 2002). Indeed, about two-thirds of the properties in the nine Housing Market Renewal Pathfinder[2] areas are private, with the remainder as social housing.

While central government has realised that the condition of the housing market is central to the success of its other regeneration initiatives in areas of low demand, there is little evidence for it to draw on when figuring out 'what works' in turning areas around. The funding provided by government to each pathfinder – approximately £2.6 million – is intended to allow them to investigate exactly what *will* work in turning housing markets around. It is in effect funding for exploration, combined with some additional funding to tackle the most egregious (and 'winnable') problems. In essence pathfinders are asked to find what an effective mix of housing improvements, demolition, compulsory purchase, and tackling anti-social behaviour might look like for reshaping local housing markets and re-shaping the communities within them. Strategic action plans for the nine Pathfinder areas are to be developed by 2005; they will combine large-scale clearance, refurbishment, and new building (National Housing Federation 2002).

The market renewal pathfinders challenge recent regeneration orthodoxy in several ways. First, they often run across local authority boundaries and encompass privately owned, privately rented, and rented social housing tenures within one pathfinder. This mix of local authorities and of housing tenures and conditions will require remarkable powers of partnership to develop wide area strategic planning as well as co-ordinating the plans of the various sub-areas within each pathfinder.

Second, the considerable differences *within* pathfinder areas point to a complicated range of varied and delicate objectives. For example, in the pathfinder area in Manchester, some 12,000 homes stood empty in mid-2003 while 30,000 were 'at risk' of abandonment. In such major urban centres, buoyant markets in the city centre contrast with whole outer districts, such as parts of Salford, where demand for housing is virtually non-existent. Low demand is similarly evident in south central Hanley, Stoke-on-Trent, while outer housing development has continued, if not to thrive, at least to modestly expand (Hetherington 2003). Within the same north Staffordshire pathfinder, the older mining villages of east Newcastle present yet another aspect of low demand.

Third, this is a 'top-down/bottom-up' approach, with a decided emphasis on the former and a considerably reduced role for local participation. The broad strategy is fixed from the outset through the partnership of agencies and consultants that have rapidly coalesced in each area. A formidable planning authority with its well-advertised powers of compulsory purchase is presented in the pathfinder prospectus to their communities. This reverses the trend toward greater and more influential participation found in NDCs and NMPs. Rapid action surveys from consultants, planning schemes and submissions are as much a focus as are consultation days for local residents. Neighbourhood action plans built around SWOT analyses with agency-led area implementation teams are rapidly being put in place. Residents' views are important and are incorporated into 'neighbourhood action plans' but have little strategic influence across what the ODPM has outlined as a fifteen-year strategy.

The implications for existing communities and neighbourhoods within renewal pathfinder areas are likely to be profound. Pathfinders are compelled to rebuild quickly, which means that before any clearance they have to have questions of 'land end use' settled at least in a broad category – designated as a commercial quarter here, a residential quarter or university quarter there. In reality, the end use of land is often obscure and subject to an array of pressures and uncertainties not documented in pathfinder plans.

Residents in renewal areas will, not surprisingly, find the process more compliant with market functions. Economic orthodoxy accepts that, in relation to abandonment and to the social problems that accompany abandonment, including loss of trust, social exclusion, and rise in crime, the housing market is the chief determinant. As a result, government policy should be directed towards 'adjustment' or economic 'stabilisation' rather than regeneration or reversal of the decline (Goodchild *et al.* 2002: 379). For example, social landlords will devise ways of promoting demand through lettings initiatives, conversion projects that open up new sources of demand, and rent adjustment. Private sector housing is subject to market price mechanisms that can be expected to reflect and absorb variations in demand. Yet the private sector is also subject to market distorting mechanisms such as negative equity and by the fact that rental patterns in low-demand areas are underpinned by housing benefit (Goodchild *et al.* 2002).

It is possible that Market Renewal Pathfinders will become a vehicle primarily for reconstituting the social class of a given area through what Wyley and Hammel (1999) call 'controlled' or 'modified' gentrification. Gentrification, in this sense, is rooted in class and is defined as the class transformation of urban neighbourhoods that suffered previous disinvestment, out-migration and decline. It is a process that is constituted with a nascent local regime 'under a devolved, privatised and "re-invented" policy framework'. Accelerated class polarisation is a likely outcome. Where such class transformation of neighbourhoods tightens the housing market in the vicinity of public housing, mixed-income redevelopment is both feasible and profitable only as long as the higher income residents do not feel threatened.

Community cohesion

Following the civil disturbances between Asian young men, the police and far right groups, in Bradford, Oldham, Burnley and Stoke-on-Trent in 2001, a clearer focus on community cohesion emerged. The series of reports that followed the disorder – the Oldham Independent Review (Ritchie 2001), the government-commissioned Cantle Report (Home Office 2001a) and the Ouseley Report (Ouseley 2001) – all highlighted the lack of integration between different 'communities' within 'communities', which severely tested current models of multi-culturalism and concepts of multicultural citizenship. They also prompted massive debate culminating in the community cohesion initiative, with a range of pathfinders across the country designed to break down barriers between culturally and physically segregated ethnic populations. Explicitly linked to social inclusiveness, the UK National Action Plan on Social Inclusion 2003–2005 (*Department for Work and Pensions 2003*) defined community cohesion as a central aspect of its wider social inclusion agenda, suggesting that areas most at risk of community tensions are also those with high factors of social exclusion.

One of the most significant findings of the Cantle Report into the disturbances was that different ethnic communities within towns and cities across the UK were living 'parallel lives':

> Whilst the physical segregation of housing estates and inner city areas came as no surprise, the team was particularly struck by the depth of polarisation of our towns and cities. The extent to which these physical divisions were compounded by so many other aspects of our daily lives, was very evident. Separate educational arrangements, community and voluntary bodies, employment, places of worship, language, social and cultural networks, means that many communities operate on the basis of a series of parallel lives. These lives often do not seem to touch at any point, let alone overlap and promote any meaningful interchanges.
>
> (Home Office 2001a: 9)

What caught both observers and government by surprise was the extent of the gulf between different ethnic and religious communities. While it had been established that the arrival of 'hyper-segregation' and the racialised ghettos of the US have not occurred in the UK (Peach 1996), nevertheless the degree of residential separation and its impact on identity and opportunity was far stronger than previously assumed (Home Office 2001a). Indeed the dimensions that Massey and Denton (1993) deployed to highlight the extent of segregation in American cities would reveal similar, if less intense, similarities in many of Britain's largest cities in relation to the distribution of different ethnic populations (or 'unevenness'), isolation, clustering, centralisation and concentration (Massey and Denton 1993: 77).

Within government thinking, housing is regarded a major determinant shaping both the clustering of cultural and ethnic communities and the relationships between those communities (Local Government Association 2002). Yet clearly, segregation goes beyond housing into separate arrangements for education, employment, language, worship and social and cultural networks (Ouseley 2001). The consequent breakdown in relations between ethnic groups led to a failure in understanding between communities, and earlier regeneration initiatives did not help to bridge the gap. Rather, the competitive nature of funding exacerbated tensions between different communities, and resulted in misunderstandings relating to the allocation of resources (Local Government Association 2002).

In the light of these findings local authorities have been required to prepare a 'local community cohesion plan', which should include 'the promotion of cross cultural contact between different communities at all levels, foster understanding and respect, and break down barriers' (Home Office 2001b: 11). Housing is recognised as integral to this, in terms of responding to the evidence of segregation and differences in tenure. Local authority housing departments are required to examine their current policies in relation to community cohesion and take appropriate action to ensure that they address the community cohesion objectives (Local Government Association 2002). Community cohesion also ties in with the National Strategy for Neighbourhood Renewal and the Neighbourhood Renewal Fund funding processes (Local Government Association 2002). This discussion is developed below.

Identity, 'cohesion', and citizenship in New Labour regeneration discourse

'Community' in New Labour regeneration

The concept of 'community' is central to New Labour's policy goals, deployed across a broad front of social regeneration policy goals.[3] Yet, in invoking 'community', the government has drawn on a long and positive historic legacy of radical local initiative over much of the twentieth century (see, for example, Piratin 1948 and Leech 2002 for two excellent accounts). During the mid-1960s and early 1970s, policy makers, informed by the growth of grass roots community movements, saw communities as a resource for tackling social inequality and deprivation (Bentley et al. 2003). The Community Development Programme, for example, provided local activists in the late 1960s with the means to tackle local corporate dominance and exploitative employment practices, enabling some local authorities to engage more energetically in shaping their local economy (CDP 1977). Although terminated by the Home Office in the early 1970s precisely because of its radicalising impact, the concept of community at that point had not acquired the norm-enforcing agency that it would a generation later. Now, according to Rose (1999: 176), under New Labour communities themselves have become governmental, creating a form of *'government through community'* (emphasis in original). Bentley et al. note that:

> The government has taken up the community discourse in its social policy agenda, developing a cross-cutting strategy that integrates the task of building stronger communities with a range of broader objectives, from reducing child poverty and health inequalities to boosting economic regeneration and public services reform.
>
> (Bentley et al. 2003: 9)

Deacon (2000) argues that the significance that is attached to the interests of the community, as opposed to those of other individuals, is distinctive of the New Labour project. Therefore, it is the responsibility of 'communities', and of individuals to their communities as active citizens, which is crucial for New Labour's project of local renewal.

It is true that within this framework the idea of a singular 'community' has largely been replaced by a more pluralist understanding of multiple communities, so that Britain is now characterised as a 'community of communities' (see also the Commission on the Future of Multi-Ethnic Britain 2000). While the recognition of difference is formally installed in regeneration policy, such as the race equality guidelines for the New Deal for Communities programme (NRU 2000), the regeneration process itself tends to cover up actual conflicts of interest and to disarm the vigorous assertion of those interests. Thus the process of partnership, with its overtones of 'cosiness' and assumptions that interests are essentially identical, undermines the expression of these different, and sometimes competing, interests. This is further aided by the application of the concept of 'community' itself, which, as Bauman suggests, 'sounds sweet ... in these insecure times' (Bauman 2001: 3). Whilst within regeneration policy and related agendas the communities being referred to are predominantly those of place, Rose suggests that the community of the Third Way is not primarily a geographical space but rather a *moral* space through which individual identities are constructed (Rose 1999: 172; our emphasis).

The regeneration of social relations within communities is central to this concept and clearly has strong links with communitarianism (Pierson *et al.* 2000). Whilst Tony Blair has repeatedly stressed that his attitude differs from Conservative calls for a return to moral values, it is founded upon a strong sense of morality, which overlaps with communitarian values at many points. The emphasis on behaviour and moral choice echoes the presumptions of communal moral failure put forward by proponents of an 'underclass' (such as Murray 1995; Field 1996), though Levitas (2000) suggests that inserting 'community' here acts as a key marker in differentiating centrist New Labour from the New Right.

Much of this has been encapsulated within the discourse of the 'Third Way', the broad philosophy and principles behind the programme of the New Labour government (see also Jordan and Jordan 2000). What is clear is that, within the Third Way framework, the regeneration of communities becomes central to the wider regeneration of society. Indeed Jordan (2001) suggests that New Labour have responded to inequality by reinterpreting social justice precisely in terms of 'opportunity' and 'community'. In this context, questions emerge about how citizens with few resources (social, economic and cultural) are able to participate effectively. Whilst the 'new localism' ensures participation through methods such as citizens' juries, questions remain about the overall level of effective and meaningful resident participation within regeneration processes (see, for example, Anastacio *et al.* 2000). There are examples where local groups have taken the initiative. The 'Getting Engaged' project, for example, in Lambeth's Vassall ward has been set up to identify the specific barriers to Black and minority ethnic involvement within local regeneration processes, with the aim of working with communities to address their own needs (Benjamin 2001).

In general, however, the pervasive deployment of 'community' throughout New Labour programmes minimises the depth of stratification around class, gender, religion and ethnicity. It rhetorically brings about the 'classless society', whilst discussions around poverty and inequality are replaced with the term 'social exclusion' (see also Lister 1998).

In urban areas where poverty is spatially concentrated, such differences and inequalities exert considerable pressure on residents' lives. Diversity is central to the local politics of regeneration here. The implementation of area-based regeneration programmes is based on the residents of neighbourhoods and communities having the capacity to act as assertive citizens and democratic agents (Imrie and Raco 2003). This can only work if the self-interests of partners and stakeholders are articulated and recognised. It is crucial, therefore, to deconstruct the concept of 'community' in terms of residential experience and to understand the significance of 'difference' for the regeneration process and its relationship to concepts of citizenship, participation, and power. This task is undertaken in the rest of the chapter.

Gender and ethnicity in regeneration processes

Whilst women predominate in informal community work, regeneration processes still largely ignore the significance of gender. The gender blindness of regeneration is now well documented (see for example Riseborough 1998). Bruegel (2000: 2) also suggests that urban regeneration policies are 'dis-engendered' and calls for a broader gendering of policy. Indeed, regeneration as a gendered process has tended to marginalise women in a variety of ways. Recently, Alsop *et al.* (2001) examined the role of young women in urban regeneration in England and found that women were under-represented at all levels within the regeneration process. They argued that the particular needs of women (as a diverse social group) have largely been invisible at both the national level of policy development and the local area-based level of programme delivery. The authors also suggest that the government's National Strategy for Neighbourhood Renewal (SEU 2000a) itself lacks a systematic and detailed analysis of gender disadvantage. Nor have the gender dimensions of economic inequality been substantively addressed within urban regeneration programmes (Grant 2002), even though the family is pivotal to the work of the Social Exclusion Unit established under New Labour (Hague *et al.* 2001). Alsop *et al.* (2001) further indicate that women are under-represented in regeneration structures. In many cases, they found no formal apparatus existed to ensure that women were heard in the regeneration process, and practical support for inclusion in terms of childcare during regeneration meetings was often overlooked. The national evaluation of the New Deal for Communities has obliquely acknowledged that, thus far, there has been virtually no recognition of gender differences within NDC programmes (NRU 2003).

In Scotland, Scott *et al.* (2000) also explored the way partnership working ignores local women in its processes. They found that, because women provided a great majority of partnership board members, there was a general assumption that women's interests were being adequately addressed – which they were not. In fact, specific goals for women were often viewed as unnecessary or counter-productive. Nor was any attention given to the different ways in which poverty and disadvantage impact on men and women. Scott *et al.* (2000) also uncovered gender-specific barriers to effective involvement in partnership governance, which included multiple home and care-based responsibilities and lack of access to childcare.

Far from regeneration dissolving gender difference and inequality, gender is central to achieving it. Moser (1993) has attempted to deconstruct the different approaches of women and men to the task of 'community management', their different relationships to the consumption needs of their community, and the difficulties they have to overcome at both personal and structural levels. She focuses particularly on the gendered nature of women's work and of women's role in the community (as carers), and suggests that men's work in the community also has a gendered character. Whereas women are involved in the community as an extension of their role in the household and therefore see themselves as community managers, men see themselves as community politicians. This has implications for women's position within the regeneration process, not only in terms of their unequal participation but also in relation to their unpaid labour.

It is also crucial to think about how gender intersects with other aspects of identity within communities, such as ethnicity. Despite evidence suggesting that women and minority ethnic groups are over-represented in areas undergoing regeneration, there is a lack of specific policy initiatives in relation to ethnicity and gender (Brownill and Darke 1998; Gill 2002). Regeneration programmes that do recognise the importance of racial and ethnic specificity (stemming from race equality guidelines[4] and race relations legislation) have still largely failed to add a gender dynamic to their analysis. This has two main outcomes. First, the needs of women from minority ethnic communities can easily become overlooked or second, their needs are based upon stereotypical assumptions about their femininity, for example, via the establishment of sewing clubs for Asian women. Gill (2002) also argues that greater attention to the needs of Black and minority ethnic women is necessary in the evaluation of regeneration programmes, alongside more effective participation of Black and minority ethnic communities in regeneration initiatives and community development.

Increasingly, regeneration programmes are at least attempting to deal with these 'real' dilemmas by engaging with the diversity of residential experience in an inclusive way, and by trying to increase the numbers of women from minority ethnic communities within regeneration processes. Even so, such engagement can be clumsy. An NDC in the East Midlands, for example, organised such an event for women from the 'Asian' community (Pierson *et al.* 2000). At first glance, this is a positive step towards inclusion. However, the event was organised through consultation with a local Muslim women's group and held in the local Muslim women's centre. This is problematic for two reasons. First, it assumes a degree of homogeneity within the 'Asian' community and fails to recognise the differences among religious and ethnic groups. Second, problems may also arise from relying on a group identified solely by religious identity, as certain women may feel excluded on the grounds of their sexuality or marital status.[5]

Yet, there are several examples contrary to this, which indicate a more dynamic and inclusive approach to participation. For example, Somerville notes that the Tassibee Project for Mirpuri Punjabi speaking women in Rotherham provides a good example of a community-controlled learning initiative, as it enabled local women to increase their confidence and self-esteem alongside more practical projects such as healthy eating advice. Ultimately, he suggests that such a project shows that 'developing a community-controlled initiative can change the nature of community itself' (Somerville 2002: 33). Mayo (2003) also notes that the Bangladeshi Youth Forum in Birmingham is further evidence of the concept of 'community' being used to positive effect, as it has allowed local youths to gather around a shared community of interest, with positive results. Recognising such ethnic diversity within communities is therefore an important dimension for inclusive community participation and, in turn, effective urban regeneration. This recognition needs to acknowledge not only diversity between different ethnic and racial groups within the community but also within each ethnic and racial group, as significant differences exist both between and within groups.

Community cohesion and citizenship

The emerging community cohesion agenda raises many interesting dimensions for thinking about our contemporary communities, the diversity of residential experience and how regeneration programmes should respond. It bears the trade-mark New Labour elements of communitarian moralism, whereby communities themselves are central for wider welfare reform and modernisation. It is also consistent with the views of commentators who argue that societies with greater social cohesion are more successful (Putnam 2000).

The community cohesion initiative also raises inescapable questions of identity, values, and citizenship. The Cantle Report notes that 'there has been little attempt to develop clear values which focus on what it means to be a citizen of a modern multi-racial Britain … many of the present problems seem to owe a great deal to the failure to communicate and agree a set of clear values that can govern behaviour' (Home Office 2001a: 18).

A further dimension of the community cohesion agenda relevant here is the extent to which it is not just about forging a sense of community but also about creating a shared sense of place:

> Community cohesion, as indicated earlier, is about helping micro-communities to gel or mesh into an integrated whole. These divided communities would need to develop common goals and a shared vision. This would seem to imply that such groups should occupy a common sense of place as well. The high levels of residential segregation found in many English towns would make it difficult to achieve community cohesion.
>
> (Home Office 2001a: 70)

The Cantle Report makes clear its intention that 'cohesion' be rooted in individuals moving beyond the pressures of residential segregation to adopt a sense of belonging in their community – their 'place'. Amin (2002) is critical of this. He argues that work on urban youth anthropologies (see, for example, Back 1996) demonstrates an already strong *territorial* sense of place amongst young people – in both majority and minority ethnic groups, which are based on turf claims defended in exclusionary ways. Amin argues, therefore, that rather than an agenda based around a unitary sense of place, what is needed are 'initiatives that exploit the potential for overlap and cross-fertilisation within spaces that in reality support multiple publics'. He goes on to criticise the very application of the term 'community' within many regeneration strategies:

> The distinctive feature of mixed neighbourhoods is that they are communities without community, each marked by multiple and hybrid affiliations of varying social and geographical reach, and each intersecting momentarily (or not) with another one for common local resources and amenities. They are not homogenous or primarily place-based communities … they are simply mixtures of social groups with varying intensities of local affiliation, varying reasons for local attachment, and varying values and cultural practices.
>
> (Amin 2002)

Whilst there are reservations about suggesting that contemporary spatial communities or neighbourhoods are 'simply mixtures of social groups' (given the persistence of structural inequality in shaping where and how people live, particularly as differentiated by ethnicity[6]), the development of common values tied to a sense of shared place may not be the best solution for creating cohesion in pluralist Britain. Amin's position here has strong links with that of Bauman who argues, in relation to ghettoization, that no

> 'collective buffer' can be forged in the contemporary ghettos for the single reason that ghetto experience dissolves solidarity and destroys mutual trust … A ghetto is not a greenhouse of community feelings. It is on the contrary a laboratory of social disintegration, atomization and anomie … To sum up: ghetto means the *impossibility of community*.
>
> (Bauman 2001: 122)

Other observers such as Kundnani note that the notion of community cohesion brings with it the end, not the enhancement, of multicultural definitions of citizenship. The Cantle Report urged that a set of core values should bring together otherwise diverse cultures with a 'greater acceptance of national institutions' (Home Office 2001a). This, argues Kundnani, marks the limit of government tolerance for the 'multiculturalist settlement', which has dominated race relations in Britain for two decades, and through which ethnic communities were relatively free to build their own parallel institutions (Kundnani 2002). What now counts as a 'national' institution remains an intriguing question, however. It could be argued that the Muslim Parliament, for example, is also a national institution of a kind.

Rather than relying upon the safety and security of community as a tool of regeneration, we need to think about alternative ways of forging understanding and cohesion, which are compatible with our diverse identities and standpoints. Lister (2003: 81) suggests some 'solutions', showing the value of working towards 'a politics of solidarity in difference', which would, Lister argues, build in difference at the very heart of the political process through representation and voice. This also requires a conception of the political subject as fluid, dynamic and shifting. 'Transversal politics' (Yuval-Davis 1997) is a similar conception, which allows for a process of rooting and shifting in which participants remain rooted in their own values but at the same time are willing to shift views in dialogue with others. Such processes may facilitate the development of a 'politics of belonging' that would transcend the older dichotomous choices of equality and difference. Two examples where this has happened are the Women's National Coalition in South Africa (Kemp *et al.* 1995) and the Northern Ireland women's coalition (Lister 2003: 84).

Conclusion

The first part of this chapter provided an overview of contemporary regeneration programmes, focusing specifically on housing in these initiatives. In doing so, the chapter has suggested that housing, when understood as a set of social relations, networks and patterns of activity, is inescapably the central instrument for the regeneration of highly disadvantaged urban areas. In appraising the flagship programmes of New Labour we noted that local citizens, within frameworks of 'participation', were being called upon to help resolve intractable social problems, the causes of which lay well outside local reach. Regeneration initiatives view these as specific to particular areas and 'neighbourhoods' and are amenable to better organisation and collaboration among mainstream services. Recent information from the field provides, in this admittedly ever-evolving story, the depressing conclusion that some initiatives, at least in some areas, are actually *decreasing* rather than augmenting social capital. Housing market renewal in particular will likely be a catalyst for unpredictable but privatised outcomes in areas of low demand. There, a mix of more affordable mortgage products and continuing local government transfer of housing stock may well create greater pressure for gentrification.

The second part of the chapter problematised the ways in which 'community' figures within New Labour regeneration measures. We have shown that, within regeneration processes, community can be used as a tool of governance with positive and negative effects. When attention is given to diversity and difference, and in fact forms the basis for action, then the discourse of community has the potential to be empowering. However, in cases where community is called upon to minimise difference and power, the exact opposite is true. This is a complex business, and individual residential experiences cannot always be neatly contained within the concept of community used by regeneration and government policy. Attempts to impose community and particular values can further alienate those within the area who do not 'fit' into the prescribed categories of identity by virtue of their sexuality, religion or other attributes. Nevertheless, regeneration policy and programmes must respond to the challenge posed by diversity. In many ways, the community cohesion agenda is one attempt at doing this. However, it too raises as many concerns as solutions, especially around the construction of values and citizenship. It is as yet too soon to tell whether the programme has helped to foster more cohesive and inclusive urban communities. In the meantime, alternative approaches such as 'transversal politics' may provide the basis for citizen organisations to find their voice within the policy process.

Notes

1 The inordinate time devoted to 'process' has parallels in the US, where 'process' tasks, that is developing appropriate mechanisms of governance and functioning working relationships among partners, dominated comprehensive community initiatives and to a degree substituted for service activity and outcomes (Chaskin 2000; Kubisch *et al.* 2001).

2 Housing Market Renewal Pathfinder covers nine sub-regions, which include some 700,000 of the estimated nearly 900,000 low demand properties in England. Most are in the north, including parts of Manchester, Salford and Hull and other cities along the M62 corridor but also include some areas in the midlands such as parts of Birmingham and Stoke-on-Trent.

3 For example, in a now infamous speech Tony Blair delivered to the Women's Institute in 2000, for which he received a slow handclap, Levitas (2000) notes that eighteen references to 'community' were made.

4 Good practice guidelines on race equality are now integral to the regeneration process and, whilst they do not provide prescriptive answers to all race equality issues, the guidance is there to support regeneration partnerships in developing ways to tackle race equality issues. For example the New Deal for Communities' Race Equality Guidance outlines the principles for ensuring the inclusion of minority ethnic groups in developing local plans around increasing employment, improving education and health, and reducing crime (NRU 2000; see also SEU 2000b), though this has not always been the case. In launching the Race Equality Guidelines for the New Deal for Communities agenda, the then Minister for Neighbourhood Renewal stated: 'This is the first time the Department has produced such detailed and comprehensive guidance on race equality issues in the regeneration field. It underlines the Government's strength of commitment to race equality. It tackles key issues such as institutional racism, racial harassment and race equality, particularly in areas with low ethnic minority populations' (DETR 2000).

5 This echoes the multiculturalist trend within social policy where the primary emphasis is on cultural practices, in which stereotypical notions of culture are often collapsed into a religious identity (Sahgal and Yuval-Davis 1992).

6 See, for example, the recent work by Deborah Phillips on Black and minority ethnic group concentration, which for some ethnic groups reflects 'persistent inequalities in housing, employment and other spheres' (Phillips 1998: 1685).

References

Alsop, R., Cilsby, S. and Craig, G. (2001) *Young, Urban and Female: Young Women and City Regeneration, Summary of Findings and Recommendations*, London: YWCA.

Ambrose, P. (2003) *Money Problems on Sea*, Brighton: Health and Social Policy Research Centre, University of Brighton.

Amin, A. (2002) 'Ethnicity and the multicultural city: living with diversity', *Environment and Planning*, 34: 959–80.

Anastacio, J., Gidley, B., Hart, L., Keith, M., Mayo, M. and Kowarzik, U. (2000) *Reflecting Realities: Participants' Perspectives on Integrated Communities and Sustainable Development*, Bristol: Policy Press in association with the Joseph Rowntree Foundation.

Baeten, G. (2001) 'Urban regeneration, social exclusion and shifting power geometries on the South Bank, London', *Geographische Zeitschrift*, 89, 2: 103–12.

Bauman, Z. (2001) *Community: Seeking Safety in an Insecure World*, Cambridge: Polity Press.

Back, L. (1996) *New Ethnicities and Urban Culture: Racisms and Multi-culture in Young Lives*, London: Routledge.

Benjamin, A. (2001) 'Ethnic barriers', *The Guardian*, 12 December, London: Guardian Newspapers.

Bentley, T., McCarthy H. and Mean, M. (2003*) Inside Out: Rethinking Inclusive Communities*, London: Demos/Barrow Cadbury Trust.

Berthoud, R. (2001) *Rich Place, Poor Place: An Analysis of Geographical Variations in Household Income within Britain*, Colchester: Institute for Economic and Social Research, University of Essex.

Blacon Management Neighbourhood Pathfinder (2002) *Delivery Plan*, Chester: Blacon Management Neighbourhood Pathfinder.

Bowers, K., Johnson, S., Hirschfield, A. and Young, C. (2003) *Investigating the Crime Reduction Claims of NDC Partnerships,* Sheffield: Northern Crime Consortium.

Bramley, G. and Pawson, H. (2002) 'Low demand for housing: incidence, causes and UK national policy implications', *Urban Studies*, 39, 3: 393–422.

Bright, J. (2002) 'The big picture lessons from the national evaluation', in *Managing Neighbourhood Change*, Neighbourhood Management National Conference report.

Brownill, S. and Darke, J. (1998) *'Rich Mix': Inclusive Strategies for Urban Regeneration*, York: Joseph Rowntree Foundation.

Bruegel, I. (2000) 'Getting explicit: gender and local economic development', *Local Economy*, 15, 1: 2–8.

Chaskin, R. (2000) *Decision Making and Action at the Neighborhood Level: An Exploration of Mechanisms and Process*, Chicago: Chapin Hall Center for Children at the University of Chicago.

Cole, I. (2003) 'Evaluating the New Deal for Communities – the UK approach to community renewal', presented at seminar on Urban Frontiers Program/Strengthening Local Communities, Sydney, July 2002.

Commission on the Future of Multi-Ethnic Britain (2000) *The Future of Multi-Ethnic Britain* (Parekh Report), London: Profile Books.

Community Development Projects (1977) *Gilding the Ghetto*, London: Home Office.

Deacon, A. (2000) 'CAVA and the moral reordering of welfare under New Labour', Workshop Paper No 10, prepared for Workshop Three on Analysing Policy Change and Implementation, Friday 11 February 2000, ESRC Research Group on Care, Values, and the Future of Welfare, Leeds: University of Leeds.

Department for Work and Pensions (DWP) (2003) *UK National Action Plan on Social Inclusion 2003–2005*, London: DWP.

Department of the Environment, Transport and the Regions (DETR) (1999) *Report of Policy Action Team 4 Neighbourhood Management*, London: The Stationery Office.

—— (2000) Press Notice 0084, 8 Februrary, London: DETR.

Field, F. (1996) *Stakeholder Welfare*, London: Institute for Economic Affairs.

Gill, F. (2002) 'The diverse experiences of Black and minority ethnic women in relation to housing and social exclusion', in P. Somerville and A. Steele (eds) *Race, Housing and Social Exclusion*, London and Philadelphia, PA: Jessica Kingsley Publishers.

Goodchild, B., Hickman, P. and Robinson, D. (2002) 'Unpopular housing in England in conditions of low demand', *Town Planning Review*, 73, 4: 373–93.

Grant, L. (2002) 'Addressing women's economic disadvantage in local economies: the limitations and benefits of partnerships', *Policy and Politics*, 30, 1: 97–113.

Hague, E., Thomas, C. and Williams, S. (2001) 'Exclusive visions? Representations of family, work and gender in the work of the British Social Exclusion Unit', *Gender, Place and Culture*, 8, 1: 73–82.

Hall, S. (2000) 'The way forward for regeneration? Lessons from the Single Regeneration Budget Challenge Fund', *Local Government Studies*, 26, 1: 1–14.

Hastings, A. (1996) 'Unravelling the process of "partnership" in urban regeneration policy', *Urban Studies*, 33, 2: 253–68.

Hetherington, P. (2003) 'Back from the brink', *The Guardian*, 24 September, London: Guardian Newspapers.

Hoban, M. and Beresford, P. (2001) 'Regenerating regeneration', *Community Development Journal*, 36, 4: 312–20.

Home Office (2001a) *Community Cohesion: A Report of the Independent Review Team* (Cantle Report), London: Home Office.

—— (2001b) *Building Cohesive Communities: A Report of the Ministerial Group on Public Order and Community Cohesion* (Denham Report), London: Home Office.

Imrie, R. and Raco, M. (2003) *Urban Renaissance? New Labour, Community and Urban Policy*, Bristol: Policy Press.

Jordan, B. (2001) 'Tough love: social work, social exclusion and the Third Way', *British Journal of Social Work*, 31: 527–46.

Jordan, B. with Jordan, C. (2000) *Social Work and the Third Way: Tough Love as Social Policy*, London: Sage.

Keenan, P., Lowe, S. and Spencer, S. (1999) 'Housing abandonment in inner cities – the politics of low demand for housing', *Housing Studies*, 14, 5: 703–16.

Kemp, A., Madlala, N., Moodley, A. and Salo, E. (1995) 'The dawn of a new day: redefining South African feminism', in A. Basu (ed.) *The Challenge of Local Feminisms*, Boulder, CO: Westview Press.

Kubisch, A., Connell, J. and Fulbright-Anderson, K. (2001) 'Evaluating complex community initiatives: theory, measurement and analysis', in J. Pierson and J. Smith (eds) *Rebuilding Community: Policy and Practice of Urban Regeneration*, Basingstoke: Palgrave.

Kundnani, A. (2002) *The Death of Multiculturalism*, London: Institute of Race Relations.

Leech, K. (2002) *Through Our Long Exile*, London: Darton, Longman and Todd.

Levitas, R. (2000) 'Community, Utopia and New Labour', *Local Economy*, 15, 3: 188–97.

Lister, R. (1998) 'From equality to social inclusion: New Labour and the welfare state', *Critical Social Policy*, 18, 2: 215–25.

—— (2003) *Citizenship: Feminist Perspectives*, 2nd edn, Basingstoke: Palgrave.

Local Government Association (2002) *Guidance on Community Cohesion*, London: LGA.

Maclennan, D. (2000) *Changing Places, Engaging People*, York: York Publishing Services.

Massey, D. and Denton, N. (1992) *American Apartheid: Segregation and the Making of the Underclass*, Cambridge, MA: Harvard University Press.

Mayo, M. (2003) 'Building heavens, havens or hells? Community as policy in the context of the post-Washington consensus', Keynote address at Communities Conference, 18–20 September 2003, Leeds: Trinity and All Saints College, University of Leeds.

Moser, C. (1993) *Gender, Planning and Development: Theory, Practice and Training*, London: Routledge.

Murray, C. (1995) 'The emerging British underclass', in R. Lister (ed.) *Charles Murray and the Underclass: The Developing Debate*, London: Institute of Economic Affairs.

National Housing Federation (2002) *Housing Market Renewal Pathfinders – The Story So Far*, London: NHF.

Neighbourhood Renewal Unit (NRU) (2000) *NDC Race Equality Guidance*, London: Office of the Deputy Prime Minister.

—— (2003) *Research Report 7 New Deal for Communities The National Evaluation Annual Report 2002–2003*, London: NRU.

Oc, T., Tiesdell, S. and Moynihan, D. (1999) 'The death and life of City Challenge: the potential for lasting impacts in a limited-life urban regeneration initiative', *Planning Practice and Research*, 12, 4: 367–81.

Office of the Deputy Prime Minister (2003) *Sustainable Communities: Building for the Future*, London: Office of the Deputy Prime Minister.

Ouseley, H. (2001) *Community Pride Not Prejudice*, Bradford: Bradford Vision.

Palmer, H. (2003) 'A hole in the ocean', *New Start*, 31, October: 12.

Peach, C. (1996) 'Does Britain have ghettos?' *Transactions – Institute of British Geographers*, 21, 1: 216–35.

Pierson J., Smith, J. and Worley, C. (2000) *New Deal for Communities and Community Participation*, Staffordshire: Housing and Community Research Unit, Staffordshire University.

Phillips, D. (1998) 'Black minority ethnic concentration, segregation and dispersal in Britain', *Urban Studies*, 35, 10: 1681–702.

Piratin, P. (1948) *Our Flag Stays Red*, London: Martin Lawrence.

Power, A. and Bergin, E. (1999) *Neighbourhood Management*, CASE paper 31, London: Centre for Analysis of Social Exclusion, London School of Economics.

Power, A. and Mumford, K. (1999) *The Slow Death of Great Cities? Urban Abandonment or Urban Renaissance*, York: York Publishing Services.

Putnam, R. (2000) *Bowling Alone: The Collapse and Revival of American Community*, London: Simon and Schuster.

Riseborough, M. (1998) 'Regeneration and the curious tale of gender blindness', *International Journal of Public Sector Management*, 11, 1: 611–21.

Ritchie, D. (2001) *Oldham Independent Review: One Oldham One Future*, Manchester: Government Office for the North West.

Robson, B., Parkinson, M., Boddy, M. and Maclennan, D. (1994) *Assessing the Impact of Urban Policy*, London: HMSO.

Rose, N. (1999) *Powers of Freedom: Reframing Political Thought*, Cambridge: Cambridge University Press.

——(2000) 'Community, citizenship and the Third Way', *American Behavioral Scientist*, 43, 9: 1395–411.

Sahgal, G. and Yuval-Davis, N. (1992) 'Introduction: fundamentalism, multiculturalism and women in Britain', in G. Sahgal and N. Yuval-Davis (eds) *Refusing Holy Orders: Women and Fundamentalism in Britain*, London: Virago: 1–25.

Scott, G., with Brown, U., Long, G. and McKenzie, J. (2000) *Women's Issues in Local Partnership Working. Social Inclusion Research Programme*, Research Findings No. 1, Edinburgh: Scottish Executive.

Smith, M. and Beazley, M. (2000) 'Progressive regimes, partnerships and the involvement of local communities: a framework for evaluation', *Public Administration*, 78, 4: 855–78.

Social Exclusion Unit (SEU) (1998) *Bringing Britain Together: A National Strategy for Neighbourhood Renewal*, Cm 4045, London: The Stationery Office.

Social Exclusion Unit (SEU) (2000a) *National Strategy for Neighbourhood Renewal*, London: Cabinet Office.

——(SEU) (2000b) *Minority Ethnic Issues in Social Exclusion and Neighbourhood Renewal: A Guide to the Work of the SEU and the Policy Action Teams So Far*, London: Cabinet Office.

——(2001) *A New Commitment to Neighbourhood Renewal National Strategy Action Plan*, London: Office of the Deputy Prime Minister.

Somerville, P. (1998) 'Explanations of social exclusion: where does housing fit in?' *Housing Studies*, 13, 6: 761–80.

——(2002) *Community Control: A Position Paper*, Lincoln: University of Lincoln.

Taylor, M. (2000) *Top Down Meets Bottom Up: Neighbourhood Management*, York: Joseph Rowntree Foundation.

Tyler, P. (2003) *Partnership Evaluation Report: Aston Pride New Deal for Communities*, Cambridge Economic Associates.

Wyley, E. and Hammel, D. (1999) 'Islands of decay in seas of renewal: housing policy and the resurgence of gentrification', *Housing Policy Debate*, 10, 4: 711–71.

Yuval-Davis, N. (1997) *Gender and Nation*, London: Sage.

11 Housing and social policy futures

Peter Somerville and Nigel Sprigings

New Labour housing policies

The New Labour Government (NLG) originally set out four main types of housing policy: making the market work; empowering individuals; ensuring best value in housing services; and strengthening communities (Armstrong 1999; Kemp 1999; Somerville 2000). Seven years on, it is timely to review the performance of NLG in the light of (among other things) the evidence, argument and analyses contained in this book.

First of all, after some initial uncertainty, it has become clear that NLG is neo-liberal in the sense that it seeks to give greater priority to ensuring a relatively unfettered operation of market forces. For example, it has continued and expanded the programme of large-scale transfer of council housing stock; it has developed new private finance initiatives; it has promoted market testing under best value; it continues to prioritise the views of owner-occupiers, and is supportive of a revival of private renting; its latest Housing Act allows private firms to become eligible for subsidy for new social housing provision. In Peck and Tickell's (2002) terms, however, NLG is an example of 'roll out' rather than 'roll back' neo-liberalism, in the sense that it is interested in re-regulation as well as deregulation. It advocates a wider and larger new role for government, for example, investing to create, enhance and equalise opportunity for all (the 'investor' state). The major new housing policies of NLG, such as the Sustainable Communities Plan (see Sprigings and Somerville, this volume), the 'Keyworker living' programme,[1] and the housing market renewal pathfinders (see Pierson and Worley, this volume) are clear illustrations of this wider role: all involve massive interventions in the housing market to correct systematic distortions (excess of demand over supply in the south, and vice versa in the north) and to ensure that the market works more efficiently (i.e. to produce an overall balance of supply and demand across the country as a whole). NLG's overriding consideration is to make the market work.

The question is, however: work for whom? Somerville (2000: 191) argued that 'making the market work' tends 'to promote the inclusion of those who can manage to access the market as "consumers", while continuing to exclude those who cannot.' The effective operation of a market does not require the participation of all possible consumers but only of a sufficiently large mass with sufficient spending capacity. In a society with a high degree of income inequality, the market can still work very well (in terms of matching supply with demand for the majority of people) even though lower income households cannot afford to enter the market. If 'making the market work' is not going to discriminate against the poor, however, greater equality of household incomes is necessary. Yet NLG has no policies to reduce income inequality as such, though some of its policies (e.g. minimum wage, working tax credit) may help towards this, to a small extent. The Sustainable Communities Plan is directed primarily at increasing the availability of housing supply for middle income groups (mainly commuters but also keyworkers), while the housing market renewal pathfinders are concerned with 'managed decline', which includes measures to increase the value of assets in these areas, encouraging possible gentrification. In both cases, the emphasis is on ensuring an overall balance between housing supply and demand, so that the price of housing in these areas will be neither too high nor too low. 'Making the market work' is not concerned with what happens to those people who cannot afford housing at this 'fair' or 'reasonable' price.

NLG's second type of housing policy, 'empowering individuals', has been very much less in evidence. For example, while retaining major individual rights such as the right to buy, NLG has introduced no new ones at all (except arguably in relation to homelessness – see below). The focus of policy has been on 'empowering' individuals primarily as users of public services and as members of communities. The policy of 'empowering individuals' has therefore been largely merged with those of Best Value and strengthening communities, and the nature of this 'empowerment' can be summed up in one word: consultation. Consultation is one of the four 'C's under Best Value (the others being concerned with service review, benchmarking and market testing), and is considered *de rigueur* for all initiatives directed at neighbourhoods or communities. Strictly speaking, however, consultation is not empowerment: at its best, it places service users and communities at the heart, but not at the head, of decision-making processes. Its aim (as with Best Value generally) is to make public services more responsive to the needs of individuals and communities (the philosophy of continuous improvement), but not necessarily to transform the relationship between government and citizens.

Beyond consultation, NLG's general approach has been described as 'steering centralism' (OPSR 2002). Essentially, this means that power is devolved to a variety of institutions and collectivities, on condition that they act in ways that NLG considers 'appropriate'. These institutions can include local authorities, housing associations and even community groups, working in partnership, with 'appropriateness' meaning efficient performance, as measured by independent inspection and audit. According to this approach, community groups such as tenants' and residents' organisations can actually take a lead in developing and running public services, but they will be subject to a more or less rigorous regulation regime.

A rather different example of 'steering centralism' has recently become clear in relation to the large-scale transfer of local authority housing. Collectively, council tenants have the power to reject their landlord's proposals to transfer their homes to another landlord such as a housing association. NLG, however, has made the transfer option look increasingly attractive, for example, by restricting investment funding for local authorities who choose to retain ownership and management of their stock, by requiring them to make all their homes 'decent' by 2010 (in England), by writing off the debt on housing that is transferred, etc. By these means, NLG seeks to 'steer' local authorities into stock transfer, even though it is tenants who have the final say, in a secret ballot. From NLG's point of view, after all, the purpose of stock transfer would appear to be to remove housing from local democratic control and subject it to more direct central influence through regulation by the Housing Corporation – i.e. a classic case of roll-back (local de-statisation), roll-out (national re-statisation) neo-liberalism.

For those for whom the market does not work, and perhaps cannot be made to work, what does NLG offer? For council tenants, it offers the long-term prospect of living in decent homes (provided that their landlord does not choose to keep their homes under council ownership and control or that they do not reject the landlord's stock transfer proposals). For private tenants, unless their home is in an area covered by one of NLG's numerous area-based initiatives, NLG offers nothing at all (houses in multiple occupation are to be licensed, but NLG rejected Des Turner's private members' bill for all private landlords to be licensed[2]). For homeless people, the Homelessness Act 2002 has extended the range of priority groups for whom local authorities have a duty to secure housing (e.g. to include sixteen- and seventeen-year-olds and a number of other so-called 'vulnerable' groups), but NLG has not correspondingly increased the funding available to meet these needs. For those requiring housing with support, NLG has introduced a new regime, Supporting People, with a single budget to fund all support costs in supported housing, which has already impacted negatively on groups that are seen to be less 'deserving' of support, such as substance misusers and ex-offenders (Somerville and Rust 2003).[3] For homeless families with children, the policy of phasing out the use of bed-and-breakfast has led to some improvement in their housing circumstances, but the use of B&B for homeless households without children may have increased. Housing provision for women fleeing domestic violence (both refuges and move-on accommodation) remains inadequate (see Smith, this volume). For disabled people, the introduction of Part M into the Building Regulations in 1999 represents a clear advance but arguably falls some way short of meeting the needs and demands of disabled people themselves (see Milner, this volume). For lower income households generally, who are unable to access affordable housing, there has been little in the way of new investment to provide such housing. It is probably fair to say that most of the affordable housing that will be provided under the Communities Plan will not be located within reach of the households that need it. Finally, for those who are not British citizens, such as asylum seekers, NLG offers an entirely segregated housing service (the National Asylum Seeker Service), with no user choice or financial support (see, for example, Pearl and Zetter 2002). In this policy, as in its policies on community cohesion, as pointed out by Cooper and by Pierson and Worley in this volume, NLG has signalled the limits of its tolerance towards those who do not conform to certain (inevitably shifting and contentious) national minimum requirements.

Contributors to this book have suggested contrasting types of explanation for housing and social policies, including those of the current UK government. In his chapter, for example, Spink explained how some policies at some times attempted, like New Labour, to make the market work through 'rational planning', while others were more ideologically driven, such as the Conservative governments of the 1980s. All governments, at all times, appeared to pay close attention to the effects of changing housing supply and demand on the national economy, and to formulate their policies, to some extent, with an eye on such economic considerations. Similarly, all governments, at all times, and subject to the demands of planning and ideology, attempted to draft their policies, and present those policies, in such a way as to achieve maximum appeal to the electorate. Implicit in Spink's account, however, is an assumption of 'path dependence' (North 1990), according to which the development of particular policies and ways of acting tends to rule out the possibility of alternative paths being taken. Thus, for example, the introduction of rent control in 1915, although intended as a temporary measure to resolve a housing crisis, 'fixed' the housing market in such a way as to secure a seventy-five-year decline of private renting. Similarly, the introduction of subsidised council housing in 1919, again intended only as a temporary measure, led to a situation in the 1970s where more than one-third of the population lived in council homes. The point is that, once such policies are adopted, they develop to a certain extent at their own momentum, and help to shape the context within which governments make their decisions – they affect what form of 'rational planning' is practicable; they change the nature of the housing market and the economy generally, and they determine, to a degree, what will appeal to the 'rational voter'. New Labour policies can therefore be understood, in part, as constrained by the 'path-breaking' policies of their Conservative predecessors, in particular the right to buy and the shift towards more marketised, but also more regulated, governance.

Joined-up policy?

A number of chapters in this book (for example, Cooper; Pierson and Worley) argue for the importance of housing as a focus for joining up policies and practices across different services. However, this could mean a number of different things.

It could mean, for example, as Bramley (1997) has argued, the end of housing policy itself, as it becomes part of economic policy or regeneration policy or merely an adjunct to another kind of policy such as planning policy or welfare policy. Or it could mean that the focus of housing management, housing service delivery and housing professionalism has changed, so that it is less concerned with the 'bread-and-butter' activities of collecting rent, letting properties and carrying out repairs, and more to do with 'joint working' with other agencies such as social services, police, schools, youth and leisure services, employment services, etc., to ensure the effective management or regeneration of neighbourhoods and of the people who live in them (as envisaged, for example, in the National Housing Federation's recent rebranding exercise for housing associations, entitled 'IN Business for Neighbourhoods'). Or it could mean, as suggested by Cooper (this volume), that a focus on place in particular is important for making sense of people's lived experience: in Habermasian terms, the colonisation of the 'lifeworld' (e.g. place-based identities) by the 'system' (which includes the 'top-down' organisation of public services) needs to be resisted and reversed, and housing or residence constitutes a crucial site on which such resistance can be organised.

Housing policy/practice can therefore be 'joined up' in at least three different senses: first, it can be subsumed within another kind of policy/practice altogether; second, housing policymakers/practitioners can work in partnership with policy-makers/practitioners in other fields, disciplines or professions, to deliver wider policy aims and objectives; and third, housing itself, as a form and set of social relations that is relatively fixed in space, can be a focus for joined up social and political activity, based on shared experience and values.

This book has, for the sake of convenience, divided the field of housing and social policy into different categories such as class, race, gender and disability, but all the contributors, especially Milner, have stressed that these categories are fluid, intersecting and overlapping. In different ways, the contributors have emphasised that each human being is different, an individual with a unique identity constructed out of different social categories, roles and experiences. Whereas Somerville, however, suggests that no particular category is central, Milner argues that the category of age, as expressed through a concept of the life course, serves as a template of some kind through which the other categories are mediated. The point is that, as beings who occupy (residential) space, we share a common material reality, which we experience very differently at different stages of our lives, irrespective of our class, race or gender. Housing can be represented as (among other things) a container of bodies, and bodies vary most dramatically according to age and impairment. Arguably, therefore, housing, as a key focus for such variation, can serve as a base from which to make sense (in a 'joined-up' way) of differences in gender, race and class. Broadly speaking, this is the approach taken in this book by Cooper, Somerville, Harrison, Smith, Milner, and Pierson and Worley.

'Community' is a concept that is most often invoked both as a justification for joined-up policy and services and as the basis on which policy and services are or should be organised. As Pierson and Worley show (this volume), NLG's flagship policies such as New Deal for Communities and neighbourhood management fit this general pattern. This means that, from NLG's point of view, these policies are to be judged not only in terms of their ability to meet the floor targets they have been set (covering employment, education and crime, as well as housing) but also in terms of how well integrated the different services are within each project and how seamlessly the project performs overall in serving its local 'community'. One strange aspect of this, however, is the issue of 'mainstreaming', which is concerned (among other things) with ensuring that the practices of joint working developed under area-based policies become part of the accepted repertoire of statutory organisations (otherwise, joint working will not be sustained when the area-based programmes are wound up, and joined up policy will gradually come to an end). It is strange because, up until now, NLG has shied away from considering the radical transformation that would be required of statutory organisations (local authorities, the National Health Service, police authorities, etc.) in order for them to achieve even a modest degree of seamlessness of performance. Instead, it has endorsed (at least in England) Local Strategic Partnerships, where these statutory organisations, together with representatives from the voluntary and community sectors, collaborate in the development of common policies (e.g. on the sharing of information) and in the delivery of relatively low budget projects. It is difficult to see how such a parsimonious and relatively permissive approach could ever achieve the root-and-branch cultural change demanded by holistic mainstreaming. It is not surprising, therefore, that Sullivan (2004) has recently described such an approach as flawed, mainly on the grounds that it does not define a clear role for local authorities – a criticism that can also be applied to neighbourhood management.

'Community' also has significance on different spatial scales, with the consequence that policy/practice might be expected to be joined up at the level of a neighbourhood, a local authority area, a region, a nation, or even a continent (e.g. Europe). NLG has increased the degree of complexity here by, for example, devolving national housing investment decisions to Regional Housing Boards. There seems little doubt that NLG intends that both local authorities and regional assemblies will have a leading role in the achievement of community governance in their territories (as envisaged, for example, in the Local Government Act 2000), where 'community governance' is understood as a process of decision-making whose scale corresponds with what identifiable communities regard as appropriate and legitimate (Clarke and Stewart, 1994). Housing policy will therefore be expected to join up with other kinds of policy not only on the scale of a neighbourhood, as with the NDCs and neighbourhood management, but also on a municipal scale, as an integral part of local authority community strategies, and on a regional scale, in ways that have yet to be determined (but perhaps fore-shadowed in ODPM's (2003) Northern Way?).[4] Clearly, in spite of some progress, joined-up working is still in its infancy.

In what sense, then, *can* housing act as a basis for joining up different policy foci and different service areas? One possibility is that it could be a source of place-based interests, arising out of asset ownership (as in the case of owner-occupation) or shared status (as tenants of the same landlord). Such interests can form 'stakes', which residents then defend, or attempt to advance, in a variety of ways, including by seeking improvements in non-housing services such as schools, parks, community centres, public transport, etc. Such joining up, however, can have negative as well as positive connotations, as discussed by Cooper and by Pierson and Worley in this volume – for example, nimbyism (to make the community of residents more exclusive) or vigilantism (to punish or to expel from the area people who are deemed to be 'undesirable'). Comprehensive community governance could be extremely efficient, effective, and democratic, but it could also be highly exclusivist, territorial, and intolerant of difference. Under such a regime, services might well improve but, at the same time, existing inequalities of class, gender, race, disability, age, etc., could become reinforced and more entrenched. The question is: how to ensure that this does not happen, and that community governance is genuinely progressive?

Values, social movements and democratic transformation

Arguably, social justice is the key aim for all housing and social policy (see Sprigings, this volume). The meaning of social justice, however, is highly contentious. People can agree to a large extent on the justice of matters such as 'due process' or the impartiality of the legal system but, when it comes to the legitimate scope of the welfare state, there is room for a wide range of opinions, from anarchism at one end to total state control at the other. How then is it possible to arrive at 'shared values' that will generate policy that is genuinely empowering for all? The answer, perhaps, lies in recognising, first, that the legitimate scope of state action has never been, is not, and probably never will be an issue on which the majority of citizens will agree. If shared values are to be agreed, therefore, they must cut across (or rather under) this great left/right political divide. State action, and political action generally, must be seen purely as a means to an end, and this end should be to ensure that people have increasing control over their own lives (see definition of empowerment in Somerville 1998: 233), and this also means that they should have decreasing control over the lives of others. Proposals for state intervention should therefore be judged against this shared value, in terms of the likely effects of the proposed intervention on personal autonomy generally.

It is of course a tall order to expect that such effects can be measured in any precise way, for example, by balancing the probable gains in autonomy for some citizens against the probable losses for others, but there seems to be no other way by which some kind of value consensus can be achieved. There has to be a general recognition that poverty, enforced worklessness, social exclusion, and so on, amount to a denial of basic human rights.

Further, in order to give social and political substance to this value of personal autonomy, there must exist a framework of 'community', within which such autonomy is recognised and respected.[5] Communities that are paranoid (against others) or demonised (by others), such as those vividly described by Cooper in this volume, are ones where such autonomy is violated on a more or less daily basis. Typically, a variety of joined up interventions, involving housing, policing, schooling, community action and general 'conscientisation' is required if such communities are to be rescued. Even then, there are problems, as Pierson and Worley note in this volume,[6] with relying on place or territory, such as a housing estate, a city, a country or whatever, as a focus for 'community', and these problems need to be addressed more directly and more honestly. Although research to date in the US and the UK suggests that community governance can be at least as impartial as what we are used to under current national institutions of criminal and social justice (see Fung and Wright 2003; Somerville 2005), there is also a risk, as Sprigings identifies in this volume, that it can go badly astray. To Cooper's discourse of 'dangerous' people and places, therefore, there can be added a newly emerging discourse of 'dangerous' communities, to which indeed Bauman (2001) is a contribution. However, it is difficult to see any more effective way of dealing with 'dangerous' communities, as with 'dangerous' people and places, other than through improved community governance. There is a need to establish, first, a rule of law at community level, and then begin the time-consuming process of building sustainable democratic life-enhancing community institutions.

The realisation of a community of shared values requires appropriate mobilisation of effective social movements. Contributors to this book have discussed a number of such movements including the tenants' movement, squatters' movements, and the movement to defend council housing. Somerville (this volume) argues that many of these movements can be understood as forms of working-class community-based protest – the housing struggles involved (for example, against rent increases or the poll tax) are intimately bound up with conditions in working-class communities. When mobilisation fixes on the specifically *housing* status of the people concerned – typically as council tenants, thus creating a council tenants' movement – its prospects for success become severely limited. Even more broadly based campaigns, however, can suffer from being primarily defensive in character. As Ruane (2004: 163) has pointed out in relation to anti-privatisation politics (of which the defend council housing movement is an example):

They focus principally upon defending *even if* the goals of extending the socialisation of the means of production are present. In the main, these broader, more far-reaching goals are not much in evidence. The main focus is upon trying to prevent threatened or potential privatisation moves or to reverse those that have already been taken. Rather, then, than attempting to bring about a popular conversion to values which are so radical they 'break the limits of compatibility of a system' (Byrne, 1997: 17), anti-privatisation protest seeks the *restoration* of values, principles and policies which increasingly appear to belong to a previous [era].

Ruane stresses, however, that it does not have to be like this: 'anti-privatisation politics can propose a revision of basic ideas, which is not merely restorative and reformist but a fundamental challenge to the emergent order' (Ruane 2004: 164). In her analysis of squatters' movements, Reeve (this volume) highlights the significance of the challenge that squatters pose to established private property rights. She argues that squatters in the 1960s and 1970s were not only engaged in a new 'politics of lifestyle' (Giddens 1991) but they also actively contested the legitimacy of the current distribution, and systems of allocation, of material resources (in particular, housing). Although focused on housing, therefore, this movement goes beyond being a defensive protest or campaign, because it questions the fundamental legitimacy of the capitalist social order, and embodies that questioning in its own forms of direct action. This is not to say that such a movement is inherently more likely to succeed than one that is primarily reactive or defensive in character. After all, the institution of private property lies at the root of our economic and political system, so the forces stacked in favour of it can appear to be overwhelming. Reeve's argument, however, does point to one possible way forward, based on the realisation of a form of primitive communism – a community in which assets are owned in common.

Of course, as Engels (1968) pointed out long ago, primitive communism is not a realistic solution to the problems thrown up by capitalist development. Squatters' movements are limited by being based on control of a single type of asset (namely, housing) but also by their predominantly localised character, which is associated with a certain fragmentation of organisation and action. Consequently, it is relatively easy for established powers, such as local authorities and national governments, to marginalise and neutralise them, through combinations of coercive and permissive measures.

A really successful counter-hegemonic mobilisation has to join up action at a local level with action at national and international levels. The movement as a whole must be effectively self-disciplined, for example, through progressive forms of community governance that guarantee, extend and enhance economic and social rights. The market must be made to work for the people, and not the other way round. Above all, decision-making processes within the movement, and consequently within society generally, need to be completely open and transparent and devolved to the lowest practicable level. Ordinary people need to be involved in decision-making as much as possible, and where they choose to have representatives acting on their behalf, those representatives should be capable of being held to account, to those who elected them, for what they do. As stated above, institutions of community governance will need to be developed to combat the effects of ghettoisation, and real community development needs to occur, across a wide range of activities, particularly employment, education and health, as well as housing. Divisions within the movement are inevitable, and these will not only have dimensions of class, gender, race, disability, age, etc., but will also be new divisions produced or highlighted by the movement itself, for example, related to failures of self-discipline and/or increased 'dangerousness' resulting from enhanced self-activity. In this context, Amin's (2002) advocacy of 'banal transgression' in order to build unity across community boundaries could be very effective but it could also be a highly risky strategy, leading to heightened tensions and occasional open conflict.

Contrary to widespread belief, there is no necessary incompatibility here between 'freedom' and 'equality', although the balance between the two will be drawn in different ways according to different political ideologies (see Sprigings, this volume). Personal autonomy needs to be protected by an agreed international framework of legally enforceable rights, and within that framework all decision-making authority needs to be sited as closely as possible to those affected by the decisions made, with the power of citizens to influence decisions being set more or less in proportion to the likely effect of those decisions on citizens (again with appropriate legal safeguards at national and international levels). This proposed extension and enhancement of democracy is based on taking the principle of equality of citizenship as far as it can go. It cannot actually guarantee equality or redistributive justice, however, and may indeed be compatible with conflicting normative approaches to redistribution. The adoption of shared values in this sense, therefore, would not put an end to politics or ideology: on the contrary, it seems likely that it would tend to revitalise politics, by providing a common foundation on which meaningful political debate can take place. A transformative community politics, as envisaged by Cooper, could develop, which recognises the depth of stratification around class, gender, religion, ethnicity, etc. (see Pierson and Worley, this volume) and which confronts directly the issues concerning 'dangerous' people, places and communities (as well as 'dangerous' politicians, bureaucrats, professionals and community 'representatives'!), but which at the same time embraces a wide variety of political approaches and ideologies.

If the way forward is to protect and enhance personal autonomy, within a framework of universal substantive human rights, then it is arguable that there is a major role for markets in achieving policy aims. The problem has been that markets have been used as a means of domination rather than liberation. The solution, therefore, is to ensure democratic control of markets, including housing markets, at local, national and global levels. One small step forward would be for governments to support and develop the fair trade movement, as discussed by Monbiot (2003).[7] Beyond this, there would have to be wide-ranging economic democratisation and expansion of community enterprise (which includes co-operative housing), so as to transform the current capitalist system into something more compatible with the values expressed above.

A final issue of justice and values is touched on by most chapters in this volume, especially those by Cooper, Smith, Harrison, Milner and Reeve, and this has to do with an understanding of social change as rooted in material relations of social class and bodily interaction. The rationale for housing and social policy is constructed on the basis of these material relations. This is perhaps most clearly seen in Reeve's chapter, where squatting is explained as a response to material conditions of housing deprivation, leading to specific policies of repression and accommodation at local and national government levels. Similarly, Cooper, while perhaps placing greater emphasis than Reeve on the discursive construction of social relations, also presents policy as being developed in the form of techniques to tackle 'dangerous' people and places. Harrison draws attention to the rich variety of the housing and social needs of different ethnic groups that have been produced but not all met by these changing material relations, while Smith emphasises the erosion of women's and children's rights in housing and social policy generally. Similarly, Milner, in relation to disabled people, criticises partial, stereotypical approaches that violate rights and fail to meet needs. All of these writers, therefore, in different ways, adhere to a common understanding of social justice as involving a challenge to dominant policy approaches, on the grounds that those approaches downplay or ignore the needs of the powerless and socially excluded. If this challenge is to succeed, we would argue that it must be based on a deep understanding of the material conditions of the individuals concerned, and on the mobilisation of forms of collective action that are most appropriate for those conditions. The latter can embrace a variety of social movements, not all of which have been discussed in this book. In order to be victorious, however, these movements will need to co-operate closely with one another on a number of different scales: corporeal, domestic, neighbourhood, village/town/city, regional, national, continental and global.

Notes

1 This involves investing £1 billion to provide housing for 'keyworkers' over three years to 2006 – see ODPM's 2004 annual report.
2 The Scottish Parliament, however, is going ahead with a Bill that proposes to set up a national register of landlords in Scotland (Lloyd 2004).
3 Moreover, this budget is already being cut even before the first round of reviews are completed. This undermines the government's ability to join-up or deliver essential services that meet the

varying strategic priorities local authorities have been required to set up in order to plan for meeting needs in their area.

4 Interestingly, the housing market renewal pathfinders seem to be pitched on a sub-regional scale, larger than a local authority but smaller than a region. They consist of clusters of communities, with no overall community governance structures.

5 This is Lister's (2003) politics of belonging that transcends equality and difference, to which Pierson and Worley refer in this volume.

6 For example, problems of territorial exclusivity and ghettoisation (Bauman 2001).

7 This could involve, for example, outlawing excessive profits or capital gains, as currently occur in the UK housing market.

References

Amin, A. (2002) 'Ethnicity and the multicultural city: living with diversity', *Environment and Planning*, 34: 959–80.

Armstrong, H. (1999) 'A new vision for housing in England', in T. Brown (ed.) *Stakeholder Housing*, London: Pluto Press: 122–32.

Bauman, Z. (2001) *Community: Seeking Safety in an Insecure World*, Cambridge: Polity Press.

Bramley, G. (1997) 'Housing policy: a case of terminal decline?' *Policy and Politics*, 25, 4: 387–407.

Byrne, P. (1997) *Social Movements in Britain*, London: Routledge.

Clarke, M. and Stewart, J. (1994) 'The local authority and the new community governance', *Regional Studies*, 28: 201–19.

Engels, F. (1968) 'Socialism: utopian and scientific', in K. Marx and F. Engels *Selected Works*, London: Lawrence and Wishart: 394–428.

Fung, A. and Wright, E.O. (eds) (2003) *Deepening Democracy: Institutional Innovations in Empowered Participatory Governance*, London and New York: Verso.

Giddens, A. (1991) *Modernity and Self-Identity: Self and Society in the Late Modern Age*, Cambridge: Polity Press.

Kemp, P. (1999) 'Housing policy under New Labour', in M. Powell (ed.) *New Labour, New Welfare State? The 'Third Way' in British Social Policy*, Bristol: Policy Press: 123–47.

Lister, R. (2003) *Citizenship: Feminist Perspectives*, 2nd edn, Basingstoke: Palgrave.

Lloyd, M. (2004) 'Coming down your street', *Inside Housing* 11 June: 43–4.

Monbiot, G. (2003) *The Age of Consent: A Manifesto for a New World Order*, London: Flamingo.

North, D.C. (1990) *Institutions, Institutional Change and Economic Performance*, Cambridge: Cambridge University Press.

Office of the Deputy Prime Minister (ODPM) (2003) *The Northern Way*, London: ODPM.

Office of Public Service Reform (OPSR) (2002) *Reforming Our Public Services. Principles into Practice*, London: The Prime Minister's Office of Public Service Reform.

Pearl, M. and Zetter, R. (2002) 'From refuge to exclusion: housing as an instrument of social exclusion for refugees and asylum seekers in the UK', in P. Somerville and A. Steele (eds) *'Race', Housing and Social Exclusion*, London: Jessica Kingsley Publishers: 226–44.

Peck, J. and Tickell, A. (2002) 'Neoliberalising space', *Antipode* 34, 3: 380–404.

Ruane, S. (2004) 'UK anti-privatisation politics', in M.J. Todd and G. Taylor (eds) *Demo-cracy and Participation: Popular Protest and New Social Movements*, London: Merlin Press: 158–75.

Somerville, P. (1998) 'Empowerment through residence', *Housing Studies* 13, 2: 233–57.

—— (2000) (with Cooper, C.) 'Housing policies', in T. Burden, C. Cooper and S. Petrie, *'Modernising' Social Policy: Unravelling New Labour's Welfare Reforms*, Aldershot: Ashgate.

—— (2005) 'Community governance and democracy', *Policy and Politics*, 33, 1.

Somerville, P. and Rust, A. (2003) *Substance Misuse in West Lindsey*, Lincoln: University of Lincoln.

Sullivan, H. (2004) 'Is enabling enough? Contrasting approaches to joined up local governance', paper presented to 54th conference of the Political Studies Association at the University of Lincoln, 6–8 April.

Index

Index

Bentley, T. *et al.* 223, 229
Berghman, J. 85, 87
Berthoud, R. 217
'Better Use of Vacant and Under-Occupied Housing' (1976) 186
Bevan, A. 178
Blackaby, B. and Chahal, K. 127
Blair, T. 85
Blakemore, K. 37
Blossfeld, H.-P. and Shavit, Y. 116
Blunkett, D. 83, 84
Bowes, A. *et al.* 125, 133, 139
Bradley, H. and Hebson, G. 103
Bramley, G. 151, 246; *et al.* 110; and Pawson, H. 225
Branson, N. 199, 200, 206
Breen, R. and Goldthorpe, J. 105
Bright, J. 224
British Crime Survey (1988) 50–1
British Standards (BS) 5619 (1978) 187
Broadwater Farm, Tottenham 224
Brownill, S. and Darke, J. 232
Bruegel, I. 231
building industry, economics of 3; and holding back of land 3, 4; risk aversion in 3
Building Regulations 21
Building Research Establishment (BRE) 182
Bull, R. and Watts, V. 183, 184
Burden, T. *et al.* 25, 75, 85, 88, 93, 95
Burnett, J. 18, 73, 74
Burrows, R. 151
Byrne, P. 120, 250

Cantle Report (2001) 84, 85–6, 228, 233–4, 235
Carroll, C. *et al.* 189
Carter, J. 174
Castells, M. 108, 112
Centre for Housing and Community Research 158
Chahal, K., and Julienne, L. 130; and Temple, B. 130
Chamba, R. *et al.* 131
Chamberlayne, P. *et al.* 94
Chartered Institute of Housing 47, 51
Chaskin, R. 236
Chicago School 75–6, 91
Children Act (1989) 167
Cholera Act (1832) 19
Christie, H. 149
Chronically Sick and Disabled Persons Act (CSDP) (1970) 184, 186
citizenship, and communities 233–5; good 67; importance of 55; and responsibility

86; rights/equality 44, 55, 63, 65, 66; and urban regeneration 233–5
Clapham, D., *et al.* 1, 16, 138; and Smith, S. 183, 184, 185
Clarke, M. and Stewart, J. 247
class 9, 10; and equality of opportunity 105–6; existence/justice of 104; and housing struggles 112–15; and housing tenure 109–12; and individual merit 104–5; individualised character of class relations 106–7; key features of 107–8; and life chances 116; Marxist approach 10, 103, 104, 120; origin vs ability/effort 105; perspectives on 103–9; political dimension 106; and power 106; and problem of legitimation 104; and regeneration policy 117–19; relative importance of 115–17, 116; and self-worth/self-identity 107; and social change 108–9; and social justice 103–4; and social mobility 103–4, 106, 110–11, 120; social/political organisation 116–17; Weberian approach 10, 103–4, 120, *see also* middle class; underclass; working class
Clydebank rent strike 113
Cohen, G.A. 49, 57
Cohen, S. 10, 70, 72, 75, 88, 98
Cole, I. 225; and Furbey, R. 36–7, 115, 178, 179, 183; and Robinson, D. 125, 134
Commission on the Future of Multi-Ethnic Britain (2000) 230
Common Lodging Houses Act (1851) 74
communitarianism 12, 57–9, 63–4, 84–7, 230
Communities Plan 245
community, cohesion/citizenship 83–7, 233–5; concept of 229, 230, 247; development of 94–8; discourse 229–31; and ethnic minorities 138; framework for 249; governance of 248; involvement of 84–7; meaning of 220–1; participation/partnership 222–3; and place 12, 80–1; pluralistic understanding of 230; significance of 247–8; social relations in 230; and Third Way 230–1; and urban regeneration 229–31, 236, *see also* neighbourhood; place; urban regeneration
Community Cohesion Task Force 84
Confederation of Cooperative Housing 115
Contact and Assessment Teams (CATs) 152
Continuing Care Retirement Community 80
Cooper, C. and Hawtin, M. 92, 95
Cope, H. 24